INDIAN SOCIAL ORGANISATION

INDIAN SOCIAL ORGANISATION

Satish Mittal
Sushil Kumar Saxena

Commonwealth

Indian Social Organisation

Edition : 2018

ISBN 978-81-311-0373-9

Published by :

COMMONWEALTH PUBLISHERS PVT. LTD.
4831/24, Prahlad Street,
Ansari Road, Darya Ganj,
New Delhi - 110002
Ph. : 23272541, 23257835
Fax : 91- 011- 23257835
e-mail : commonwealthbooks@gmail.com

Typesetting by :

Dimple Computers
Delhi

Printed at :
Roshan Offset Printers
Delhi

Preface

The term "social organisation" means the systematic ordering of social relations. It implies the interdependence of parts, which is an essential and important feature of all enduring collectivities such as, groups, communities, and societies. These interdependent parts consist of a set of roles and social positions, values, norms and beliefs found in society. The social values of a society are usually based on religious beliefs. Behaviour is based on values, and hence religious beliefs play an important role in determining social behaviour. There are many religious groups in India and the country has declared itself to be secular. This means that all religions are to be treated equally by the state.

When we speak of social organisation, we talk about the arrangement of actions which conform with the norms and values of society. Thus, to understand the social organisation of a particular society, we need to study the systematic ordering of social relations, including changes that have taken place over time in them. In any description of social organisation of a people we need to refer to the ideological basis of the way the people act.

This book is intended to provide a detailed description of the social organisation of different religious groups living in India. Written in a lively and accessible style, it would be of great value for the students, teachers, researchers, anthropologists and the general public alike.

Authors

Contents

1

Indian Social System

Indian society is multifaceted to an extent perhaps unknown in any other of the world's great civilisations. Virtually no generalisation made about Indian society is valid for all of the nation's multifarious groups. Comprehending the complexities of Indian social structure has challenged scholars and other observers over many decades. The ethnic and linguistic diversity of Indian civilisation is more like the diversity of an area as variable as Europe than like that of any other single nation-state. Living within the embrace of the Indian nation are vast numbers of different regional, social, and economic groups, each with different cultural practices. Particularly noteworthy are differences between social structures in the north and the south, especially in the realm of kinship systems. Throughout the country, religious differences can be significant, especially between the Hindu majority and the large Muslim minority; and other Indian groups—Buddhists, Christians, Jains, Jews, Parsis, Sikhs, and practitioners of tribal religions—all pride themselves on being unlike members of other faiths.

Access to wealth and power varies considerably, and vast differences in socioeconomic status are evident everywhere. The poor and the wealthy live side by side in urban and rural areas. It is common in city life to see a prosperous, well-fed man or woman chauffeured in a fine car pass gaunt street dwellers huddled beneath burlap shelters along the roadway. In many villages, solid cement houses of landowners rise not far from the flimsy thatched shacks of landless labourers. Even when not so obvious, distinctions of class are found in almost every settlement in India.

Urban-rural differences can be immense in the Indian Society. Nearly 74 percent of India's population dwells in villages, with agriculture providing support for most of these rural residents. In villages, mud-plastered walls ornamented with traditional designs, dusty lanes, herds of grazing cattle, and the songs of birds at sunset provide typical settings for the social lives of most Indians. In India's great cities, however, millions of people live amidst cacophony—roaring vehicles, surging crowds, jammed apartment buildings, busy commercial establishments, loudspeakers blaring movie tunes—while breathing the poisons of industrial and automotive pollution. Gender distinctions are pronounced. The behaviour expected of men and women can be quite different, especially in villages, but also in urban centers. Prescribed ideal gender roles help shape the actions of both sexes as they move between family and the world outside the home.

Crosscutting and pervading all of these differences of region, language, wealth, status, religion, urbanity, and gender is the special feature of Indian society that has received most attention from observers: caste. The people of India belong to thousands of castes and castelike groups—hierarchically ordered, named groups into which members are born. Caste members are expected to marry within the group and follow caste rules pertaining to diet, avoidance of ritual pollution, and many other aspects of life.

The study of Indian society necessitates that we try to understand the basic elements which provide the blueprint for thought and action. How are relationships organised through the history and in the contemporary times? What the rules and norms for individual and social conduct and from where they derive legitimacy are some of the issues which need to be understood. Indian society is extremely diverse in terms of societies, cultures and social behaviour. Sociologists, however, point to caste system as an organising principle of Indian society. It is seen to be providing the basic frame around which relationships across groups are organised. Legitimacy for the caste divisions is derived from Hinduism the great religion of the Indian continent. Sociologists, however, also point out that earlier social science understandings were derived from great Hindu texts that these act as the guiding principles for social behaviour. The contextual realities vary a great deal.

Social Hierarchy in Indian Society

India is a hierarchical society. Within Indian culture, whether in the north or the south, Hindu or Muslim, urban or village, virtually all things, people, and groups of people are ranked according to various essential qualities. If one is attuned to the theme of hierarchy in India, one can discern it everywhere. Although India is a political democracy, in daily life there is little advocacy of or adherence to notions of equality.

Castes and castelike groups--those quintessential groups with which almost all Indians are associated—are ranked. Within most villages or towns, everyone knows the relative rankings of each locally represented caste, and people's behaviour toward one another is constantly shaped by this knowledge. Between the extremes of the very high and very low castes, however, there is sometimes disagreement on the exact relative ranking of castes clustered in the middle.

Castes are primarily associated with Hinduism but also exist among other Indian religious groups. Muslims sometimes expressly deny that they have castes—they state that all Muslims are brothers under God—but observation of Muslim life in various parts of India reveals the existence of castelike groups and clear concern with social hierarchy. Among Indian Christians, too, differences in caste are acknowledged and maintained.

Throughout India, individuals are also ranked according to their wealth and power. For example, there are "big men" (*bare admi*) and "little men" (*chhote admi*) everywhere. "Big men" sit confidently on chairs, while "little men" come before them to make requests, either standing or crouching down on their haunches, certainly not presuming to sit beside a man of high status as an equal. Even men of nearly equal status who might share a string cot to sit on take their places carefully—the higher-ranking man at the head of the cot, the lower-ranking man at the foot.

Within families and kinship groupings, there are many distinctions of hierarchy. Men outrank women of the same or similar age, and senior relatives outrank junior relatives. Several other kinship relations involve formal respect. For example, in northern India, a daughter-in-law of a household shows deference to a daughter of a household. Even among young siblings in a household, there is constant acknowledgment of age differences: younger siblings never address an older sibling by name, but rather by respectful terms for elder brother or elder sister. However, an older sibling may address the younger by name.

Even in a business or academic setting, where colleagues may not openly espouse traditional observance of caste or class ranking behaviour, they may set up fictive kinship relations, addressing one another by kinship terms reflecting family or village-style hierarchy. For example, a younger colleague might respectfully address an older colleague as *chachaji* (respected father's younger brother), gracefully acknowledging the superior position of the older colleague.

VARNA SYSTEM

In the Indian social system, Varna is only a reference category and not a functioning unit of social structure, and only refers broadly to the ascribed status of different jatis. It is also a classificatory device. In it, several jatis with similar ascribed ritual status are clustered together and are hierarchically graded. The three upper levels—the Brahman, the Kshatriya, and the Vaishya—are considered twice-born, as in addition to biological birth they are born a second time after initiation rites. The Sudra, the fourth level, includes a multiplicity of artisans and occupationally-specialised jatis who pursue clean, i.e. non-polluting occupations. Though the Varna hierarchy ends here, but there is a fifth level which accommodates those following supposedly unclean occupations that are believed to be polluting. They are *Antyaja,* i.e., outside the Varna system. They constitute what are known as the Dalit.

Origin of the Varna

There are several passages in the oldest Vedic literature dealing with the origin of the varnas. The four orders of society are believed to have originated from the self-sacrifice of *Purusha*—the creator, the primeval being. *Purusha* is said to have destroyed himelf so that an appropriate social order could emerge. The oldest is the hymn in the *purusha-sakta* of the Rig-Veda which says that the Brahmana Varna represented the mouth of the purusha,- which word may be translated as the "the Universal Man", referring perhaps to mankind as a whole,—the Rajanya (i.e. Kshatriya) his arms, the Vaisya his thighs and the Sudra his feet.

But it has been shown that there are other passages, apart from the Purusha-Sukta, in which the division of society in to Varnas, though not in the rigid form of later times, is mentioned. Thus, in Rig-Veda, the three varnas, the Brahma, Kshatam, and Visah are mentioned; while in Rig-Veda, the four varnas are referred to thus: "One to high sway (i.e. Brahmana), one to exalted glory (i.e. the Kshatriya), one to pursue his gain (i.e. the Valsya) and one to his labour (i.e. the Sudra),- all to regard their different vocations, all moving creatures hath the Dawn awakened. Haug's opinion on the origin of the institution of caste seems to be correct. "It has been of late asserted" he observes, "that the original parts of the Vedas do not know the system of caste. But this conclusion was prematurely arrived at without sufficiently weighing the evidence. It is true that caste system is not to be found in such a developed state; the duties assigned to the several castes are not so clearly defined as in the law books and Puranas. But nevertheless the system is already known in the earlier parts of the Vedas, or rather presupposes. The barriers only were not as insurmountable as in later times.

S.C.Dube gives the Triguna theory of the origin of the Varna system i.e. the philosophic speculation of ancient India identified three *gunas*—inherent qualities—in human beings, animate and inanimate objects, and in human actions: *sattva, rajas,* and *tamas. Sattva* consisted of noble thoughts and deeds, goodness and virtue, truth and wisdom. *Rajas,* on the other hand, were characterised by high-living and luxury, passion and some indulgence, pride, and valour. At the bottom was *tamas*, with the attributes of coarseness and dullness, overindulgence without taste, the capacity to carry out heavy work without much imagination. Those with *sattvic* qualities were classified as Brahman, those with *rajasic* as Kshatriya and Vaishya, and those with *tamsic* qualities as Sudra. Another third theory takes account of ethnic admixture, culture contact, and functional specialisation. Any of these three components cannot singly explain the origin of the Varna. In the initial stage of the evolution of Hindu society-the Vedic stage-race and complexion were important factors, but in its fully evolved form it was only a make-believe phenomenon, not a biological reality. Aryanisation was the result of culture contact, but it was not a one-way process involving donor-recipient relations. The Vratya pre-Aryan traditions asserted themselves and in the process modified the Aryan scheme of social organisation, rituals, beliefs, world-view, and its ethos. Groups were incorporated *en masse* into the emerging social order, adopting some new features, retaining some old characteristics, and imparting their imprint on the wider society.

Reverting to the *Purusha-Sakta*, an allegorical meaning is by the whole *sakta* with reference to the *Purusha* and the creation of varnas from his limbs. The *Purusha* is described as being himself "this whole universe, whatever has been and whatever shall be" Further, we are also told that the moon sprang from his mind (*manas*), the Sun from his eyes, Indra and Agni were created out of his mouth, and air or wind from his breath. Again, from his navel arose the atmosphere (*antariksham*), from his head the sky, from his feet the earth (*bhumi*), and from his ear the four quarters (*disah)*; in this manner, the worlds were created.

There is a great deal of theorising in the Epic and the Dharma-Sastra literature on the problem of the origin and development of varnas; There were no distinct castes or classes of men in the *Krita* Yuga, according to the Mahabharata At another place, the sage Bhrigu says that only a few Brahmanas were first created by the great Brahman. But later on, the four divisions of mankind Brahmana, Kshatriya, Vaisya and Sudra developed. The complexion (*varnah*) of the Brahmanas was white (*sita*) that of Kshatriyas red (*lohitah*), that of the Viasyas yellow (*pitakah)*, and that of the Sudras black (*asitah)*—thus does the rishi Bhrigu explain his theory of the origin of the varnas to Bharadwaja.

At first the whole world consisted of **Brahmanas.** Created equally by Brahman, men have, on account of their acts, been divided into various varnas. The theory goes on to explain how the four varnas and other castes (*jatayah*) arose out of the one original class of Dvijas (twice-born). Those who found excessive pleasure in enjoyment became possessed of the attributes of harshness and anger; endowed with courage, and unmindful of their own dharma, (*tyakta-sva-dharmah*), those Dvijas possessing the quality of redness (*raktangah*), became Kshatriyas. Those again, who, unmindful of the duties laid down for them, became endued with both the qualities of Redness and Darkness *(pitah)* and followed the occupations of cattle breeding and agriculture, became Vaisyas. Those Dvijas, again, who were given to untruth and injuring other creatures, possessed of cupidity (*lubdhah*), who indiscriminately followed all sorts of occupations for their maintenance (*sarva-karmo'pa-jivinah*), who had no purity of behaviour (*saucha-paribhrashtah*), and who thus, nursed within them the quality of Darkness (*krishnah*) Became sudras. Thus "divided by there occupations, the Dvijas, (who were, in the first instance, all Brahmanas) due to falling away from the duties of their own order, became members of the other three varnas. None of them, therefore, is prohibited from carrying out all the activities of dharmas and yajnas. Further, those who, through their ignorance, fell away from their prescribed duties and led a loose life (svachchandacharacheshtitah), endied in reducing themselves to the various lower castes (jatayah), viz. the Pisachas (feinds), the Raksasas (globilins), the Pretas (the evil-spirited), and the various mlechchha (barbarian or outcast)jatis (castes).

The theory that the four varnas proceeded from the limbs of the creator is also held by Manu-Smriti. And, in order to protect this whole universe (*sarvasya)*, differential duties and occupations have been assigned to the different varnas (prithak-karmani) by him. Manu then goes on to eulogise the Brahmana varna as the supreme creation of God. He further positively asserts that the Brahmana, Kshatriya, Vaisya and sudra are the only varnas in existence; there is no fifth varna; and with this, Yajnavalkya, Baudhayana and Vasishtha also agree.

Manu's theory of the origin of mixed castes is, in certain respects, different from that of the Mahabharata. Sons begotten by twice-born men (dvijas, i.e. Brahmanas, Kshatriyas and Vaisyas) of wives from the immediate lower class belong no doubt to the varna of their fathers respectively but they are censured on account of the fauly inherent in their mothers (*matri-dosha*). Such is the traditional (*sanatana*) law (*vidhih)* applicable to children of a wife from a varna only one degree lower than her husband's. The real mixture of varnas (varnas-samkarah) therefore arises with offsprings born of a woman two or three degrees lower. Thus the son born of a Brahmana father and a Vaisya mother would be called an Ambashtha; that born of a Brahmana father and a sudra mother would be called Nishada, and so on. The mixture of varnas takes place in other ways also. Of a Kshatriya father and Brahmana mother spring issues belonging to the Suta caste; children born of a Vaisya father and Kshatriya mother or a Brahmana mother belong to Magadha and Videha castes respectively; and so on And, inter-marriages between these new castes give rise to newer and newer castes, so that the process goes on multiplying.

Duties of the Varna

The division into four Varnas is here correlated to the duties of each Varna. Their origin is a symbolic representation of the rank and functions of the four Varnas. In the cultural body-image the head, the arms, the thighs, and the feet are ranked in descending order, so are the traditional functions.

The *Purusha-Sukta* has been interpreted as having an allegorical significance behind it from another point of view. Thus, the mouth of the *Purusha* from which the Brahmanas are created is the seat of speech; the Brahmanas therefore are created to be teachers and instructors of mankind.

According to Manu, a Brahman should always and assiduously study the Veda alone and teach the Vedas. It is also the privilege of a Brahman to officiate as a priest and as a means of livelihood permitted to receive gifts from a worthy person of the three higher varnas. This is known as *pratigraha.*

The arms are symbol of valour and strength; the Kshatriya's mission in this world is to carry weapons and protect people. Thus, defence and war, administration and government were the functions assigned to the Kshatriya. It is difficult to interpret that portion of the hymn which deals with the creation of the Vaisyas from the thighs of the Purusha. But the thigh may have been intended to represent the lower portion of the body, the portion which consumes food, and therefore the Vaisya may be said to be created to provide food to the people. Trade, commerce and agriculture were the work of the Vaishya. The creation of the Sudra from the foot symbolises the fact that the Sudra is to be the "footman", the servant of other varnas. The Sudra ranked the lowest by serving others though crafts and labour.

The whole social organisation is here conceived symbolically as one human being-the "Body Social", we may say—with its limbs representing the social classes based on the principle of division of labour. The Mahabharata states the same thing thus: Our obeisance to That (*Purusha*) who consists of Brahmanas in the mouth, Kashtras in the arms, Vaishya in the entire regions, stomach and thighs, and Sudras in the feet.

Responsibilities and Status

In the above mentioned fourfold classification of duties according to Dharmashastras, there was an ascending order of responsibilities. While Brahmin was given the highest position he was also entrusted with maximum responsibilities. The entire task of preserving Dharma was mainly the responsibility of the Brahmin. The next social status in Varna hierarchy was given to the Kshatriya as he had the responsibility of defending the nation in times of war and administering law and order in the society. He provided social justice with the help of the Brahmin scholar. The Vaishyas and Sudras had lesser responsibilities and therefore were assigned lower status. The Sudra gradually came to be so much looked down upon that he could not touch a Brahmin. The Sudra could not be initiated into the Vedic study and the only ashram out of the four that he was entitled to, was that of the householder.

Characteristics of Caste System

Caste may be defined as a hereditary endogamous group which decides the individual's status in the social stratification and his profession. Caste is also defined as an aggregate of persons whose share of obligations and privileges is fixed by birth, sanctioned and supported by magic and or religion. Ketkar defines caste as a social group having two characteristics-memberships confirmed to those who are born of members and includes all persons so born and the members are forbidden by an inexorable social law to marry outside the group. According to Cooley when a class is somewhat strictly hereditary, we may call it caste. When status is wholly predetermined, so that men are born to their lot in life without any hope of changing it, then class takes the form of caste.

According to G.S. Ghurye, caste in India is a Brahminic child of the Indo-Aryan culture, cradled in the land of the Ganges country. Abbe Dubbois first propounded the political theory of the origin of Caste in India. However, the complex social structure based upon castes appears impossible that the aim of caste system would have been to maintain the dominance of the Brahmin priests over Hindu society according to Majumdar.

The traditional theory attributes the origin of the caste system to the creator Brahma who created the four varnas. According to Hutton, the caste system originated in the religious customs and rituals of the non-Aryan group particularly the theory of Manu. The traditions of endogamy, untouchability etc. has their roots in Manu. According to Majumdar, caste system was developed to save Aryan Race and culture from intermixing with other races.

There are various characteristics which determine the caste of a person. These are given below:

1. *Determination by birth*: The membership of a caste is determined by birth. A person remains the member of a caste unto which they are born and this does not undergo change even if change takes place in his status, occupation, education, wealth, etc.
2. *Rules and regulations concerning food:* Each individual caste has its own laws which govern the food habits of its members. Generally, there are no restrictions against fruit, milk, butter, dry fruit, etc. but kachcha food (bread, etc.) can be accepted only from a member of one's own or of a higher caste.
3. *Definite occupation*: In the Hindu scriptures there are mention of the occupations of all varnas. According to Manu, the functions of the Brahmins, Kshatriyas, Vaishyas and the Sudras are definite. The function of the Brahmins is to study the Vedas, teach, guide and perform religious rituals, to give and receive alms. Sudras have to do menial work for all the other varnas.

Having developed from the varna system, the occupations in caste system are definite.

4. *Endogamous group*: The majority of persons marry only within their own caste. Brahmins, Kshatriyas, Sudras and Vaishyas all marry within their respective castes. Westermarck has considered this to be a chief characteristic of the caste system. Hindu community does not sanctify inter-caste marriage even now.

5. *Rules concerning status and touchability*: The various castes in the Hindu social organisation are divided into a hierarchy of ascent and descent one above the other. In this hierarchy the Brahmins have the highest and the untouchables the lowest place. This sense of superiority is much exaggerated and manifests in the south. The very touch and sometimes even the shadow of a member of the lower caste is enough to defile an individual of a high caste. In Kerala, a Namboodari Brahmin is defiled by the touch of a Nayar, but in the case of a member of a Tiyyar caste a distance of 36 feet must be kept to avoid being defiled and in the case of a member of the Pulayana caste the distance must be ninety six feet. The stringent observation of the system of untouchability has resulted in some low castes of the Hindu society being called 'untouchables' who were, consequently, forbidden to make use of places of worship, cremation grounds, educational institutions, public roads and hotels etc., and were disallowed from living in the cities.

Mobility of the Varnas

There seems to be a constant upward and downward social mobility between the different Varnas. Yajnavalkya speaks of two kinds of such mobility. When a lower Varna changed into a higher varna, it was known as *jatyutkarsa* or uplift of the caste. On the other hand, if a person belonging to a higher varna gradually descended into a lower Varna, it was known as *jatyapakarsa* or the degeneration of the caste. Provisions for both these processes of social mobility in stratification were laid by different Dharmasastras with minor distinctions about the conditions. It was particularly based upon two conditions, firstly, upon the following of the vocation of some other Varna for five to six generations and secondly, marrying into different Varnas for as much period. It may be easily guessed that in practice such mobility happened only in exception, since the process had to be covered for several generations, but it is clear that the Dharmasastras did prescribe change of Varnas by means of interaction between the Varnas both upwards and downwards. This can be through marriage and education.

While varna dharma had to be followed in normal circumstances, in abnormal circumstances the Dharmasastras prescribe what is known as *Apad* Dharma or that which is worthy of following in exceptional circumstances. Manu enumerate ten means of maintaining oneself in *apad* (distress) *viz,* learning, arts and crafts, work for wages, service i.e., carrying out another's orders, rearing cattle, sale of commodities, agriculture, contentment, alms, money-lending. Out of these some cannot be followed by Brahmin or a Kshatriya when there is no distress.

The Dharmasastras maintained that Brahmins doing certain things are to be treated as Sudras. Without studying the Veda but works hard to master something else is quickly reduced to the status of a Sudra together with his family. Thus, *Apad* Dharma does not mean the license to do whatever one likes to do in the times of trouble. There are numerous cases of so many notable persons who refused to change their allotted duties even in the face of extremely adverse circumstance. Again, even when such a change was permitted, it was always looked down and never appreciated.

Caste Structure and Kinship

Caste structure is intimately related to the kinship system amongst the Hindus in India. The sole reason for this relationship lies in the endogamous nature of caste system. Caste is basically a closed system of stratification, since members are recruited on the criteria of ascribed status. In other words, an individual becomes a member of a caste in which he or she is born. Thus it is an ascribed status. Even if there is social mobility in the caste system through the process of Sankritisation, urbanisations, etc it is only a positional change rather than a structural change.

A person remains the member of his/her caste irrespective of his/her individual status. Any movement in the structure occurs in the social mobility of the caste group in the local hierarchy of the society, which is only a shifting of its position from one level to another.

Kinship is a method or a system by which individuals as members of society relate themselves with other individuals of that society. There are two types of kinship bonds. One is consanguinal and the other is affinal. Consanguinal ties are ties of blood such as, between mother-daughter, mother-son, father-daughter, etc. Affinal ties are ties through marriage, such as, between husband-wife, husband-wife's brother, etc.

Kinship in India is largely an analysis of the internal structure of the sub-caste. Sub-caste is the largest segment of a caste and it performs nearly all the functions of caste like endogamy, social control, etc. For example, the Brahmin caste has several sub-castes like endogamy, social control, etc. For example, the Brahmin caste has several sub-castes like the Gaur Brahmins, the Kanyakubjis, the Saraswat Brahmins, etc. It is these segments of the main caste of Brahmins which form the effective functioning group within which social interaction, marriage etc. takes place. However, these segments are also subdivided and have a regional connotation too, like the Sarjupari Brahmins of North India are those who originally lived beyond the river Saryu or Ghaghara.

The effective caste group is the caste population of a single village while the effective sub caste group within which marriage and kinship takes place is composed of the people belonging to the region around the village having several scores of settlements. Due to the practice of endogamy and restriction in social intercourse a person marries within the sub-caste group, or at the most caste group in India; which extends generally, beyond the village to a larger region.

Kinship system found in various parts of India differs from each other in many respects. However, generally speaking, we can distinguish between the kinship system in the Northern region, the Central region and the southern region.

North India is in it self a very large region, having innumerable types of kinship systems. This region includes the region between the Himalayas in the North and the Vindhyas in the South. In this region a person marries outside the village since all the members of one's caste in a village are considered to be brothers and sisters, or uncles and aunts. Marriage with a person inside the village is forbidden. In fact, an exogamous circle with a radius of four miles can be drawn round a man's village.

Hypergamy is practiced in this region according to which a man takes a wife from a clan, which is lower in status to his own clan. That is, a girl goes in marriage from a lower status group to a higher status group within a sub-caste. The effect of the hypergamy and village exogamy is that it spatially widens the range of ties. Several villages become linked to each other through affinal and matrilateral links. In his study of the Ramkheri village in Madhya Pradesh, Adrian Mayer not only described the Rajput caste and other sub-castes of the village but also the regions around it as well.

The clans, lineages, and kutumbs are all part of the internal structure of the caste at the same time being part of the kinship organisation. These groups are all the time increasing and branching off with time.

The organisation of family in the northern region is mainly patriarchal patrilineal and patrilocal. The lineage is traced through the male, i.e., patrilineal system is followed in this region. It is patriarchal because authority lies with the male head of the family and it is patrilocal because after marriage the bride is brought to reside in the father's house of the bride-groom.

Generally, in most of the castes in the north such as the Jats, an agricultural caste of South Punjab, Delhi and Haryana the "four-clan" rule of marriage is followed. According to this rule,

1. A man cannot marry in the clan to which his father (and he himself) belongs:
2. To which his mother belongs;
3. To which his father's mother belongs; and
4. To which his mother's mother belongs

In the northern region, therefore, marriage with cousins, removed even by two or three degrees is viewed as an incestuous union. In most parts of the region, as mentioned earlier, village exogamy is practiced by most of the castes, especially the Brahmin, kshatriya and Vaishya castes. This rule is known in Delhi, Haryana and Punjab, as the rule of Sassan.

In Central India which includes Rajputana the Vindhyas, Gujrat, Maharashr and Orrissa we find the general practice of caste endogamy. Hypergmy is most characteristic of the Rajputs of this region and village exogamy is also found in this region. However, in this region especially in Gujarat and Maharashtra amongst some caste communities we find cross-cousin marriages being practised. Here there is a tendency for a man to marry his mother's brother's daughter. But marriage with the father's sister's daughter is taboo. The preference for a single type of cross-cousin marriage seems to move away from the taboo of marrying cousins of any class in the northern region. Thus, in many ways this preference suggests a closer contact with the practices of the southern region.

The southern region comprises states like Karnatak, Andhra Pradesh, Tamil Nadu and Kerala where the Dravidian languages are spoken. This region is distinct from the northern and central regions of India in the sense that here we find basically preferential rules of marriage. Here a man knows whom he has to marry while in most areas in the north a man knows whom he cannot marry.

Most of the parts of the Southern region except some, like the Malabar, follow the patrilineal family system. Here also we find exogamous social groups called *gotras.* The difference between the exogamous clans in the north is that a caste in a village is held to be of one patriclan and therefore, no marriage is allowed within a village.

Sometimes even a group of villages are supposed to be settled by one patrilineage and marriage between them is prohibited.

In the South, there is no identification of a *gotra* with one village or territory. More than one inter-marrying clans may live in one village territory and practice inter-marriage for generations. Thus the social groups; which are formed due to this kind of marriage pattern in the South shows a centripetal tendency (of moving towards a centre) as against the centrifugal (of moving away from the centre) tendency of social groups found in north Indian villages. In the South, a caste is divided in to a number of *gotras*. The first marriage creates obligations about giving and receiving daughters. Hence, within exogamous clans, small endogamous circles are found to meet inter-family obligations and a number of reciprocal alliances are found in South Indian villages.

Apart from castes, which are patrilineal in the southern region, we also find some castes, such as the Nayars of Malabar district who follow matrilineal system of kinship. Their household is made up of a woman, her sisters and brothers, her daughters and sons and her daughter's daughters and sons. Amongst them, property passes from the mother to the daughter. But the authority even in this system lies with the brother, who manages the property and takes care of his sister's children; Husbands only visit their-wives in this system. The Nayar matrilineal house is called a *Tharavad.* Nayar is a broad category of castes of which not all of them follow the same kinship system.

The relationship between the caste structure and the kinship system is so inter-twined that we cannot understand one without understanding the details of the other. In this section we have explained the regional variations found in the relationship between the caste structure and related kinship pattern.

Sub-Caste

A sub-caste is considered a smaller unit within a caste. In the village setting usually we find that there is only one sub-caste living there. A larger number of sub-castes indicate the late arrivals to a village. Thus for all practical purposes a sub-caste represents the caste in the village. In the wider setting of a region, however, we find many sub-castes. One example from Maharastra is of Kumbhar (potters). The subcaste is the smallest endogamous groups and it has some mechanisms like *panchayats* to regulate the behaviour of members in the traditional setting. In a village, the difference between caste and sub-caste does not come to the surface but in a region, the difference is visible.

Four Stages of Life

It is the *dharma* of a Hindu to pass through four different *ashram* (stages) in their life. The first Ashram is called *brahmacharya ashram* (the educational stage) from which the fourth Varna, Sudra and women of the first three varna are barred. It ends at marriage. The second stage of life is called the *grihasthashram.* During this a man rears a family, earns a living and performs his daily personal and social duties. After this a man gradually enters the third stage of life called the *vanaprashthashram.* During this stage the householder relinquishes his duties in the household, and devotes his time to religious pursuits. His links with his family are weakened. During this ashram a man retires into the forest with or without his wife leaving behind the householder's cares and duties. The final phase of Hindu's life begins with the stage known as the *sanyasashram.* In this stage one attempt to totally withdraw oneself from the world and its cares by going to the forest and spending the rest of life in pursuit of *moksha*. Like the Varna system, the *varnashram* is a model that is not compulsory but recommended.

Purushartha

The Hindu scriptures declare four goals in human life and they are called the *purushartha.* The term *purushartha* not only denotes what the objectives of life should be but it also means what the objectives of life are as the result of the psychological tendencies of the individual. The *purushartha* consists of dharma, *Artha, Kama* and *Moksha* in the same order.

First, every human being needs to obey the law of nature by strictly following dharma. Dharma is the stability of the society, the maintenance of social order, and the general welfare of mankind. And whatever conduces to the fulfilment of this purpose is called 'dharma'.

Artha is the acquisition of wealth, is regarded as the primary purpose of life, as without it, human existence is impossible. One has to live before one can live well. *Artha* is the foundation upon which the whole structure of life has been built and all the other purushrthas can be achieved only by the fulfilment of this primary purpose in life. The acquisition of wealth is through dharmic actions and wealth needs to be used in the preservation of dharma.

Kama means desires, desires of varying degrees. It is from dharma that artha and kama result. Man recognises here that *artha* and *kama* satisfy the psychological tendencies of man and they form essentially the two fundamental aspirations of every individual. It is implied what one desires need to be within the threshold of one's wealth and within dharmic values!

Now the word *moksha* means the ultimate freedom from birth and death or the deliverance of the soul from bondage. From the *advaitic* point of view, *moksha* results from the extinction of false knowledge (ignorance). The self-knowledge is the aim and end of man's misery and bondage.

In support of the realisation of self, the Upanishads outline several additional explanations. The universe has the natural tendency to guide the realisation by the human soul. The natural forces of the universe maintain the balance between the material objects, living plants, conscious animals, and intelligent human beings. The transition from human consciousness into divine (transcendental) consciousness is a long and laborious process. Ordinarily, within the span of a single lifetime, it is not feasible to transit from human to divine. Life is a continuous journey, carried over and continued through the succeeding lives till the attainment of SELF realisation.

According to Hindu *sastra-karas* (i,e,. those who have written the *sastrasm* the scientific treatises) have taken man into influence his life and its conduct: He is considered in relation to : (i) *dela,* (place, region) which may be said to be the regional approach to the study of society; (ii) *kala* (time) which, we may say, constitutes the historical approach to the study of society, (iii) *srama* (effort) which takes in to account man with reference to his nurture and development in the contemporary environment; and (iv) *guna* (natural traits), which refers to the natural inherent psycho-biological equipment of man.

In sharp contrast with such attitude, the Hindu, in his *sastric* discussions of social life and practices, first raises the fundamental question of the significance of man's existence on earth, gives consideration to basic questions of the relation between man and the possible ultimate purpose and fulfilment of his existence, and, upon such bases, seeks to define and formulate his relations with every other thing, person, event and circumstance in the world.

Thus, for the Hindu, the individual's relations with the ultimate principle of the Universal or Primal Cause defines his relations with other men, with his family, with the group or society in which he lives or with which he comes in contact, with his village and his country; and, indeed, with the entire animate and inanimate creation. The whole of the life of an individual is, for the Hindu, a kind of schooling and self-discipline. Now, during the course of this schooling and self discipline, he has to pass through four stages, four grades of training, as it were called the *Ashrams.* And, in regard to the *Ashrams*, too, every item and stage and phase has to be defined in terms of the already defined relations between man and God. Here, therefore, practically we start with supernatural basis; upon this we erect the superstructure of man's earthly career. The earthly existence has thus to be defined primarily in terms of dharma; and dharma has to be interpreted in the concrete in terms of karma. The *ashram* scheme, therefore, defines our dharma in and through a life of worldliness, of *samsara,* before it, and beyond its pale; and, in practice it seeks to delineate the implications of dharma in terms of karma. This scheme of transition from one stage to another is prescribed for men of upper castes only, women are supposed to help and support their husbands in proper fulfillment of these goals.

In order to understand the psycho-moral basis of the *ashrams* proper, it is advisable that we should look in to the theory of the *purushartha* which concern themselves with the understanding, justification, management and conduct of affairs of the individual's *purushartha* are four, viz, *dharma, artha, kama* and *moksa*. We speak of this life in relation to the group, in and through the *asramas*. The *purushartha* as the 'psycho-moral' bases of the *asrama* theory, because, on the one hand, the individual receives a psychological training through the *asramas* in terms of lessons in the use and management of the *purushartha;* while, on the other hand, in actual practice, he has to deal with the society in accordance with these lessons. It is in the light of the understanding of the meaning and place of the *purushartha* in the asrama scheme that we shall be able to comprehend the right method, way and outlook for the management of each of the asramas.

It is usual to translate these terms dharma, artha, kama and moksa in English by such words as morality, wealth, desires or passion, and salvation respectively. But the Sanskrit terms are potent with deeper meanings than these English words singly convey. Thus, the word dharma is derived from the Sanskrit root *dhri* meaning 'to hold together, to preserve.' The social implications and meaning of dharma as a principle for maintaining the stability of society is brought out by God Sri Krishna in three verses in the Mahabharata: In advising Arjuna as to what is dharma he explains that " dharma is created for the well-being of all creation", and further that "all that is free from doing harm to any created being is certainly dharma; for, indeed, dharma is created to keep all creation free from any harm" Sri Krisna proceeds, next, to give a still more comprehensive view of dharma: " Dharma is so called because it protects (dharanat) all; dharma preserves all that is created. Dharma, then, is surely that principle which is capable of preserving the universe". *Artha,* on the other hand, is to be understood as referring to all the means necessary for acquiring worldly properity, such as wealth or power. And k*ama* refers to all the desires in man for enjoyment and satisfaction of the life of the senses, including the sex drive to which the word *kama* more prominently refers. The term refers to the native impulses, instincts and desires of man, his natural mental tendencies, and finds its equivalent, we may say, in the use of the English terms "desires", "needs", "basic or primary motives", "urges", or "drives" and the collective use of the term *kama* would refer to the totality of the innate desires and drives of man. The term is also often used in a broader sense to include socially acquired motivation too. Dharma, *artha* and *kama,* therefore, refer respectively to the moral, material and mental resourees, accessories and energies available to man.

Of these three, *artha* and *kama* refer to two of man's earthly belongings, while dharma stands on a higher level. At its lowest level of manifestation, *kama* is understood in the sense of pure sex drive, and is said to be one of the six "enemies" of human being.

But it is equally true that a human being cannot conduct his life without *artha* which constitutes the material means of living, and *kama* which helps the propagation of the species. Therefore, it is needed that the correct quality and quantity, the place, and the time of *artha* and *kama*, have to be determined and laid down by the wise sages. This is done in terms of dharma, which defines, for man, the proper quantum, place and season, for the right functioning of *artha* and *kama*. By attending to his dharma, therefore, a person is able to live a proper life even though it may be lived in terms of artha and kama.

In the opinion of Manu, the good of humanity lies in a harmonious management or co-ordination of the three (*trivarga*), viz, *dharma, artha* and *kama*. Says he: "some declare that the good of man consists in dharma, and *artha*; others opine that it is to be found in *kama* and *artha;* some say that dharma alone will give it; while the rest assert that *artha* alone is the chief good of man here below (on earth). But the correct position is that the good of man consists in the harmonious co-ordination of the three".

Now, *artha* and *kama* have to be practised by the individual with reference to one or more other individuals. So also, the practice of dharma cannot be possibly conceived as existing apart from the relation between he individual and the group, except when the dharma directed is entirely in the interest of the *moksha* of the individual, as in the case of the *samnyasin* (the recluse), in whose case *artha* and *kama* become transformed and get merged in to *moksha*. Thus, on the whole, the *purusharthas* are concerned both with the individual as well as the group. They enunciate and justify the kinds of relation between the individual and the group; they define the just relations between activities of the individual and those of the group; they also state explicitly and by implication, the improper relations between the individual and the group with a view to enabling the individual to avoid them. Thus, the *purushartha* control both the individual and the group, and also their-relations.

Here, it is to be remembered that when we refer to *artha* and *kama* as *purusharthas,* we refer to them in their proper proportions, that is to say, only in the best sense of these words. *Artha* refers to the problem and activities connected with the finding, making, gathering, conserving and organising of the material necessities of life and all that accompanies the same. Similarly, *kama* refers to the sex and the reproductive aspect, its understanding, its right functions, its functioning, its organisation and management both with reference to the individual and the group. As we have pointed out above, *Kama* in the wider sense refers to all the innate desires and urges of man. Dharma seems to be the arbiter, the conscience keeper, the director, the interpreter, of the properties that govern the right functioning and management of the relations between the inner man and the outer man and between the individual and the group. Dharma is, therefore, the holder of the balance in terms of which *artha* and *kama* have to be dealt with weighed, practiced and apportioned. *Moksha,* on the other hand, seems to be concerned mainly with the individual. It refers, perhaps, to the appeal of the inner man to the individual, unaffected by the group. It is perhaps too personal an outlook that defines the struggle and hope and justification within the individual for *moksha.* But, from the Hindu's point of view, we must also remember, that the inner personality of the individual, at its best, is identified by him not only with the group, nor only with the society, nor with the nation, nor the race, nor even with he entire human race, but with the whole creation, animate and inanimate, seen and unseen, which includes all these and is still much more than all these. In the light of these considerations, the goal of *moksha* does not possess the narrow individual outlook, for the Hindu nor is it to be pursued exclusively and directly by an individual unless and until he has duly satisfied all his social debts (*rinah*) or obligations.

Purity and Pollution

Many status differences in Indian society are expressed in terms of ritual purity and pollution. Notions of purity and pollution are extremely complex and vary greatly among different castes, religious groups, and regions. However, broadly speaking, high status is associated with purity and low status with pollution. Some kinds of purity are inherent, or inborn; for example, gold is purer than copper by its very nature, and, similarly, a member of a high-ranking Brahman, or priestly, caste is born with more inherent purity than a member of a low-ranking Sweeper caste. Unless the Brahman defiles himself in some extraordinary way, throughout his life he will always be purer than a Sweeper. Other kinds of purity are more transitory—a Brahman who has just taken a bath is more ritually pure than a Brahman who has not bathed for a day. This situation could easily reverse itself temporarily, depending on bath schedules, participation in polluting activities, or contact with temporarily polluting substances.

Purity is associated with ritual cleanliness—daily bathing in flowing water, dressing in properly laundered clothes of approved materials, eating only the foods appropriate for one's caste, refraining from physical contact with people of lower rank, and avoiding involvement with ritually impure substances. The latter include body wastes and excretions, most especially those of another adult person. Contact with the products of death or violence are typically polluting and threatening to ritual purity.

During her menstrual period, a woman is considered polluted and refrains from cooking, worshiping, or touching anyone older than an infant. In much of the south, a woman spends this time "sitting outside," resting in an isolated room or shed. During her period, a Muslim woman does not touch the Quran. At the end of the period, purity is restored with a complete bath. Pollution also attaches to birth, both for the mother and the infant's close kin, and to death, for close relatives of the deceased.

Members of the highest priestly castes, the Brahmans, are generally vegetarians (although some Bengali and Maharashtrian Brahmans eat fish) and avoid eating meat, the product of violence and death. High-ranking Warrior castes (Kshatriyas), however, typically consume nonvegetarian diets, considered appropriate for their traditions of valour and physical strength.

A Brahman born of proper Brahman parents retains his inherent purity if he bathes and dresses himself properly, adheres to a vegetarian diet, eats meals prepared only by persons of appropriate rank, and keeps his person away from the bodily exuviae of others (except for necessary contact with the secretions of family infants and small children).

If a Brahman happens to come into bodily contact with a polluting substance, he can remove this pollution by bathing and changing his clothing. However, if he were to eat meat or commit other transgressions of the rigid dietary codes of his particular caste, he would be considered more deeply polluted and would have to undergo various purifying rites and payment of fines imposed by his caste council in order to restore his inherent purity.

In sharp contrast to the purity of a Brahman, a Sweeper born of Sweeper parents is considered to be born inherently polluted. The touch of his body is polluting to those higher on the caste hierarchy than he, and they will shrink from his touch, whether or not he has bathed recently. Sweepers are associated with the traditional occupation of cleaning human faeces from latrines and sweeping public lanes of all kinds of dirt. Traditionally, Sweepers remove these polluting materials in baskets carried atop the head and dumped out in a garbage pile at the edge of the village or neighbourhood. The involvement of Sweepers with such filth accords with their low-status position at the bottom of the Hindu caste hierarchy, even as their services allow high-status people, such as Brahmans, to maintain their ritual purity.

Members of the Leather-worker (Chamar) caste are ascribed a very low status consonant with their association with the caste occupation of skinning dead animals and tanning the leather. Butchers (Khatiks, in Hindi), who kill and cut up the bodies of animals, also rank low on the caste hierarchy because of their association with violence and death.

However, castes associated with ruling and warfare—and the killing and deaths of human beings—are typically accorded high rank on the caste hierarchy. In these instances, political power and wealth outrank association with violence as the key determinant of caste rank.

Maintenance of purity is associated with the intake of food and drink, not only in terms of the nature of the food itself, but also in terms of who has prepared it or touched it. This requirement is especially true for Hindus, but other religious groups hold to these principles to varying degrees. Generally, a person risks pollution—and lowering his own status—if he accepts beverages or cooked foods from the hands of people of lower caste status than his own. His status will remain intact if he accepts food or beverages from people of higher caste rank. Usually, for an observant Hindu of any but the very lowest castes to accept cooked food from a Muslim or Christian is regarded as highly polluting.

In a clear example of pollution associated with dining, a Brahman who consumed a drink of water and a meal of wheat bread with boiled vegetables from the hands of a Sweeper would immediately become polluted and could expect social rejection by his caste fellows. From that moment, fellow Brahmans following traditional pollution rules would refuse food touched by him and would abstain from the usual social interaction with him. He would not be welcome inside Brahman homes—most especially in the ritually pure kitchens—nor would he or his close relatives be considered eligible marriage partners for other Brahmans.

Generally, the acceptance of water and ordinary foods cooked in water from members of lower-ranking castes incurs the greatest pollution. In North India, such foods are known as *kaccha khana*, as contrasted with fine foods cooked in butter or oils, which are known as *pakka khana*. Fine foods can be accepted from members of a few castes slightly lower than one's own. Local hierarchies differ on the specific details of these rules.

Completely raw foods, such as uncooked grains, fresh unpeeled bananas, mangoes, and uncooked vegetables can be accepted by anyone from anyone else, regardless of relative status. Toasted or parched foods, such as roasted peanuts, can also be accepted from anyone without ritual or social repercussions. Thus, a Brahman may accept gifts of grain from lower-caste patrons for eventual preparation by members of his own caste, or he may purchase and consume roasted peanuts or tangerines from street vendors of unknown caste without worry.

Water served from an earthen pot may be accepted only from the hands of someone of higher or equal caste ranking, but water served from a brass pot may be accepted even from someone slightly lower on the caste scale. Exceptions to this rule are members of the Waterbearer (Bhoi, in Hindi) caste, who are employed to carry water from wells to the homes of the prosperous and from whose hands members of all castes may drink water without becoming polluted, even though Waterbearers are not ranked high on the caste scale.

These and a great many other traditional rules pertaining to purity and pollution constantly impinge upon interaction between people of different castes and ranks in

India. Although to the non-Indian these rules may seem irrational and bizarre, to most of the people of India they are a ubiquitous and accepted part of life. Thinking about and following purity and pollution rules make it necessary for people to be constantly aware of differences in status. With every drink of water, with every meal, and with every contact with another person, people must ratify the social hierarchy of which they are a part and within which their every act is carried out. The fact that expressions of social status are intricately bound up with events that happen to everyone every day—eating, drinking, bathing, touching, talking—and that transgressions of these rules, whether deliberate or accidental, are seen as having immediately polluting effects on the person of the transgressor, means that every ordinary act of human life serves as a constant reminder of the importance of hierarchy in Indian society.

There are many Indians, particularly among the educated urban elite, who do not follow traditional purity and pollution practices. Dining in each others' homes and in restaurants is common among well-educated people of diverse backgrounds, particularly when they belong to the same economic class. For these people, guarding the family's earthen water pot from inadvertent touch by a low-ranking servant is not the concern it is for a more traditional villager. However, even among those people whose words and actions denigrate traditional purity rules, there is often a reluctance to completely abolish consciousness of purity and pollution from their thinking. It is surely rare for a Sweeper, however well-educated, to invite a Brahman to dinner in his home and have his invitation unself-consciously accepted. It is less rare, however, for educated urban colleagues of vastly different caste and religious heritage to enjoy a cup of tea together. Some high-caste liberals pride themselves on being free of "casteism" and seek to accept food from the hands of very low-caste people, or even deliberately set out to marry someone from a significantly lower caste or a different religion. Thus, even as they deny it, these progressives affirm the continuing significance of tràditional rules of purity, pollution, and hierarchy in Indian society.

Social Interdependence

One of the great themes pervading Indian life is social interdependence. People are born into groups—families, clans, subcastes, castes, and religious communities—and live with a constant sense of being part of and inseparable from these groups. A corollary is the notion that everything a person does properly involves interaction with other people. A person's greatest dread, perhaps, is the possibility of being left alone, without social support, to face the necessary challenges of life. This sense of interdependence is extended into the theological realm: the very shape of a person's life is seen as being greatly influenced by divine beings with whom an ongoing relationship must be maintained.

Social interaction is regarded as being of the highest priority, and social bonds are expected to be long lasting. Even economic activities that might in Western culture involve impersonal interactions are in India deeply imbedded in a social nexus. All social interaction involves constant attention to hierarchy, respect, honor, the feelings of others, rights and obligations, hospitality, and gifts of food, clothing, and other desirable items. Finely tuned rules of etiquette help facilitate each individual's many social relationships.

Western visitors to India are sometimes startled to find that important government and business officials have left their posts—often for many days at a time—to attend a cousin's wedding or participate in religious activities in a distant part of the country. "He is out of station and will be back in a week or two," the absent official's office-mates blandly explain to the frustrated visitor. What is going on is not laziness or hedonistic recreation, but is the official's proper recognition of his need to continually maintain his social ties with relatives, caste fellows, other associates, and God. Without being enmeshed in such ties throughout life, a person cannot hope to maintain long-term efficacy in either economic or social endeavour. Social bonds with relatives must be reinforced at family events or at rites crucial to the religious community. If this is not done, people who could offer vital support in many phases of life would be alienated.

In every activity, there is an assumption that social ties can help a person and that their absence can bring failure. Seldom do people carry out even the simplest task on their own. From birth onward, a child learns that his "fate" has been "written" by divine forces and that his life will be shaped by a plan decided by more powerful beings. When a small child eats, his mother puts the mouthfuls of food into his mouth with her own hand. When a boy climbs a tree to pluck mangoes, another stands below with a basket to receive them. When a girl fetches water from the well in pots on her head, someone at her home helps her unload the pots. When a farmer stacks sheaves of grain onto his bullock cart, he stands atop the cart, catching the sheaves tossed up to him by his son.

A student applying to a college hopes that he has an influential relative or family friend who can put in a good word for him with the director of admissions. At the age of marriage, a young person expects that parents will take care of finding the appropriate bride or groom and arranging all the formalities. At the birth of a child, the new mother is assured that the child's kin will help her attend to the infant's needs. A businessman seeking to arrange a contract relies not only on his own abilities but also on the assistance of well-connected friends and relatives to help finalise the deal. And finally, when facing death, a person is confident that offspring and other relatives will carry out the appropriate funeral rites, including a commemorative feast when, through gifts of clothing and food, continuing social ties are reaffirmed by all in attendance.

2

Religious Communities in India

It is impossible to kno4w India without understanding its religious beliefs and practices, which have a large impact on the personal lives of most Indians and influence public life on a daily basis. Indian religions have deep historical roots that are recollected by contemporary Indians. The ancient culture of South Asia, going back at least 4,500 years, has come down to India primarily in the form of religious texts. The artistic heritage, as well as intellectual and philosophical contributions, has always owed much to religious thought and symbolism. Contacts between India and other cultures have led to the spread of Indian religions throughout the world, resulting in the extensive influence of Indian thought and practice on Southeast and East Asia in ancient times and, more recently, in the diffusion of Indian religions to Europe and North America. Within India, on a day-to-day basis, the vast majority of people engage in ritual actions that are motivated by religious systems that owe much to the past but are continuously evolving. Religion, then, is one of the most important facets of Indian history and contemporary life.

A number of world religions originated in India, and others that started elsewhere found fertile ground for growth there. Devotees of Hinduism, a varied grouping of philosophical and devotional traditions, officially numbered

687.6 million people, or 82 percent of the population in the 1991 census. Buddhism and Jainism, ancient monastic traditions, have had a major influence on Indian art, philosophy, and society and remain important minority religions in the late twentieth century. Buddhists represented 0.8 percent of the total population while Jains represented 0.4 percent in 1991.

Islam spread from the West throughout South Asia, from the early eighth century, to become the largest minority religion in India. In fact, with 101.5 million Muslims (12.1 percent of the population), India has at least the fourth largest Muslim population in the world (after Indonesia with 174.3 million, Pakistan with 124 million, and Bangladesh with 103 million; some analysts put the number of Indian Muslims even higher—128 million in 1994,[1] which would give India the second largest Muslim population in the world).

Sikhism, which started in Punjab in the sixteenth century, has spread throughout India and the world since the mid-nineteenth century. With nearly 16.3 million adherents, Sikhs represent 1.9 percent of India's population.

Christianity, represented by almost all denominations, traces its history in India back to the time of the apostles and counted 19.6 million members in India in 1991. Judaism and Zoroastrianism, arriving originally with traders and exiles from the West, are represented by small populations, mostly concentrated on India's west coast. A variety of independent tribal religious groups also are lively carriers of unique ethnic traditions.

The listing of the major belief systems only scratches the surface of the remarkable diversity in Indian religious life. The complex doctrines and institutions of the great traditions, preserved through written documents, are divided into numerous schools of thought, sects, and paths of devotion. In many cases, these divisions stem from the teachings of great masters, who arise continually to lead bands of followers with a new revelation or path to salvation. In contemporary India, the migration of large numbers of people to urban centers and the impact of modernisation have led to the emergence of new religions, revivals, and reforms within the great traditions that create original bodies of teaching and kinds of practice. In other cases, diversity appears through the integration or acculturation of entire social groups—each with its own vision of the divine—within the world of village farming communities that base their culture on literary and ritual traditions preserved in Sanskrit or in regional languages. The local interaction between great traditions and local forms of worship and belief, based on village, caste, tribal, and linguistic differences, creates a range of ritual forms and mythology that varies widely throughout the country. Within this range of differences, Indian religions have demonstrated for many centuries a considerable degree of tolerance for alternate visions of the divine and of salvation.

Religious tolerance in India finds expression in the definition of the nation as a secular state, within which the government since independence has officially remained separate from any one religion, allowing all forms of belief equal status before the law. In practice it has proven difficult to divide religious affiliation from public life. In states where the majority of the population embrace one religion, the boundary between government and religion becomes permeable; in Tamil Nadu, for example, the state government manages Hindu temples, while in Punjab an avowedly Sikh political party usually controls the state assembly. One of the most notable features of Indian politics, particularly since the 1960s, has been the steady growth of militant ideologies that see in only one religious tradition the way toward salvation and demand that public institutions conform to their interpretations of scripture. The vitality of religious fundamentalism and its impact on public life in the form of riots and religion-based political parties have been among the greatest challenges to Indian political institutions in the 1990s.

India is a land of several religious communities. As hordes of people came to India in search of fertile lands, better resources and opportunities, and to escape from cruel regimes, they also brought with them their cultures, a component of which is religion. Broadly speaking. Indian religions may be divided into two categories: first, those which are of local origin, and second, those which were introduced from other parts of the world. Under the first category, we may place Hinduism, and those religious movements that emerged on the Indian soil and later became independent religions, such as Buddhism, Jainism, and Sikhism. Placed under the second category are Zoroastrianism. Judaism, Christianity, and Islam. In India, none of them could remain isolated. Rather, continuous interactions took place (and are taking place even now) between the local religious communities and those which came from outside. From these interactions there came up composite culture of India.

We shall study the characteristics of each of the religions found in India in a time sequence, i.e., beginning with the oldest religion and moving to those that are relatively younger.

Hinduism

About eighty-three per cent of India's population is Hindu. Besides India, Hindus are found in other countries of Asia, Africa, the Caribbean Islands, Fiji, and the United Kingdom.

Hinduism is one of the most ancient religions of the world. Its roots can be traced^ back to the Indus Valley

Civilisation, around 3000 B.C. Archaeologists point out that the worship of Shiva and the mother goddess *(shakti)* came into existence in the pre-Aryan period (3000-2000 B.C.). Having such a long history, it is obvious that Hinduism has developed over a period of time and is bound to show a far greater diversity in its thoughts and practices than any other religion.

The doctrines of Hinduism are not contained in any one sacred book. Hinduism does not have a single historical founder. Hindus worship innumerable gods and goddesses. But at the same time, they also have the concept of one God, from whom everything emerges and in whom everything dissolves. At one end, if Hinduism is polytheistic (consists of many gods and goddesses), at the other, it is monotheistic (the concept of one God). It is interesting that one need not believe in the existence of god in order to be a Hindu. Contradictory beliefs are contained in Hinduism. There are no particular beliefs or practices that are common to all Hindus. Hinduism comprises a vast body of sacred literature such as the Vedas, Upanishads, Dharmashastra, Puranas, Darsanas, Agamas and Tantras, etc. These texts deal with the philosophical issues; some of them deal with the performance of rituals in temples and households. As is true of the philosophical matters, in rituals also, there is a great deal of variation.

Hinduism is intimately connected with Hindu society with the result that it is difficult to say where one ends and the other begins. Because of this, some authors say that Hinduism may be understood as a way of life. The social basis of Hinduism is found in caste system, which according to Rig Veda has a divine origin. The four social categories, called *varna,* emerged from the body *of the purusa,* the first being who was sacrificed in a ritual. Social categories that at one time were regarded as untouchable were not part of this scheme. This model of caste with four varnas known as the *chaturvarna* system.

However, in reality, there are not four but innumerable castes that are endogamous, i.e., marry within. They are known as*jatis*. Each of them has a monopoly over an occupation and claims to fall in one or the other *varna.* When Hindu sacred and legal texts speak of caste, it is mostly *varna* that they have in view and very rarely *jati.* The concepts of purity and pollution are central to Hinduism, and thus caste system, although the strictness with which they are observed differs from one caste society to another.

Certain concepts central to Hinduism are *dharma, karma,* and *moksa.* The word *dharma* means 'duty', and each individual is advised to live according to the duty laid down for one's caste, sex, and age. The net balance of good and bad deeds in previous births is called *karma.* It determines whether one will be born a human or animal, or will be released forever from the cycle of birth and death. The permanent release from the world is called *mokṣa* (salvation'), which should be the aim of every Hindu. But one should think of one's salvation after having accomplished one's household duties as successfully as possible.

In the course of its history, Hinduism has undergone many changes. Certain Hindu institutions, such as untouchability, *sati* (i.e., a woman following her husband to death), human sacrifice, female infanticide (i.e., killing of female children), were severely criticised by the British. One of the great reformers of the nineteenth century was Raja Ram Mohan Roy, who founded a religious society called Brahmo Samaj in 1828. Dayananda Saraswati, who founded Arya Samaj in 1875, also worked for a revival of Vedic Hinduism.

Vedas and Polytheism

Hinduism in India traces its source to the Vedas, ancient

hymns composed and recited in Punjab as early as 1500 B.C. Three main collections of the Vedas—the Rig, Sama, and Yajur—consist of chants that were originally recited by priests while offering plant and animal sacrifices in sacred fires. A fourth collection, the Atharva Veda, contains a number of formulas for requirements as varied as medical cures and love magic. The majority of modern Hindus revere these hymns as sacred sounds passed down to humanity from the greatest antiquity and as the source of Hindu tradition.

The vast majority of Vedic hymns are addressed to a pantheon of deities who are attracted, generated, and nourished by the offerings into the sacred flames and the precisely chanted mantras (mystical formulas of invocation) based on the hymns. Each of these deities may appear to be the supreme god in his or her own hymns, but some gods stand out as most significant. Indra, god of the firmament and lord of the weather, is the supreme deity of the Vedas. Indra also is a god of war who, accompanied by a host of storm gods, uses thunderbolts as weapons to slay the serpent demon Vritra (the name means storm cloud), thus releasing the rains for the earth. Agni, the god of fire, accepts the sacrificial offerings and transmits them to all the gods. Varuna passes judgment, lays down the law, and protects the cosmic order. Yama, the god of death, sends earthly dwellers signs of old age, sickness, and approaching mortality as exhortations to lead a moral life. Surya is the sun god, Chandra the moon god, Vayu the wind god, and Usha the dawn goddess.

Some of the later hymns of the Rig Veda contain speculations that form the basis for much of Indian religious and philosophical thought. From one perspective, the universe originates through the evolution of an impersonal force manifested as male and female principles. Other hymns describe a personal creator, Prajapati, the Lord of creatures, from whom came the heavens and the earth and all the other gods. One hymn describes the universe as emerging from the sacrifice of a cosmic man (*purusha*) who was the source of all things but who was in turn offered into the fire by gods. Within the Vedic accounts of the origin of things, there is a tension between visions of the highest reality as an impersonal force, or as a creator god, or as a group of gods with different jobs to do in the universe. Much of Hinduism tends to accept all these visions simultaneously, claiming that they are all valid as different facets of a single truth, or ranks them as explanations with different levels of sophistication. It is possible, however, to follow only one of these explanations, such as believing in a single personal god while rejecting all others, and still claim to be following the Vedas. In sum, Hinduism does not exist as a single belief system with one textual explanation of the origin of the universe or the nature of God, and a wide range of philosophies and practices can trace their beginnings somewhere in the hymns of the Vedas.

By the sixth century B.C., the Vedic gods were in decline among the people, and few people care much for Indra, Agni, or Varuna in contemporary India. These gods might appear as background characters in myths and stories about more important deities, such as Shiva or Vishnu; in some Hindu temples, there also are small statues of Vedic deities. Sacrificial fire, which once accompanied major political activities, such as the crowning of kings or the conquest of territory, still forms the heart of household rituals for many Hindus, and some Brahman families pass down the skill of memorising the hymns and make a living as professional reciters of the Vedas. One of the main legacies of Brahmanical sacrifice, seen even among traditions that later denied its usefulness, was a concentration on precise ritual actions and a belief in sacred sound as a powerful tool for manifesting the sacred in daily life

Karma and Liberation

The Upanishads, originating as commentaries on the Vedas between about 800 and 200 B.C., contain speculations on the meaning of existence that have greatly influenced Indian religious traditions. Most important is the concept of *atman* (the human soul), which is an individual manifestation of *brahman*. *Atman* is of the same nature as *brahman*, characterised either as an impersonal force or as God, and has as its goal the recognition of identity with *brahman*. This fusion is not possible, however, as long as the individual remains bound to the world of the flesh and desires. In fact, the deathless *atman* that is so bound will not join with *brahman* after the death of the body but will experience continuous rebirth. This fundamental concept of the transmigration of *atman*, or reincarnation after death, lies at the heart of the religions emerging from India.

Indian religious tradition sees karma as the source of the problem of transmigration. While associated with physical form, for example, in a human body, beings experience the universe through their senses and their minds and attach themselves to the people and things around them and constantly lose sight of their true existence as *atman*, which is of the same nature as *brahman*. As the time comes for the dropping of the body, the fruits of good and evil actions in the past remain with *atman*, clinging to it, causing a tendency to continue experience in other existences after death. Good deeds in this life may lead to a happy rebirth in a better life, and evil deeds may lead to a lower existence, but eventually the consequences of past deeds will be worked out, and the individual will seek more experiences in a physical world. In this manner, the bound or ignorant *atman* wanders from life to life, in heavens and hells and in many different bodies. The universe may expand and be destroyed numerous times, but the bound *atman* will not achieve release.

The true goal of *atman* is liberation, or release (*moksha*), from the limited world of experience and realisation of oneness with God or the cosmos. In order to achieve release, the individual must pursue a kind of discipline (yoga, a "tying," related to the English word yoke) that is appropriate to one's abilities and station in life. For most people, this goal means a course of action that keeps them rather closely tied to the world and its ways, including the enjoyment of love (*kama*), the attainment of wealth and power (*artha*), and the following of socially acceptable ethical principles. From this perspective, even manuals on sexual love, such as the *Kama Sutra* (Book of Love), or collections of ideas on politics and governance, such as the *Arthashastra* (Science of Material Gain), are part of a religious tradition that values action in the world as long as it is performed with understanding, a *karma-yoga* or selfless discipline of action in which every action is offered as a sacrifice to God. Some people, however, may be interested in breaking the cycle of rebirth in this life or soon thereafter. For them, a wide range of techniques has evolved over the thousands of years that gives Indian religion its great diversity. The discipline that involves physical positioning of the body (hatha-yoga), which is most commonly equated with yoga outside of India, sees the human body as a series of spiritual centers that can be awakened through meditation and exercise, leading eventually to a oneness with the universe. Tantrism is the belief in the Tantra (from the Sanskrit, context or continuum), a collection of texts that stress the usefulness of rituals, carried out with a strict discipline, as a means for attaining understanding and spiritual awakening. These rituals include chanting powerful mantras; meditating on complicated or auspicious diagrams (mandalas); and, for one school of advanced practitioners, deliberately violating social norms on food, drink, and sexual relations.

A central aspect of all religious discipline, regardless of its emphasis, is the importance of the guru, or teacher. Indian religion may accept the sacredness of specific texts and rituals but stresses interpretation by a living practitioner who has personal experience of liberation and can pass down successful techniques to devoted followers. In fact, since Vedic times, it has never been possible, and has rarely been desired, to unite all people in India under one concept of orthodoxy with a single authority that could be presented to everyone. Instead, there has been a tendency to accept religious innovation and diversity as the natural result of personal experience by successive generations of gurus, who have tailored their messages to particular times, places, and peoples, and then passed down their knowledge to lines of disciples and social groups. As a result, Indian religion is a mass of ancient and modern traditions, some always preserved and some constantly changing, and the individual is relatively free to stress in his or her life the beliefs and religious behaviours that seem most effective on the path to deliverance.

BUDDHISM

Buddhism began with the life of Siddhartha Gautama, a prince from the small Shakya Kingdom located in the foothills of the Himalayas in Nepal. Brought up in luxury, the prince abandoned his home and wandered forth as a religious beggar, searching for the meaning of existence. The stories of his search presuppose the Jain tradition, as Gautama was for a time a practitioner of intense austerity, at one point almost starving himself to death. He decided, however, that self-torture weakened his mind while failing to advance him to enlightenment and therefore turned to a milder style of renunciation and concentrated on advanced meditation techniques. Eventually, under a tree in the forests of Gaya (in modern Bihar), he resolved to stir no farther until he had solved the mystery of existence. Breaking through the final barriers, he achieved the knowledge that he later expressed as the Four Noble Truths: all of life is suffering; the cause of suffering is desire; the end of desire leads to the end of suffering; and the means to end desire is a path of discipline and meditation. Gautama was now the Buddha, or the awakened one, and he spent the remainder of his life traveling about northeast India converting large numbers of disciples. At the age of eighty, the Buddha achieved his final passing away (*parinirvana*) and died, leaving a thriving monastic order and a dedicated lay community to continue his work.

By the third century B.C., the still-young religion based on the Buddha's teachings was being spread throughout South Asia through the agency of the Mauryan Empire. By the seventh century A.D., having spread throughout East Asia and Southeast Asia, Buddhism probably had the largest religious following in the world.

For centuries Indian royalty and merchants patronised Buddhist monasteries and raised beautiful, hemispherical stone structures called stupas over the relics of the Buddha in reverence to his memory. Since the 1840s, archaeology has revealed the huge impact of Buddhist art, iconography, and architecture in India. The monastery complex at Nalanda in Bihar, in ruins in 1993, was a world center for Buddhist philosophy and religion until the thirteenth century. But by the thirteenth century, when Turkic invaders destroyed the remaining monasteries on the plains, Buddhism as an organised religion had practically disappeared from India. It survived only in Bhutan and Sikkim, both of which were then independent Himalayan kingdoms; among tribal groups in the mountains of northeast India; and in Sri Lanka. The reasons for this disappearance are unclear, and they are many: shifts in royal patronage from Buddhist to Hindu religious institutions; a constant intellectual struggle with dynamic Hindu intellectual schools, which eventually triumphed; and slow adoption of popular religious forms by Buddhists while Hindu monastic communities grew up with the same style of discipline as the Buddhists, leading to the slow but steady amalgamation of ideas and trends in the two religions.

Buddhism began a steady and dramatic comeback in India during the early twentieth century, spurred on originally by a combination of European antiquarian and philosophical interest and the dedicated activities of a few Indian devotees. The foundation of the Mahabodhi Society (Society of Great Enlightenment) in 1891, originally as a force to wrest control of the Buddhist shrine at Gaya from the hands of Hindu managers, gave a large stimulus to the popularisation of Buddhist philosophy and the importance of the religion in India's past.

A major breakthrough occurred in 1956 after some thirty years of Untouchable, or Dalit, agitation when Bhimrao Ramji Ambedkar, leader of the Untouchable wing within the Congress, announced that he was converting to Buddhism as a way to escape from the impediments of the Hindu caste system. He brought with him masses of Untouchables—also known as Harijansor Dalits—and members of Scheduled Castes, who mostly came from Maharashtra and border areas of neighboring states and from the Agra area in Uttar Pradesh. By the early 1990s, there were more than 5 million Buddhists in Maharashtra, or 79 percent of the entire Buddhist community in India, almost all recent converts from low castes. When added to longtime Buddhist populations in hill areas of northeast India (West Bengal, Assam, Sikkim, Mizoram, and Tripura) and high Himalayan valleys (Ladakh District in Jammu and Kashmir, Himachal Pradesh, and northern Uttar Pradesh), and to the influx of Tibetan Buddhist refugees who fled from Tibet with the Dalai Lama in 1959 and thereafter, the recent converts raised the number of Buddhists in India to 6.4 million by 1991. This was a 35.9 percent increase since 1981 and made Buddhism the fifth largest religious group in the country.

The forms of Buddhism practiced by Himalayan communities and Tibetan refugees are part of the Vajrayana, or "Way of the Lightning Bolt," that developed after the seventh century A.D. as part of Mahayana (Great Path) Buddhism. Although retaining the fundamental importance of individual spiritual advancement, the Vajrayana stresses the intercession of bodhisattvas, or enlightened beings, who remain in this world to aid others on the path.

Most other Buddhists in India follow Theravada Buddhism, the "Doctrine of the Elders," which traces its origin through Sri Lankan and Burmese traditions to scriptures in the Pali language, a Sanskritic dialect in eastern India. Although replete with miraculous events and legends, these scriptures stress a more human Buddha and a democratic path toward enlightenment for everyone. Ambedkar's plan for the expanding Buddhist congregation in India visualised Buddhist monks and nuns developing themselves through service to others. Convert communities, by embracing Buddhism, have embarked on social transformations, including a decline in alcoholism, a simplification of marriage ceremonies and abolition of ruinous marriage expenses, a greater emphasis on education, and a heightened sense of identity and self-worth.

Traditions of Enlightened Masters

A number of avowedly Hindu monastic communities have grown up over time and adopted some of the characteristics associated with early Buddhism and Jainism, while remaining dedicated to the Hindu philosophical traditions. One of the oldest and most respected of the Hindu orders traces its origin to the teacher Shankara (788-820), believed by many devotees to have lived hundreds of years earlier. Shankara's philosophy is a primary source of Vedanta, or the "End of the Veda," the final commentary on revealed truth, which is one of the most influential trends in modern Hinduism.

His interpretation of the Upanishads portrays *brahman* as absolutely one and without qualities. The phenomenal world is illusion (*maya*), which the embodied soul must transcend in order to achieve oneness with *brahman*. As a wandering monk, Shankara traveled throughout India, combating Buddhist atheism and founding five seats of learning at Badrinath (Uttar Pradesh), Dwaraka (Gujarat), Puri (Orissa), Sringeri (Karnataka), and Kanchipuram (Tamil Nadu). In the 1990s, those seats are still held by successors to Shankara's philosophy (Shankara Acharyas), who head an order of orange-clad monks that is highly respected by the Hindu community throughout India. Activities of the *acharyas*, including their periodic trips away from their home monasteries to visit and preach to devotees, receive exposure in regional and national media. Their conservative viewpoints and pronouncements on a variety of topics, although not binding on most believers, attract considerable public attention.

The initiation of a renunciant usually depends on the judgment of an *acharya* who determines whether a candidate is dedicated and prepared or not; he then gives to the disciple training and instructions including the initiate's own secret formula or mantra. After initiation, the disciple may remain with his teacher or in a monastery for an indefinite period or may wander forth in a variety of careers. The Ramanandi order in North India, for example, includes holy men (sadhus) who practice ascetic disciplines, militant members of fortified temples, and priests in charge of temple administration and ritual.

There are other orders of renunciants who lead still more austere existences, including naked ascetics who wander begging for their food and assemble for spectacular parades at major festivals. A few dedicated seekers still withdraw to the fastness of the Himalayas or other remote spots and work on their meditation and yoga in total obscurity. Others beg in populated areas, sometimes engaging in fierce austerities such as piercing their bodies with pins and knives. They are a reminder to all people that the path of renunciation waits for anyone who has the dedication and the courage to leave the world behind.

Another kind of renunciation appears in the cult of Shridi Sai Baba, who achieved national and international fame in the twentieth century. He wasa holy man (died 1918)—who appeared in 1872 in Maharashtra and lived a humble life that blended meditation and devotional techniques from a variety of sources. This saint has a small but dedicated following throughout India.

A later saint was Satya Narayana Raju, who renamed himself as Satya Sai Baba, born in 1926 in Andhra Pradesh. At age thirteen, he experienced the first of several seizures that resulted in a changed personality and intense devotional activity, leading to his statement that he is the second incarnation of Sai Baba. By 1950 he had set up a retreat at Puttaparti in what later became Andhra Pradesh and was accepting disciples. His fame spread along with numerous apocryphal stories of his ability to perform miracles. The cult has expanded to include publishing, social service, and education institutions and includes an international association of thousands of believers.

Jainism

The oldest continuous monastic tradition in India is Jainism, the path of the Jinas, or victors. This tradition is traced to Vardhamana Mahavira (599-527 B.C.), the twenty-fourth and last of the Tirthankaras (Sanskrit for fordmakers). According to legend, Mahavira was born to a ruling family in the town of Vaishali, located in the modern state of Bihar. At the age of thirty, he renounced his wealthy life and devoted himself to fasting and self-mortification in order to purify his consciousness and discover the meaning of existence. He never again dwelt in a house, owned property, or wore clothing of any sort. Following the example of the teacher Parshvanatha (ninth century B.C.), he attained enlightenment and spent the rest of his life meditating and teaching a dedicated group of disciples who formed a monastic order following rules he laid down. His life's work complete, he entered a final fast and deliberately died of starvation.

The ancient belief system of the Jains rests on a concrete understanding of the working of karma, its effects on the living soul (*jiva*), and the conditions for extinguishing action and the soul's release. According to the Jain view, the soul is a living substance that combines with various kinds of nonliving matter and through action accumulates particles of matter that adhere to it and determine its fate. Most of the matter perceptible to human senses, including all animals and plants, is attached in various degrees to living souls and is in this sense alive. Any action has consequences that necessarily follow the embodied soul, but the worst accumulations of matter come from violence against other living beings. The ultimate Jain discipline, therefore, rests on complete inactivity and absolute nonviolence (ahimsa) against any living beings. Some Jain monks and nuns wear face masks to avoid accidently inhaling small organisms, and all practicing believers try to remain vegetarians. Extreme renunciation, including the refusal of all food, lies at the heart of a discipline that purges the mind and body of all desires and actions and, in the process, burns off the consequences of actions performed in the past. In this sense,

Jain renunciants may recognise or revere deities, but they do not view the Vedas as sacred texts and instead concentrate on the atheistic, individual quest for purification and removal of karma. The final goal is the extinguishing of self, a "blowing out" (nirvana) of the individual self.

By the first century A.D., the Jain community evolved into two main divisions based on monastic discipline: the Digambara or "sky-clad" monks who wear no clothes, own nothing, and collect donated food in their hands; and the Svetambara or "white-clad" monks and nuns who wear white robes and carry bowls for donated food. The Digambara do not accept the possibility of women achieving liberation, while the Svetambara do. Western and southern India have been Jain strongholds for many centuries; laypersons have typically formed minority communities concentrated primarily in urban areas and in mercantile occupations. In the mid-1990s, there were about 7 million Jains, the majority of whom live in the states of Maharashtra (mostly the city of Bombay, or Mumbai in Marathi), Rajasthan, and Gujarat. Karnataka, traditionally a stronghold of Digambaras, has a sizable Jain community.

The Jain laity engage in a number of ritual activities that resemble those of the Hindus around them. Special shrines in residences or in public temples include images of the Tirthankaras, who are not worshiped but remembered and revered; other shrines house the gods who are more properly invoked to intercede with worldly problems. Daily rituals may include meditation and bathing; bathing the images; offering food, flowers, and lighted lamps for the images; and reciting mantras in Ardhamagadhi, an ancient language of northeast India related to Sanskrit. Many Jain laity engage in sacramental ceremonies during life-cycle rituals, such as the first taking of solid food, marriage, and death, resembling those enacted by Hindus. Jains may also worship local gods and participate in local Hindu or Muslim celebrations without compromising their fundamental devotion to the path of the Jinas. The most important festivals of Jainism celebrate the five major events in the life of Mahavira: conception, birth, renunciation, enlightenment, and final release at death.

At a number of pilgrimage sites associated with great teachers of Jainism, the gifts of wealthy donors made possible the building of architectural wonders. Shatrunjaya Hills (Siddhagiri) in Gujarat is a major Svetambara site, an entire city of about 3,500 temples. Mount Abu in Rajasthan, with one Digambara and five Svetambara temples, is the site of some of India's greatest architecture, dating from the eleventh through thirteenth centuries A.D. In Karnataka, on the hill of Sravana Belgola, stands the monolithic seventeen-meter-high statue of the naked Bhagwan Bahubali (Gomateshvara), the first person in the world believed by the faithful to have attained enlightenment, so deep in meditation that vines are growing around his legs. At this site every twelve years, a major concourse of Jain ascetics and laity participate in a purification ceremony in which the statue is anointed from head to toe. Carved in 981, the statue is considered the holiest Jain shrine. In addition to its lavish patronage of shrines, the Jain community, with its long scriptural tradition and wealth gained from trade, has always been known for its philanthropy and especially for its support of education and learning. Prestigious Jain schools are located in most major cities. The largest concentrations of Jains are in Maharashtra (more than 965,000) and Rajasthan (nearly 563,000), with sizable numbers also in Gujarat and Madhya Pradesh.

SIKHISM

Sikhism has about 20 million believers worldwide but has an importance far beyond those numbers because Sikhs have played a disproportionately large role in the armed forces and public affairs in India for the last 400 years. Although most Indian Sikhs (79 percent) remain concentrated in the state of Punjab, nearly 3.5 million Sikhs live outside the state, while about 4 million live abroad. This Sikh diaspora, driven by ambition and economic success, has made Sikhism a world religion as well as a significant minority force within the country.

Early History

Sikhism began with Guru Nanak (1469-1539), a member of a trading caste in Punjab who seems to have been employed for some time as a government servant, was married and had two sons, and at age forty-five became a religious teacher. At the heart of his message was a philosophy of universal love, devotion to God, and the equality of all men and women before God. He set up congregations of believers who ate together in free communal kitchens in an overt attempt to break down caste boundaries based on food prohibitions. As a poet, musician, and enlightened master, Nanak's reputation spread, and by the time he died he had founded a new religion of "disciples" (*shiksha* or sikh) that followed his example.

Nanak's son, Baba Sri Chand, founded the Udasi sect of celibate ascetics, which continued in the 1990s. However, Nanak chose as his successor not his son but Angad (1504-52), his chief disciple, to carry on the work as the second guru. Thus began a lineage of teachers that lasted until 1708 and amounted to ten gurus in the Sikh tradition, each of whom is viewed as an enlightened master who propounded directly the word of God. The third guru, Amar Das (1479-1574), established missionary centers to spread the message and was so well respected that the Mughal emperor Akbar visited him. Amar Das appointed his son-in-law Ram Das (1534-81) to succeed him, establishing a hereditary succession for the position of guru. He also built a tank for water at Amritsar in Punjab, which, after his death, became the holiest center of Sikhism.

By the late sixteenth century, the influence of the Sikh religion on Punjabi society was coming to the notice of political authorities. The fifth guru, Arjun Das (1563-1606), was executed in Lahore by the Mughal emperor Jahangir (1605-27) for alleged complicity in a rebellion. In response, the next guru, Hargobind (d. 1644), militarised and politicised his position and fought three battles with Mughal forces. Hargobind established a militant tradition of resistance to persecution by the central government in Delhi that remains an important motif in Sikh consciousness. Hargobind also established at Amritsar, in front of the Golden Temple, the central shrine devoted to Sikhism, the Throne of the Eternal God (Akal Takht) from which the guru dispensed justice and administered the secular affairs of the community, clearly establishing the tradition of a religious state that remains a major issue. The ninth guru, Tegh Bahadur (1621-75), because he refused Mughal emperor Aurangzeb's order to convert to Islam, was brought to Delhi and beheaded on a site that later became an important *gurdwara* (abode of the guru, a Sikh temple) on Chandni Chauk, one of the old city's main thoroughfares.

These events led the tenth guru, Gobind Singh (1666-1708), to transform the Sikhs into a militant brotherhood dedicated to defense of their faith at all times. He instituted a baptism ceremony involving the immersion of a sword in sugared water that initiates Sikhs into the Khalsa (*khalsa*, from the Persian term for "the king's own," often taken to mean army of the pure) of dedicated devotion. The outward signs of this new order were the "Five Ks" to be observed at all times: uncut hair (*kesh*), a long knife (*kirpan*), a comb (*kangha*), a steel bangle (*kara*), and a special kind of breeches not reaching below the knee (*kachha*). Male Sikhs took on the surname Singh (meaning lion), and women took the surname Kaur (princess). All made vows to purify their personal behaviour by avoiding intoxicants, including alcohol and tobacco. In modern India, male Sikhs who have dedicated themselves to the Khalsa do not cut their beards and keep their long hair tied up under turbans, preserving a distinctive personal appearance recognised throughout the world.

Much of Guru Gobind Singh's later life was spent on the move, in guerrilla campaigns against the Mughal Empire, which was entering the last days of its effective authority under Aurangzeb (1658-1707). After Gobind Singh's death, the line of gurus ended, and their message continued through the *Adi Granth* (Original Book), which dates from 1604 and later became known as the *Guru Granth Sahib* (Holy Book of the Gurus). The *Guru Granth Sahib* is revered as a continuation of the line of gurus and as the living word of God by all Sikhs and stands at the heart of all ceremonies.

Most of the Sikh gurus were excellent musicians, who composed songs that conveyed their message to the masses in the saints' own language, which combined variants of Punjabi with Hindi and Braj and also contained Arabic and Persian vocabulary. Written in Gurmukhi script, these songs are one of the main sources of early Punjabi language and literature. There are 5,894 hymns in all, arranged according to the musical measure in which they are sung. An interesting feature of this literature is that 937 songs and poems are by well-known *bhakti* saints who were not members of the lineage of Sikh gurus, including the North Indian saint Kabir and five Muslim devotees. In the *Guru Granth Sahib*, God is called by all the Hindu names and by Allah as well. From its beginnings, then, Sikhism was an inclusive faith that attempted to encompass and enrich other Indian religious traditions.

The belief system propounded by the gurus has its origins in the philosophy and devotions of Hinduism and Islam, but the formulation of Sikhism is unique. God is the creator of the universe and is without qualities or differentiation in himself. The universe (*samsar*) is not sinful in its origin but is covered with impurities; it is not suffering, but a transitory opportunity for the soul to recognise its true nature and break the cycle of rebirth. The unregenerate person is dominated by self-interest and remains immersed in illusion (*maya*), leading to bad karma. Meanwhile, God desires that his creatures escape and achieve enlightenment (nirvana) by recognising his order in the universe. He does this by manifesting his grace as a holy word, attainable through recognition and recitation of God's holy name (*nam*). The role of the guru, who is the manifestation of God in the world, is to teach the means for prayer through the *Guru Granth Sahib* and the community of believers. The guru in this system, and by extension the *Guru Granth Sahib*, are coexistent with the divine and play a decisive role in saving the world.

Where the *Guru Granth Sahib* is present, that place becomes a *gurdwara*. Many Sikh homes contain separate rooms or designated areas where a copy of the book stands as the center of devotional ceremonies. Throughout Punjab, or anywhere there is a substantial body of believers, there are special shrines where the *Guru Granth Sahib* is displayed permanently or is installed daily in a ceremonial manner. These public *gurdwaras* are the centers of Sikh community life and the scene of periodic assemblies for worship. The typical assembly involves group singing from the *Guru Granth Sahib*, led by distinguished believers or professional singers attached to the shrine, distribution of holy food, and perhaps a sermon delivered by the custodian of the shrine.

As for domestic and life-cycle rituals, well into the twentieth century many Sikhs followed Hindu customs for birth, marriage, and death ceremonies, including readings from Hindu scriptures and the employment of Brahmans as officiants. Reform movements within the Sikh community have purged many of these customs, substituting instead readings from the *Guru Granth Sahib* as the focus for rituals and the employment of Sikh ritual specialists. At major public events—weddings, funerals, or opening a new business—patrons may fund a reading of the entire *Guru Granth Sahib* by special reciters.

Twentieth-Century Developments

The existence of the Khalsa creates a potential division within the Sikh community between those who have undergone the baptism ceremony and those who practice the system laid down in the *Guru Granth Sahib* but who do not adopt the distinctive life-style of the Khalsa. Among the latter is a sect of believers founded by Baba Dayal named the Nirankaris, who concentrate on the formless quality of God and his revelation purely through the guru and the *Guru Granth Sahib*, and who accept the existence of a living, enlightened teacher as essential for spiritual development. The dominant tendency among the Sikhs since the late nineteenth century has been to stress the importance of the Khalsa and its outward signs.

Revivalist movements of the late nineteenth century centered on the activities of the Singh Sabha (Assembly of Lions), who successfully moved much of the Sikh community toward their own ritual systems and away from Hindu customs, and culminated in the Akali (eternal) mass movement in the 1920s to take control of *gurdwaras* away from Hindu managers and invest it in an organisation representing the Sikhs. The result was passage of the Sikh Gurdwara Act of 1925, which established the Central

Gurdwara Management Committee to manage all Sikh shrines in Punjab, Haryana, and Himachal Pradesh through an assembly of elected Sikhs. The combined revenues of hundreds of shrines, which collected regular contributions and income from endowments, gave the committee a large operating budget and considerable authority over the religious life of the community. A simultaneous process led to the Akali Dal (Eternal Party), a political organisation that originally coordinated nonviolent agitations to gain control over *gurdwaras*, then participated in the independence struggle, and since 1947 has competed for control over the Punjab state government. The ideology of the Akali Dal is simple—single-minded devotion to the guru and preservation of the Sikh faith through political power—and the party has served to mobilise a majority of Sikhs in Punjab around issues that stress Sikh separatism.

There is no official priesthood within Sikhism or any widely accepted institutional mechanism for policy making for the entire faith. Instead, decisions are made by communities of believers (*sangat*) based on the *Guru Granth Sahib* —a tradition dating back to the eighteenth century when scattered bodies of believers had to fight against persecution and manage their own affairs. Anyone may study the scriptures intensively and become a "knower" (*giani*) who is recognised by fellow believers, and there is a variety of training institutes with full-time students and teachers.

Leaders of sects and sectarian training institutions may feel free to issue their own orders. When these orders are combined with the prestige and power of the Central Gurdwara Management Committee and the Akali Dal, which have explicitly narrow administrative goals and are often faction-ridden, a mixture of images and authority emerges that often leaves the religion as a whole without clear leadership. Thus it became possible for Sant Jarnail Singh

Bhindranwale, head of a training institution, to stand forth as a leading authority on the direction of Sikhism; initiate reforms of personal morality; participate in the persecution of Nirankaris; and take effective control of the holiest Sikh shrine, the Golden Temple in Amritsar, Punjab, in the early 1980s. His takeover of the Golden Temple led to a violent siege and culminated in the devastation of the shrine by the army in 1984. Later terrorist activities in Punjab, carried out in the name of Sikhism, were performed by a wide range of organisations claiming to represent an authoritative vision of the nature and direction of the community as a whole.

ISLAM

Islam is India's largest minority religion, with Muslims officially comprising 12.1 percent of the country's population, or 101.6 million people as of the 1991 census. The largest concentrations—about 52 percent of all Muslims in India—live in the states of Bihar (12 million), West Bengal (16 million), and Uttar Pradesh (24 million), according to the 1991 census. Muslims represent a majority of the local populations only in Jammu and Kashmir (not tabulated in 1991 but 65 percent in 1981) and Lakshadweep (94 percent). As a faith with its roots outside South Asia, Islam also offers some striking contrasts to those religions that originated in India.

Origins and Tenets

Islam began with the ministry of the Prophet Muhammad (570-632), who belonged to a merchant family in the trading town of Mecca in Arabia. In his middle age, Muhammad received visions in which the Archangel Gabriel revealed the word of God to him. After 620 he publicly preached the message of these visions, stressing the oneness of God (Allah), denouncing the polytheism of his fellow Arabs, and calling for moral uplift of the population. He attracted a dedicated band of followers, but there was intense opposition from the leaders of the city, who profited from pilgrimage trade to the shrine called the Kaaba. In 622 Muhammad and his closest supporters migrated to the town of Yathrib (now renamed Medina) to the north and set up a new center of preaching and opposition to the leadership of Mecca. This move, the hijrah or hegira, marks the beginning of the Islamic calendar and the origin of the new religion of Islam. After a series of military engagements, Muhammad and his followers were able to defeat the authorities in Mecca and return to take control of the city. Before his death in 632, Muhammad was able to bring most of the tribes of Arabia into the fold of Islam. Soon after his death, the united Arabs conquered present-day Syria, Iraq, Egypt, and Iran, making Islam into a world religion by the end of the seventh century.

Islam means submission to God, and a Muslim is one who has submitted to the will of God. At the center of the religion is an intense concentration on the unity of God and the separation between God and his creatures. No physical representation of God is allowed. There are no other gods. The duty of humanity is to profess the simple testimony: "There is no god but God (Allah), and Muhammad is his Prophet." Obedience to God's will rests on following the example of the Prophet in one's own life and faithfulness to the revelations collected into the most sacred text, the Quran. The Five Pillars of Islam are reciting the profession of faith; praying five times a day; almsgiving to the poor; fasting (abstaining from dawn to dusk from food, drink, sexual relations, and smoking) during the month of Ramazan (the ninth month of the Islamic calendar, known as Ramadan in Arab countries), the holy month when God's revelations were received by Muhammad; and making the pilgrimage (hajj) to Mecca at least once during one's life if possible. People who obey God's commandments and live a good life will go to heaven after death; those who disobey will go to hell. All souls will be resurrected for a last judgment at the end of the world. Muslims view themselves as followers of the same tradition preserved in the Judaic and Christian scriptures, accept the prophetic roles of Ibrahim (Abraham), Musa (Moses), and Isa (Jesus), and view Islam as the final statement of revealed truth for the entire world.

Regulation of the Muslim community rests primarily on rules in the Quran, then on authenticated tales of the conduct (*sunna*) of the Prophet Muhammad, then on reasoning, and finally on the consensus of opinion. By the end of the eighth century, four main schools of Muslim jurisprudence had emerged in Sunni Islam to interpret the sharia (Islamic law). Prominent among these groups was the Hanafi school, which dominated most of India, and the Shafii school, which was more prevalent in South India. Because Islam has no ordained priesthood, direction of the Muslim community rests on the learning of religious scholars (ulama) who are expert in understanding the Quran and its appended body of commentaries.

Early leadership controversies within the Muslim community led to divisions that still have an impact on the body of believers. When Muhammad died, leadership fell to his father-in-law, Abu Bakr, who became the first caliph (*khalifa*, or successor), a position that combined spiritual and secular power. A separate group advocated the leadership of Ali, the cousin and son-in-law of the Prophet, who had married his daughter Fatima. Leadership could have fallen to Ali's son Husayn, but, in the power struggle that followed, in 680 Husayn and seventy-two followers were murdered at Karbala (now in modern Iraq).

This leadership dispute formed the most crucial dividing point in Islamic history: the victorious party went on to found the Umayyad Dynasty (661-750), which had its headquarters at Damascus, leading the majority of Muslims in the Sunni path. The disaffected Shiat Ali (or Party of Ali) viewed only his line as legitimate and continued to follow descendants of Husayn as their leader. Among the followers of this Shiapath, there is a party of "Seveners" who trace the lineage of imams down to Ismail, the Seventh Imam and eldest son of the Sixth Imam. The Ismailis are the largest Shia group in India, and are concentrated in Maharashtra and Gujarat. A second group, the "Twelvers" (the most numerous Shia group worldwide), traces the lineage of imams through twelve generations, believing that the last or Twelfth Imam became "hidden" and will reappear in the world as a saviour, or Mahdi, at some time in the future.

The division between Sunni and Shia dates back to purely political struggles in the seventh century, but over time between the two major communities many divisive differences in ritual and legal interpretations have evolved. The vast majority of Muslims are Sunni, and in contemporary India 90 percent of Muslims follow this path. Sunnis have recognised no legitimate caliph after the position was abolished in Turkey in 1924, placing the direction of the community clearly with the ulama.

Public worship for the average Muslim consists of going to a mosque (*masjid*)—normally on Fridays, although mosques are well attended throughout the week—for congregational prayers led by a local imam, following the public call to prayer, which may be intoned from the top of a minaret (*minar*) at the mosque. After leaving their footwear at the door, men and women separate; men usually sit in front, women in back, either inside the mosque or in an open courtyard. The prayer leader gives a sermon in the local regional language, perhaps interspersed with Arabic or Farsi (sometimes called Persian or Parsi) quotations, depending on his learning and the sophistication of the audience. Announcements of events of interest that may include political commentary are often included. Then follow common prayers that involve responses from the worshipers who stand, bow, and kneel in unison during devotions.

Islamic Traditions in India

Muslims practice a series of life-cycle rituals that differ from those of Hindus, Jains, or Buddhists. The newborn baby has the call to prayer whispered into the left ear, the profession of faith whispered into the right ear, honey or date paste placed in the mouth, and a name selected. On the sixth day after birth, the first bath occurs. On the seventh day or a multiple of the seventh, the head is shaved, and alms are distributed, ideally in silver weighing as much as the hair; a sacrifice of animals imitates the sheep sacrificed instead of Ishmael (Ismail) in biblical times. Religious instruction starts at age four years, four months, and four days, beginning with the standard phrase: "In the name of God, the Beneficent, the Merciful." Male circumcision takes place between the ages of seven and twelve. Marriage requires a payment by the husband to the wife and the solemnisation of a marital contract in a social gathering. Marriage ceremonies include the donning of a nose ring by the bride, or in South India a wedding necklace, and the procession of the bridegroom. In a traditional wedding, males and females attend ceremonies in different rooms, in keeping with the segregation of sexes in most social settings. After death the family members wash and enshroud the body, after which it is buried as prayers from the Quran are recited. On the third day, friends and relatives come to console the bereaved, read the Quran, and pray for the soul of the deceased. The family observe a mourning period of up to forty days.

The annual festivals of Islam are based on a lunar calendar of 354 days, which makes the Islamic holy year independent of the Gregorian calendar. Muslim festivals make a complete circuit of the solar year every thirty-three years.

The beginning of the Islamic calendar is the month of Muharram, the tenth day of which is Ashura, the anniversary of the death of Husayn, the son of Ali. Ashura, a major holiday, is of supreme importance for the Shia. Devotees engage in ritualised mourning that may include processions of colorful replicas of Husayn's tomb at Karbala and standards with palms on top, which are carried by barefoot mourners and buried at an imitation Karbala. In many areas of India, these parades provide a dramatic spectacle that draws large numbers of non-Muslim onlookers. Demonstrations of grief may include bouts of self-flagellation that can draw blood and may take place in public streets, although many families retain personal mourning houses. Sunni Muslims may also commemorate Husayn's death but in a less demonstrative manner, concentrating instead on the redemptive aspect of his martyrdom.

The last day of Ramazan is Id al Fitr (Feast of Breaking the Fast), another national holiday, which ends the month of fasting with almsgiving, services in mosques, and visits to friends and neighbors. Bakr Id, or Id al Zuha (Feast of Sacrifice), begins on the tenth day of the Islamic month of Dhul Hijjah and is a major holiday. Prescribed in the Quran, Id al Zuha commemorates Ibrahim's willingness to sacrifice Ishmael (rather than Ishaq—Isaac—as in the Judeo-Christian tradition) according to God's command, but it is also the high point of the pilgrim's ritual cycle while on the hajj in Mecca. All of these festivals involve large feasts, gifts given to family and neighbors, and the distribution of food for charitable purposes.

A significant aspect of Islam in India is the importance of shrines attached to the memory of great Sufi saints.

Sufism is a mystical path (*tariqat*) as distinct from the path of the sharia. A Sufi attains a direct vision of oneness with God, often on the edges of orthodox behaviour, and can thus become a *pir* (living saint) who may take on disciples (*murids*) and set up a spiritual lineage that can last for generations. Orders of Sufis became important in India during the thirteenth century following the ministry of Muinuddin Chishti (1142-1236), who settled in Ajmer, Rajasthan, and attracted large numbers of converts to Islam because of his holiness. His Chishtiyya order went on to become the most influential Sufi lineage in India, although other orders from Central Asia and Southwest Asia also reached to India and played a large role in the spread of Islam. Many Sufis were well known for weaving music, dance, intoxicants, and local folktales into their songs and lectures. In this way, they created a large literature in regional languages that embedded Islamic culture deeply into older South Asian traditions.

In the case of many great teachers, the memory of their holiness has been so intense that they are still viewed as active intercessors with God, and their tombs have become the site of rites and prayers by disciples and lay people alike. Tales of miraculous deeds associated with the tombs of great saints have attracted large numbers of pilgrims attempting to gain cures for physical maladies or solutions to personal problems. The tomb of the *pir* thus becomes a *dargah* (gateway) to God and the focus for a wide range of rituals, such as daily washing and decoration by professional attendants, touching or kissing the tomb or contact with the water that has washed it, hanging petitions on the walls of the shrine surrounding the tomb, lighting incense, and giving money.

The descendants of the original *pir* are sometimes seen as inheritors of his spiritual energy, and, as *pirs* in their own right, they might dispense amulets sanctified by contact with them or with the tomb. The annual celebration of the *pir* 's death is a major event at important shrines, attracting hundreds of thousands of devotees for celebrations that may last for days. Free communal kitchens and distribution of sweets are also big attractions of these festivals, at which Muslim fakirs, or wandering ascetics, sometimes appear and where public demonstrations of self-mortification, such as miraculous piercing of the body and spiritual possession of devotees, sometimes occur. Every region of India can boast of at least one major Sufi shrine that attracts expressive devotion, which remains important, especially for Muslim women.

The leadership of the Muslim community has pursued various directions in the evolution of Indian Islam during the twentieth century. The most conservative wing has typically rested on the education system provided by the hundreds of religious training institutes (*madrasa*) throughout the country, which have tended to stress the study of the Quran and Islamic texts in Arabic and Persian, and have focused little on modern managerial and technical skills. Several national movements have emerged from this sector of the Muslim community. The Jamaati Islami (Islamic Party), founded in 1941, advocates the establishment of an overtly Islamic government through peaceful, democratic, and nonmissionary activities. It had about 3,000 active members and 40,000 sympathisers in the mid-1980s. The Tablighi Jamaat (Outreach Society) became active after the 1940s as a movement, primarily among the ulama, stressing personal renewal, prayer, a missionary and cooperative spirit, and attention to orthodoxy. It has been highly critical of the kind of activities that occur in and around Sufi shrines and remains a minor if respected force in the training of the ulama. Other ulama have upheld the legitimacy of mass religion, including exaltation of *pirs* and the memory of the Prophet. A powerful secularising drive led to the founding of Aligarh Muslim University (founded in 1875 as the

Muhammadan Anglo-Oriental College)—with its modern curriculum—and other major Muslim universities. This educational drive has remained the most dominant force in guiding the Muslim community.

ZOROASTRIANISM

According to the 1991 census, there were 79,382 members of the Zoroastrian faith. Some 79 percent lived in Maharashtra (primarily in Bombay) and most of the rest in Gujarat. Zoroastrians are primarily descendants of tenth-century immigrants from Persia who preserved the religion of Zoroaster, a prophet of Iran who taught probably in the sixth century B.C. Although the number of Parsis steadily declined during the twentieth century as a result of emigration and low birth rates, their religion is significant because of the financial influence wielded by this mostly trading community and because they represent the world's largest surviving group of believers in this ancient faith.

Originally, the Parsis were shipbuilders and traders located in the ports and towns of Gujarat. Their freedom from food or occupational restrictions based on caste affiliation enabled them to take advantage of the numerous commercial opportunities that accompanied the colonial expansion of trade and control. Substantial numbers moved to Bombay, which served as a base for expanding their business activities throughout India and abroad. A combination of Western commercial contacts and English-language education during the colonial period made the Parsis arguably the most cosmopolitan community in India. Socially, they were equally at home with Indians and Westerners; Parsi women enjoyed freedom of movement earlier than most high-caste Hindu or upper-class Muslim women. In contemporary India, Parsis are the most urban, elite, and wealthy of any of the nation's religious groups. Their role in the development of trade, industry, finance, and philanthropy has earned them an important place in the country's social and economic life, and several have achieved high rank in government.

The source of Parsi religion is a body of texts called the *Avesta*, which includes a number of sections in archaic language attributed to Zoroaster himself, and which preserve the cult of the fire sacrifice as the focus of ritual life. The supreme spirit is Ahura Mazda (or Ohrmazd), whose will is manifest in the world through the actions of bountiful immortals or good spiritual attributes that support life and love. Opposing the supreme spirit is the force of evil, Angra Mainyu (or Ahriman), which is the cause of all destruction and corruption in the world. Equipped with free will, humans can choose sides in this struggle and after death will appear at the bridge of judgment. People who choose to do good deeds go to heaven, those who commit evil go to hell. The opposed cosmic forces battle through the history of the universe, until at the end of time there will be a final judgment and a resurrection of the dead to a perfect world.

The extensive ritual life of devout Parsis revolves around sacred fires, of which there are three grades dependent on extensive ceremonial preparation. The highest two grades can only be maintained in fire temples by hereditary priests, who undergo extensive purificatory rites and wear special face masks to prevent polluting the flames with breath or saliva, while the third grade of fire can exist in the household. The most important rite for most lay people is the Navjote, which occurs between the seventh and fifteenth year of life, and initiates the young person into the adult community. The ceremony involves purifying bathing, reciting *Avesta*-based scriptures, and being invested with a sacred shirt (*sudrah*) and waist thread (*kusti*) that should always be worn thereafter. Marriage is also an important rite, complete with scriptural recitations. At death, great care is taken to avoid pollution from the body, and funeral services usually take place within twenty-four hours. The dead are then disposed of by exposure to vultures on large, circular "towers of silence" (*dakhma*). Most rituals take place in the home or in special pavilions; congregational worship at fire temples is limited to spring and autumn festivals.

The towns of Sanjan, Nausari, and Udvada in Gujarat are of prime importance to Parsis, having long served as community centers before mass migration to Bombay in the nineteenth century. Bombay is home to 70 percent of India's Parsis, where the management of Parsi affairs rests in the hands of a *panchayat*, the assembly that serves as a charitable and educational organisation providing a comprehensive social welfare system at the local level.

JUDAISM

Trade contacts between the Mediterranean region and the west coast of India probably led to the presence of small Jewish settlements in India as long ago as the early first millennium B.C. In Kerala a community of Jews tracing its origin to the fall of Jerusalem in A.D. 70 has remained associated with the cities of Cranganore and Kochi (formerly known as Cochin) for at least 1,000 years. The Pardesi Synagogue in Kochi, rebuilt in 1568, is in the architectural style of Kerala but preserves the archaic ritual style of the Sephardic rite, with Babylonian and Yemenite influence as well. The Jews of Kochi, concentrated mostly in the old "Jew Town," were completely integrated into local culture, speaking Malayalam and taking local names while preserving their knowledge of Hebrew and contacts with Southwest Asia. A separate community of Jews, called the Bene Israel, had lived along the Konkan Coast in and around Bombay, Pune, and Ahmadabad for almost 2,000 years. Unlike the Kochi Jews, they became a village-based society and maintained little contact with other Jewish communities. They always remained within the orthodox Jewish fold, practicing the Sephardic rite without rabbis, with the synagogue as the center of religious and cultural life. A third group of Jews immigrated to India, beginning at the end of the eighteenth century, following the trade contacts established by the British Empire. These Baghdad Jews came mostly from the area of modern Iraq and settled in Bombay and Calcutta, where many of them became wealthy and participated in the economic leadership of these growing cities.

The population of the Kochi Jews, always small, had decreased from 5,000 in 1951 to about fifty in the early 1990s. During the same period, the Bene Israel decreased from about 20,000 to 5,000, while the Baghdad Jews declined from 5,000 to 250. Emigration to Australia, Israel, Britain, and North America accounts for most of this decline. According to the 1981 Indian census, there were 5,618 Jews in India, down from 5,825 in 1971. The 1991 census showed a further decline to 5,271, most of whom lived in Maharashtra and Mizoram

CHRISTIANITY

The first Christians in India, according to tradition and legend, were converted by Saint Thomas the Apostle, who arrived on the Malabar Coast of India in A.D. 52. After evangelising and performing miracles in Kerala and Tamil Nadu, he is believed to have been martyred in Madras and buried on the site of San Thomé Cathedral. Members of the Syro-Malabar Church, an eastern rite of the Roman Catholic Church, adopted the Syriac liturgy dating from fourth century Antioch. They practiced what is also known as the Malabar rite until the arrival of the Portuguese in the late fifteenth century. Soon thereafter, the Portuguese attempted to latinise the Malabar rite, an action which, by the mid-sixteenth century, led to charges of heresy against the Syro-

Malabar Church and a lengthy round of political machinations. By the middle of the next century, a schism occurred when the adherents of the Malankar rite (or Syro-Malankara Church) broke away from the Syro-Malabar Church. Fragmentation continued within the Syro-Malabar Church up through the early twentieth century when a large contingent left to join the Nestorian Church, which had had its own roots in India since the sixth or seventh century. By 1887, however, the leaders of the Syro-Malabar Church had reconciled with Rome, which formally recognised the legitimacy of the Malabar rite. The Syro-Malankara Church was reconciled with Rome in 1930 and, while retaining the Syriac liturgy, adopted the Malayalam language instead of the ancient Syriac language.

Throughout this period, foreign missionaries made numerous converts to Christianity. Early Roman Catholic missionaries, particularly the Portuguese, led by the Jesuit Saint Francis Xavier (1506-52), expanded from their bases on the west coast making many converts, especially among lower castes and outcastes. The miraculously undecayed body of Saint Francis Xavier is still on public view in a glass coffin at the Basilica of Bom Jesus in Goa. Beginning in the eighteenth century, Protestant missionaries began to work throughout India, leading to the growth of Christian communities of many varieties.

The total number of Christians in India according to the 1991 census was 19.6 million, or 2.3 percent of the population. About 13.8 million of these Christians were Roman Catholics, including 300,000 members of the Syro-Malankara Church. The remainder of Roman Catholics were under the Catholic Bishops' Conference of India. In January 1993, after centuries of self-government, the 3.5-million-strong Latin-rite Syro-Malabar Church was raised to archepiscopate status as part of the Roman Catholic Church. In total, there were nineteen archbishops, 103 bishops, and about 15,000 priests in India in 1995.

Most Protestant denominations are represented in India, the result of missionary activities throughout the country, starting with the onset of British rule. Most denominations, however, are almost exclusively staffed by Indians, and the role of foreign missionaries is limited. The largest Protestant denomination in the country is the Church of South India, since 1947 a union of Presbyterian, Reformed, Congregational, Methodist, and Anglican congregations with approximately 2.2 million members. A similar Church of North India has 1 million members. There are 473,000 Methodists, 425,000 Baptists, and about 1.3 million Lutherans. Orthodox churches of the Malankara and Malabar rites total 2 million and 700,000 members, respectively.

All Christian churches have found the most fertile ground for expansion among Dalits, Scheduled Castes, and Scheduled Tribe groups. During the twentieth century, the fastest growing Christian communities have been located in the northeast, among the Khasis, Mizos, Nagas, and other hill tribes. Christianity offers a non-Hindu mode of acculturation during a period when the state and modern economy have been radically transforming the life-styles of the hill peoples. Missionaries have led the way in the development of written languages and literature for many tribal groups. Christian churches have provided a focus for unity among different ethnic groups and have brought with them a variety of charitable services.

Tribal Religions

Among the 68 million citizens of India who are members of tribal groups, the religious concepts, terminologies, and practices are as varied as the hundreds of tribes, but members of these groups have one thing in common: they are under constant pressure from the major organised religions. Some of this pressure is intentional, as outside missionaries work among tribal groups to gain converts.

Most of the pressure, however, comes from the process of integration within a national political and economic system that brings tribes into increasing contact with other groups and different, prestigious belief systems. In general, those tribes that remain geographically isolated in desert, hill, and forest regions or on islands are able to retain their traditional cultures and religions longer. Those tribes that make the transition away from hunting and gathering and toward sedentary agriculture, usually as low-status labourers, find their ancient religious forms in decay and their place filled by practices of Hinduism, Islam, Christianity, or Buddhism.

One of the most studied tribal religions is that of the Santal of Orissa, Bihar, and West Bengal, one of the largest tribes in India, having a population estimated at 4.2 million. According to the 1991 census, however, only 23,645 people listed Santal as their religious belief.

According to the Santal religion, the supreme deity, who ultimately controls the entire universe, is Thakurji. The weight of belief, however, falls on a court of spirits (*bonga*), who handle different aspects of the world and who must be placated with prayers and offerings in order to ward off evil influences. These spirits operate at the village, household, ancestor, and subclan level, along with evil spirits that cause disease, and can inhabit village boundaries, mountains, water, tigers, and the forest. A characteristic feature of the Santal village is a sacred grove on the edge of the settlement where many spirits live and where a series of annual festivals take place.

The most important spirit is Maran Buru (Great Mountain), who is invoked whenever offerings are made and who instructed the first Santals in sex and brewing of rice beer. Maran Buru's consort is the benevolent Jaher Era (Lady of the Grove).

A yearly round of rituals connected with the agricultural cycle, along with life-cycle rituals for birth, marriage and burial at death, involves petitions to the spirits and offerings that include the sacrifice of animals, usually birds. Religious leaders are male specialists in medical cures who practice divination and witchcraft. Similar beliefs are common among other tribes of northeast and central India such as the Kharia, Munda, and Oraon.

Smaller and more isolated tribes often demonstrate less articulated classification systems of the spiritual hierarchy, described as animism or a generalised worship of spiritual energies connected with locations, activities, and social groups. Religious concepts are intricately entwined with ideas about nature and interaction with local ecological systems. As in Santal religion, religious specialists are drawn from the village or family and serve a wide range of spiritual functions that focus on placating potentially dangerous spirits and coordinating rituals.

Unlike the Santal, who have a large population long accustomed to agriculture and a distinguished history of resistance to outsiders, many smaller tribal groups are quite sensitive to ecological degradation caused by modernisation, and their unique religious beliefs are under constant threat. Even among the Santal, there are 300,000 Christians who are alienated from traditional festivals, although even among converts the belief in the spirits remains strong. Among the Munda and Oraon in Bihar, about 25 percent of the population are Christians. Among the Kharia of Bihar (population about 130,000), about 60 percent are Christians, but all are heavily influenced by Hindu concepts of major deities and the annual Hindu cycle of festivals. Tribal groups in the Himalayas were similarly affected by both Hinduism and Buddhism in the late twentieth century. Even the small hunting-and-gathering groups in the union territory of Andaman and Nicobar Islands have been under severe pressure because of immigration to this area and the resulting reduction of their hunting area.

Modern Changes in Religions

The process of modernisation in India, well under way during the British colonial period (1757-1947), has brought with it major changes in the organisational forms of all religions. The missionary societies that came with the British in the early nineteenth century imported, along with modern concepts of print media and propaganda, an ideology of intellectual competition and religious conversion. Instead of the customary interpretation of rituals and texts along received sectarian lines, Indian religious leaders began devising intellectual syntheses that could encompass the varied beliefs and practices of their traditions within a framework that could withstand Christian arguments.

One of the most important reactions was the Arya Samaj (Arya Society), founded in 1875 by Swami Dayananda (1824-83), which went back to the Vedas as the ultimate revealed source of truth and attempted to purge Hinduism of more recent accretions that had no basis in the scriptures. Originally active in Punjab, this small society still works to purify Hindu rituals, converts tribal people, and runs centers throughout India. Other responses include the Ramakrishna order of renunciants established by Swami Vivekananda (1863-1902), which set forth a unifying philosophy that followed the Vedanta teacher Shankara and other teachers by accepting all paths as ultimately leading toward union with the undifferentiated *brahman*. One of the primary goals of the Ramakrishna movement has been to educate Hindus about their own scriptures; the movement also runs book stores and study centers in all major cities. Both of these paths are directly modeled on the institutional and intellectual forms used by European missionaries and religious leaders.

During the 1930s and 1940s, again responding to institutional models from Europe, the more activist

Rashtriya Swayamsevak Sangh (RSS—National Volunteer Organisation) emerged to protect Hinduism. The RSS had been founded in 1925 by Keshav Baliram Hedgewar (1889-1944), a native of Maharashtra who was concerned that Hinduism was in danger of extinction from its external foes and needed a strong, militant force of devotees to protect it. Members believe that the Indian nation is the divine mother to whom the citizen devotes mind and body through *karma-yoga*, or disciplined service. Training consists of daily early morning meetings at which the saffron, white, and green Indian flag and the swallow-tailed, red-ocher RSS banner are raised as rows of members salute silently. There are then group drills in gymnastic exercises, sports, discussions of patriotic themes from a primarily Hindu viewpoint, group singing of nationalist songs, and a final assembly with saluting. Throughout India in the early 1990s, there were cells (*shakha*) of fifty to 100 members from all walks of life (the RSS rejects class differences) who were devoted to the nation. Although it has attracted hundreds of thousands of members from all over India, the RSS has never projected itself as a political party, always remaining a national club that is ready to send its members to trouble spots for the defense of the nation and the national culture, embodied in Hinduism. The Jana Sangh, established in 1951, was the RSS's political arm until it joined the Janata Party in 1977 and its membership split away in 1980 to form the BJP.

Another activist organisation is the Vishwa Hindu Parishad (VHP—World Hindu Council), founded in 1964. The VHP runs schools, medical centers, hostels, orphanages, and mass movements to support Hinduism wherever it is perceived as threatened. This ultraconservative organisation played a role in the extensive agitation for the demolition of a mosque in Ayodhya, leading to the destruction of the structure during a huge demonstration in 1992. As a result of the VHP's complicity in the affair, the Ministry of Home

Affairs imposed a two-year ban on the Vishwa Hindu Parishad under the Unlawful Activities Act. When the ban expired in December 1994, the government reimposed it for two additional years.

The spread of Hindu "communal" (that is, religious) sentiment parallels a similar rise in religious chauvinism and "fundamentalist" ideologies among religious minorities, including Muslims and Sikhs. Against this background of agitation, the periodic outbreak of communal riots in urban areas throughout India contributes to an atmosphere of religious tension that has been a hallmark of the national political scene during the twentieth century. Hindu-Muslim riots, especially in North India, reached a peak during the partition of India in 1947 and periodically escalated in urban areas in the early 1990s. This strife typically involves low-income groups from both communities in struggles over land, jobs, or local resources that coalesced around a religious focus after seemingly trivial incidents polarised the two communities. In practice, although members of other religious communities are the victims of violence, rioters are rarely motivated by religious instructors, although fundamentalist agitators are often implicated. The situation in North India became complicated during the 1980s by Sikh terrorism connected with the crisis in Punjab, the widespread anti-Sikh riots after Prime Minister Indira Gandhi's assassination in November 1984 by her Sikh bodyguards, and a series of terrorist or counterterrorist actions lasting into the 1990s. In all of these cases, many observers believe that religion has appeared as a cover for political and economic struggles.

The perception that one's religion is in danger receives periodic reinforcement from the phenomenon of public mass religious conversion that receives coverage from the news media. Many of these events feature groups of Scheduled Caste members who attempt to escape social disabilities through conversion to alternative religions, usually Islam, Buddhism, or Christianity. These occasions attract the attention of fundamentalist organisations from all sides and heighten public consciousness of religious divisions. The most conspicuous movement of this sort occurred during the 1950s during the mass conversions of Mahars to Buddhism. In the early 1980s, the primary example was the conversion of Dalits to Islam in Meenakshipuram, Tamil Nadu, an event that resulted in considerable discussion in the media and an escalation of agitation in South India. Meanwhile, conversions to Christianity among tribal groups continue, with growing opposition from Hindu revivalist organisations.

Alongside the more publicised violent outbreaks, there have been major nonviolent changes, as new sectarian movements continue to grow and as established movements change. For example, the Radhasoami Satsang movement of North India, which includes adherents in Punjab and Uttar Pradesh, encompasses yogic ideas on the relationship between humans and the universe, the *bhakti* saint tradition including select Sikh influences, and the veneration of the enlightened guru. The dominant tendency of these new religions, following the example of the great teachers of the past that was reiterated by Mahatma Gandhi and most modern gurus, remains nonviolence to all living beings and acceptance of the remarkable diversity of Indian religion.

3

Social Organisation among Hindus

Religion is a system of beliefs, emotional attitudes and practices, by means of which a group of people attempt to cope with the ultimate problems of life. Religion and social life are interrelated and it plays an important role in social control. Religious values impose a certain type of behaviour. The rituals of religion make one to have respect for the sacred. Religion also has a bearing on other social institutions. It lays down norms and values, which should guide the relationships within a family and other social groups. The sacred texts often indicate how a people should be governed. Religious beliefs also have an effect on economic behaviour, e.g. the concept of *artha* and the protestant ethic. Religion has acted both as hindrance and help in social change. Where religion has tended to be traditional, it has resisted change. However, where it has moved with the time it has often advocated change.

Generally speaking, the process of doing things in an orderly fashion is called organisation. When we speak of social organisation, we talk about the arrangement of actions which conform with the norms and values of society. Thus, to understand the social organisation of a particular society, in this case Hindu society, we need to study the systematic ordering of social relations, including changes that have taken place over time in them.

Religious Concepts

Hinduism is one of the oldest religions in the world. It is a religion followed by several racial and ethnic groups. The Hindu sacred texts deal with the ethical behaviour of an individual of a family and of society in general. They also discuss and prescribe rules of administration, politics, statesmanship, legal principles and statecraft. The rules of conduct apply to personal and social life. Here, we will discuss only some religious concepts, which provide an understanding of the ways in which Hindu society is organised.

A life of righteousness for a Hindu is possible through the fourfold scheme of practical endeavour. It comprises the concepts of *dharma, artha, kama* and *moksha.*

i) *Dharma* is honest and upright conduct or righteous action.

ii) *Artha* means a righteous and honest pursuit of economic activities.

iii) *Kama* is the fulfillment of one's normal desires.

iv) *Moksha* is liberation, that is absorption of the self into eternal bliss.

Related to these four concepts are the concepts of *karma* and *samsara.*

Depending upon one's deeds *(karma)* one is able to reach the stage of *moksha* or liberation. The stage of *moksha* or liberation is a term for describing the end of the cycle of birth and rebirth. The cycle of birth and rebirth is known as *samsara.* The Hindus believe that each human being has a soul and that this soul is immortal. It does not perish at the time of death. The process of birth and rebirth goes on until *moksha* is attained. This cycle of transmigration is also known as *samsara,* which is the arena where the cycle of birth and rebirth operates. One's birth and rebirth in a particular state of existence is believed by the Hindus to be dependent on the quality of one's deeds *(karma)*.

For a Hindu, the issue of liberation is of paramount significance. Let us discuss a little more about these two concepts, i.e., *Karma* and *Samsara*.

The concepts of *dharma, artha, kama* and *moksha* are related to tenets of *karma* and *samsara*. *Karma* is a word used for all activity or work. *Samsara* is the term used for the arena where the cycle of birth and rebirth continues to operate until one attains liberation. This is also called the theory of reincarnation or *punarjanma*. Actions are divided into good or bad on the basis of their intrinsic worth. Good deeds bring fame, merit and are the path to heaven. Bad deeds bring notoriety and lead to punishment and life in hell. It is recognised that an individual's overall position in a future life depends on the way he or she lives the present one. This belief, which gave a positive or negative value to certain actions, developed into a general theory of actions and is called the *karma* theory. The concept of karma is fully developed and woven into the belief in re-birth, which in turn is related to the belief concerning heaven, hell, and *moksha*. An individual's fate after death is determined by the sum total of grades and attributes of his or her actions or deeds *(karma)* during his or her life. Better birth and status is obtained if there is a surplus of many good deeds in a person's life. Otherwise one's status falls in the next life. Another related belief-is that the world moves in a cyclical process (birth and death follow one another). By following one's *karma* prescribed within the fourfold scheme of *dharma, artha, kama, moksha* an individual strives to get out of this otherwise infinite cyclical process of birth and death. Depending on one's previous and present *karma*, one prospers or suffers in this world. Later after death he either gains heaven or is punished with life in hell. Thus a human being after death may become a denizen or inhabitant of heaven or hell, may be reborn as an animal, or even be reborn as a tree. All this depends on one's *karma*. An individual usually wanders through many births till he or she finds final release or *moksha*.

Relevance to Hindu Social Structure

The belief in *karma* and *dharma* has direct relevance to Hindu social organisation, which is based on an arrangement of castes into a graded order. This hierarchy, in turn, is linked with the quality of one's *karma*. One can say that if one's actions are good, one will be born in a higher caste in the next birth. Hindu society is supposed to be governed by rather strict rules of caste behaviour. There are, on the other hand, some general rules governing the behaviour of all members irrespective of caste. Castes coexist with different norms of behaviour and a continuity with the past in terms of one's actions in the previous birth. Whatever position one may be born into, one must fulfil the functions, without attachment, without hatred and resentment. Whatever may be one's *dharma*, its performance through one's *karma* brings blessings.

Each person has a duty *(dharma)* appropriate to one's caste and one's station in life. As mentioned before, the term *dharma* refers to honest and upright conduct or righteous action. *Dharma* has two aspects; one normative and the other naturalistic. The normative aspect refers to duty or path to be followed. The naturalistic meaning implies the essential attributes or nature, for example, the dharma or nature of water is to flow. The Hindus believe that one must follow one's *dharma* to achieve ultimate liberation from the cycle of births and deaths in this world. An individual belongs to a family and a caste group and has to perform his or her *dharma* (in the sense of its naturalistic aspect) accordingly. The main aim of following one's *dharma* is to eventually achieve *moksha* or liberation.

Dharma relates not only to the caste but also to the different stages in one's life. As part of following one's *dharma* a Hindu goes through the life cycle rituals which are carried out in the context of marriage, family and caste. Let us now look at the size and spread of the Hindu community in India.

THE HINDU COMMUNITY

Hinduism is one of the most ancient religions of the world. Its earliest literary productions were the four Vedas. These comprise hymns and ritual ceremonies of the early Aryan settlers, who were a pastoral and agricultural people. The Vedic period covers about 2500 B.C. to 600 B.C. The Upanishadic teachings, also of this period, contain philosophical reflection of human life. The period of the Epics succeeded that of the Upanishads. In the *Ramayana* and *Mahabharata* philosophical doctrines were often presented in the form of stories and parables. Many other doctrines followed including the *Bhakti* movement of Ramanuja, Vaishnavism, Saktism, Brahmo and Arya Samaj, Ramakrishna, and Aurobindo. Thus, Hindu doctrine developed in several stages.

Demographically the Hindus are the largest percentage of the population of India comprising 82.64 percent in 1981. Even though the absolute number of people who follow Hinduism increased from 549 million in 1981 to 672 million (82.4 percent) in 1991, there was a marginal decrease in terms of percentage points (Census of India 1991). We find that in some states of India the percentage of Hindus is somewhat higher or much lower than the national average. In 1981, those above it included Himachal Pradesh (95.4), Orissa (95.4) and Madhya Pradesh (92.9). In 1991, in ten States the percentage of Hindus was above the national average. Himachal Pradesh (95.8 percent) has the highest concentration of Hindus. In 1981 those below the national average included the States of West Bengal (76.9), Sikkim (67.2), Manipur (60.0), Kerala (58.1), Punjab (36.9), Jammu and Kashmir (32.2), Meghalaya (18.0) and Nagaland (14.4). In comparison, a total of four States had Hindu population less than 50 percent in 1991 with the lowest being in Meghalaya (5.04 percent). The low figures are due to other religious denominations being higher. The percentage increase for 1971-81 among Hindus was highest in Nagaland (88.4) followed by Sikkim (47.2). Total population rose by 24.69 per cent during 1971-81 and for Hindus the rise was 24.15 per cent. This was in keeping with high fertility and low mortality rates found in this community.

Marriage System

Before we discuss specific institutions of the Hindus in India, let us emphasise how widely spread this community is. Consequently, in the areas of marriage or family, there are regional variations. What you will read in these pages is a generalisation covering the common elements and mentioning in passing about the variations. By and large, to marry and raise a family is a sacramental activity for the Hindus. Let us first look at the institution of marriage and then at the family in the Hindu community.

Marriage is a sacred duty for all Hindus. It is an obligatory sacrament because the birth of a son is considered by many Hindus as necessary for obtaining *moksha.* In order to perform important rituals towards gods and ancestors, the sacred texts decree that it is obligatory for a Hindu to be married and have male descendants. Today, a large number of Hindus may, however, not believe in and practice these traditional ideas and associated customs.

Marriage is considered to be one of the sacraments sanctifying the body, mind and soul of the groom and bride. Therefore at the proper age and time, every Hindu woman and man is expected to get married. A wife is considered to be instrumental in helping her husband fulfil the four kinds of *purushartha,*namely, d*harma, artha, kama* and *moksha.* According to this view of marriage, a man is thought to be incomplete without wife and children.

When we discuss Hindu marriage, we should also speak of the eight forms of marriage, which describe the ways marriages are traditionally consecrated among the Hindus.

Eight Forms of Hindu Marriage

Before enumerating these eight forms, let us make it clear that here we are not talking about the usual usage in sociology regarding the forms of marriage. In sociology we discuss monogamy, polygamy and group marriage etc. under the topic of forms of marriage. In that respect, it will suffice to note here that monogamy (i.e., a man is married to one woman at a time) is the usual form of marriage among the Hindus. But various forms of polygamy are also found in the Hindu community. A widow is allowed to remarry among lower castes.

Higher castes usually prohibit widow marriage. The Hindu Marriage Act of 1955 permits divorce on the grounds of insanity, leprosy, adultery, etc. Coming back to the forms of marriage among the Hindus, only the first four of the following eight forms bring purification to ancestors on the sides of father and mother, the remaining four forms produce no such value. The eight forms are given below.

1. *The Brahma form*: It comprises the gift or giving away of the daughter by the father to a man, who has learnt the Veda.
2. *The Daiva form*: It involves the giving away of the daughter by the father to a priest, who duly officiates at a sacrifice, during the course of

3. *The Arsha form*: It consists of the daughter being given away by the father to a man after receiving a cow and a bull from the bridegroom, not with an intention of selling the child, but in accordance with the requirement of the *dharma*.
4. *The Prajapatya form*: In this form of marriage, the father gives away his daughter to the bridegroom and addresses the couple to perform their *dharma* together.
5. *The Asura form*: It involves a payment by the bridegroom to the bride's father for obtaining a wife.
6. *The Gandharva form*: Here the bride and the bridegroom agree to marry at their own consent. Such a decision to marry is consequently consecrated by going through the sacred rites of marriage.
7. *The Rakshasa form*: This is described as a marriage, through force.
8. *The Paishacha form:* In this form, a man first seduces a woman (who may be intoxicated or mentally retarded) and subsequently marries her.

Of these eight forms of marriage, the giving away the daughter by her father described in the first four is considered as the ideal form. The right to give a maiden in marriage is held by the father, the grandfather, the brothers, the kinspersons and the mother, in that order.

The Hindus lay stress on pre-marital chastity on the part of both the male and the female. The marital bond is also to be respected through mutual fidelity. There are also forms of endogamy (marriage within a certain group) and exogamy (marriage outside the group) for which rules are laid down. These rules are designed to regulate the Hindu marriage in the sense of specifying the choice of spouses within specific groups.

Endogamy

The widest category of endogamy for a Hindu is his or her *varna*. Within each *varna* are several castes and sub-castes which are considered to be the categories for endogamy in the region. We do also come across some inter-caste/ inter-subcaste marriages in contemporary times. Yet, these are few and far between. The rule of caste/ subcaste endogamy is the prescribed mode followed by most of the Hindus all over India.

Exogamy

As regards the rule of exogamy, a Hindu is enjoined not to marry within his own gotra. The word *'gotra'* in this context denotes one's extended family or the clan. The *gotra* of a family, is usually named after the ancestor who founded the family. People with a common ancestor are not allowed to marry each other. At present, the rule of exogamy is usually defined in terms of prohibition of marriage within five generations on the mother's side and seven generations on the father's side. However this rule can be circumvented by letting someone of a different *gotra* do the *kanyadaan,* that is the rite of giving the daughter away in marriage. There is a clearly defined limit upto which persons are considered to be related in such a way that their marriage cannot be permitted.

There are marked differences in north India and south India in this regard. In north India, a marriage between both the cross and parallel cousins is prohibited while in south India, cross-cousins are allowed to marry. Thus, the *gotra* rule, as understood in north India, does not apply to the Hindus of south India.

The most common form of marriage is that the bridegroom and his group goes to the bride's home. There the bride is given away by the father or her guardian with due rituals and ceremonies. Variations, of course, occur according to the region and caste.

THE HINDU FAMILY

For a Hindu, the event of marriage signifies the completion of the *brahmacharya ashrama* i.e., the stage of a celibate-life. Marriage heralds the beginning of the householder stage *(grihastha)*. Now, begins the process of the preservation and continuity of the *kula* or the family. A Hindu home symbolises the continuity of its living members, past members that are no more and future members that are yet to come. The living members are considered to be the trustees of the home. It is supposed to belong to the ancestors and includes the interests of the male descendants of the family. The individual as such does not belong to the home. One only performs one's *dharma*. The home is the place where *dharma* and *karm*a are practised by the people who are enjoined to remain detached yet conduct the affairs of the world. For a Hindu, his or her life in the stage of a householder is lived and regulated in terms of *dharma* and *karma*. In performing these two activities, one also performs one's *artha* and *kama*. This process leads one towards the final goal, *moksha*.

Form of Hindu Family

The most striking feature of a Hindu family is its jointness. That is to say the unit of residence is often not confined to the parents and their children only. It usually includes three generations living under the same roof and sharing the family property in common.

Whether living in a nuclear or a joint family most Hindu families prefer that each member goes through some basic life-cycle rituals. These sacraments have been prescribed by the sacred texts and are meant for purifying body and mind. The sacraments are supposed to help make the human being into a social being. Some of them purify a human being in the present life and others help in the life-after-death. From birth to death, the sacraments (rituals) help in organising and disciplining the life of the Hindus, and enabling them to perform the *dharma* in accordance with their status. There is diversity in the observance of the sacrament. Depending on the region and caste, different numbers of sacraments are observed. There are rituals from which women are excluded.

Yet other rituals have special significance for them. Thus for a female the nuptial ceremony is regarded as being of equal significance to the sacrament of *upanayan* (the stage when a male child is initiated into the study of the Veda).

Relations among Family Members

As the concepts of *dharma* and *karma* are so much a part of the Hindu way of life both at normative and behavioural levels, we find that each member in the family has his or her prescribed *sacred duty.* General principles of differentiation on the basis of age and sex regulate the relations within the Hindu family, in terms of precedence, obedience and subservience.

Males are more respected than females, and members senior in age command more respect than the younger members. For example, the father is respected more than the mother and has greater authority. The father's mother by virtue of her age, is respected by all members who are younger to her. It is considered ideal for a man and wife to live with all their married sons in a joint family. They are to be respected and cared for by the sons and their wives and children. It is expected that the sons and their wives will perform their duties to the satisfaction of the parents, and thereby earn their blessings and religious merit.

The sons have a right in their fathers' ancestral property. The age old rules of inheritance which are still customary gave ownership and inheritance rights to males, while they give only maintenance rights to females. These customary rules continue to prevail even today. The Hindu Succession Act and the Hindu Adoptions and Maintenance Act, 1956, however, introduced some changes. The Act makes the husband legally responsible for the maintenance of his wife and children. According to this Act (which is also applicable to Jains, Buddhists and Sikhs), the property of a Hindu comes down to his sons, daughters, widow and mother. Daughters legally have a share equal to that of sons in their father's property. In actual practice customs and tradition continue to be so powerful that very few women are able to take advantage of their rights. From being a member of the primary group, such as the family, one goes on to being a part of one's lineage and subcaste/caste. The largest category of this belongingness for a Hindu can be expressed in terms of the idea of *varna*. Let us now understand the *varna* system among the Hindus.

Stages of Life

The Life of a Hindu is considered to be divisible into four stages, namely

i) *brahmacharya ashram*

ii) *grihastha ashram*

iii) *vanaprastha ashram*

iv) *sanyasa ashram*

It is the *dharma* of a Hindu to pass through these stages in one's life. The male members of Brahman, Kshatriya and Vaishya *varna* pass through four different *ashram* (stages) in their life. The first *ashram* is called *brahmacharya ashram* (the educational stage) from which the fourth *varna,* viz., *Sudra* and women of the first three *varna* are barred

Brahmacharyashram ends (after studentship) at marriage. Celibacy is prescribed till marriage.

The second stage of life is called the *grihasthashram*. During this a man rears a family, earns a living and performs his daily personal and social duties. Following this a man gradually enters the third stage of life called the *vanaprashthashram*. During this stage the householder relinquishes his duties in the household, and devotes his time to religious pursuits. His links with his family are weakened. During this *ashram* a man retires into the forest with or without his wife leaving behind the householder's cares and duties. The final phase of a Hindu's life begins with the stage known as the *sanyasashram*. In this stage one attempts to totally withdraw oneself from the world and its cares by going to the forest and spending the rest of life in pursuit of *moksha*. The four stages of a Hindu's life just described are together called the *varnashrama* system. There is an ideal scheme, which correlates the *vamashrama* phases to ages at which a particular *ashram* begins. However, it is the endeavour that is important and not the age at which this begins. Thus Hinduism permits young unmarried sanyasi, as well as those who never go beyond *grihasthashrama*. Thus there is nothing compulsory about living life in the *varnashram* scheme. It is, however, highly recommended.

At present most Hindus do not systematically go through the *varnashrama*. They do, however, accept these stages to be the ideal ways in which a Hindu should spend his life. Like the four *varna*, the four stages of life are models. In real life, we find that occupations associated with each *varna* are not followed precisely in accordance with what is written in the sacred texts. Today a Brahman may be employed in a shoe company, selling shoes to all the customers irrespective of their *varna* or caste. As we said before, the Hindus are divided into castes or *jati* which are hereditary groups.

Jati System

Jati or castes are hereditary groups in *hierarchical* relation to one another, similar to the hierarchy among *varna*. Brahman castes are the highest while untouchable castes are the lowest. Those between these two extremes are placed according to regional hierarchies.

A caste group can be seen as an extended kin group because members of a caste marry among themselves. Caste endogamy is also explained by the term *beti vyavahar* as against *roti vyavahar*. *Beti vyavahar* refers to the practice of giving and taking of the daughters *(beti)* of different families within a caste. *Roti vyavahar* means only the giving and taking of food *(roti)* with certain categories of people. It is possible to have *roti vyavahar* with people of castes other than one's own. Lower castes accept cooked food and water from higher castes but the opposite is traditionally not permitted. There are certain rules and conditions which regulate the type of food which is accepted when offered to a person of higher caste. The caste groups claim their superior status by showing the evidence of their dietary practices in terms of acceptance/non-acceptance of food and water from particular castes. Besides food, there are also customary discriminatory practices related to different caste groups. For example, the untouchable castes were not permitted to enter certain parts of upper caste streets or houses and temples. This is a typical example of the idea of purity and pollution on which the ideology of caste is supposed to be based. When we consider a caste to be high or low on the basis of its purity or pollution level, we refer to it as a ritual hierarchy of castes. The level of purity/ pollution is judged by the prevalent practices relating to acceptance/non-acceptance of food, entry to sacred places and widow-remarriage. In all these hierarchically arranged caste-groups, the scheme of *dharma, artha, kama* and *moksha* is followed without hatred or resentment towards the lower or the higher group. In other words, people born into a caste accept the sacred duty *(dharma)* of their caste and do not question the right to the higher caste-people to social privileges. Within their own caste they organise themselves for fulfilling several purposes. Let us say a few words about caste councils, which have specific functions in regulating the behaviour of their caste members.

Caste Councils and Caste Associations

Generally each caste has its council. The leaders in the council are usually the elderly members of the caste. Caste councils act as a judiciary for caste groups and help settle disputes related to marriage, separation, divorce or any other untoward behaviour of their caste members. The caste councils are localised covering many villages.

Caste associations are recent phenomena. They are engaged in various activities. For example, they run educational institutions, cooperatives, hospitals, old age homes and orphanages. From time to time they print and distribute among their members pamphlets containing information about new rules of behaviour regarding marriage ceremonies, gifts, widow remarriage, etc. They also publicise the nature of punishment to be meted out to defaulters. These associations are generally regional. They also act as political pressure groups. The caste councils and caste associations regulate the behaviour of caste members.

Interdependence

There is interdependence among caste groups. A member of a caste not only interacts within his own caste but also with other castes. Both aspects are very important for the socio-economic and political organisation of the Hindus. We shall now discuss a little about the inter-caste relationships. For the Hindus, the caste system is a coherent and comprehensive system with rituals and occupational hierarchy. The occupational division of castes also helps to maintain equilibrium in the economic sphere. Being religiously oriented, members of different castes accept their rituals and occupational position. Within the framework of caste ideology, they perform their *dharma* and *karma* and endeavour to improve their present and future life. In both the ritual and economic spheres, members of different castes are dependent on one another. Members of different castes are vertically organised which is more manifest in the rural society. The context of Hindu social organisation is to be seen as a system of interdependence among the members of different caste groups. The *jajmani* system is an important aspect of this interdependence.

Jajmani System

In rural areas of India, it was found that a village generally comprises several Hindu castes, each living in different clusters. These castes have relationships of giving and taking of services among one another. Usually the peasant castes are numerically preponderant. Due to their numerical majority and also their economic power they have been called dominant castes by sociologists. The dominant caste needs services of the carpenters, blacksmith, potter, barber, washerman for various farming and ritual activities. The peasants pay in cash and kind for these services from other castes. The castes providing these services depend for their livelihood on the patronage of the dominant caste. In turn, the servicing castes also give support to their patrons in matters of political group formation. The relationship of patron and client among these interacting caste groups usually continue from generation to generation. Thus, the villagers are bound in a system of the exchange of services. Without this exchange the normal day-to-day life may not run smoothly. This is why this aspect is a very important part of Hindu social organisation.

The interdependence among caste groups is also evident in the ritual sphere apart from politico-economic activities. Pilgrimage, worship, recitation of holy texts, life cycle ritual ceremonies, fairs and festivals are rituals which bring together members of different castes. Without a whole series of interaction among them, these activities are just not possible. The instance of a Hindu wedding (one of the life cycle ritual ceremonies) is a case which illustrates this point. Here, a Brahman priest is needed to perform the sacred rites, the barber is required for the shaving and bathing, the drummer beats the drums, the washerman brings freshly laundered clothes, the untouchable takes the charge of sweeping the floor, the gardeners bring flowers and so on.

We can also look at the temple activities as an example of interdependence among castes. Members of different castes perform their respective sacred duties (*sva-dharma*) for the up-keep of the temple. The priestly castes perform the worship, the goldsmith caste provides ornaments for the idols, other castes provide services like cooking, tailoring, filling water, playing drums and so on. Among the Hindus, temples do not figure as prominently in terms of organised systems, as such institutions as the Mosque and Church of the Muslims and Christians respectively. People belonging to different castes organise and perform their duties to earn religious merit and improve their life after death. Each person considers his or her contribution to the temple as one's duty and improves his or her *karma*. No task is less or more important when performed in the context of one's caste membership and one's *ashram* in life. This shows that the ritual aspect of social activities of caste groups forms an important part of social organisation. This aspect is most reflected in collective behaviour at festivals, fairs and pilgrimages. This is the reason why we are now going to discuss here the festivals, fairs and pilgrimages among the Hindus.

Festivals and Pilgrimages

Festivals, pilgrimages and other ceremonial occasions are usually linked with religion. As such they show how both personal identity of the individuals as well as collective identity of the groups are highlighted by the patterns of interaction during these events. Festivals manifest the social cohesion and solidarity of the community. We begin our discussion of this aspect of social organisation by describing festivals, fairs and pilgrimages among the Hindus.

Festivals

Most of the Hindu festivals are linked to the arrival of particular seasons. For example, the festival of *Diwali* marks the arrival of winter season while that of *Holi* signifies the beginning of summer season. Some festivals are associated with eclipses and movements of the heavenly bodies such as the moon and other planets. Many festivals are held in the honour of the deities like Krishna, Siva, Durga, Lakshmi and Rama, e.g., *Dussehra, Durgapuja, Janmashtami,* etc. Local festivals have their roots in the ecology of the region, celebrating myths associated with plants like coconuts, *tulsi (basil),* the sacred tree, or with animals, like elephants, snakes and monkeys. There are regional festivals connected with the agricultural cycle such as the occasion of first ploughing, sowing or harvest. Among the artisans, carpenter, blacksmith and brass-workers, people worship the deity called Vishwakarma.

We shall not go into the ritualistic aspect of these festivals. The emphasis here is on the role these festivals play in social life of the people. During festivals, people in a locality get together and their participation in a common activity enhances their feeling of belonging to a community. These occasions also provide the chance to people for buying and selling special commodities. By preparing special food and wearing special clothes, people bring about the feelings of freshness and change in their day-to-day life. This regenerates them for carrying the routine activities. Recurrence of festivals and associated rituals strengthens their faith in the stability and integrity of their social order.

Festivals like *Holi, Diwali* and *Dussehra* are celebrated on a scale, which includes participation of Hindus as well as non-Hindus. They provide occasions for a meeting across religions.

Associated with festivals are fairs, which are held at prescribed times on a holy spot. Sometimes, fairs assume independent significance and attract the participation of cross-section of society. Some famous fairs such as the fair of Sonepur or Pushkar draw people from all over the country. In these fairs, craftsmen bring their special artware, artists come to present their shows, agricultural surplus is brought for selling, brisk trading summer season in cattle, horses, elephants. Each fair is both and movements a secular occasion and people participate in both with equal enthusiasm.

Pilgrimage

Not very different from a fair is a pilgrimage. The cultural unity of the Hindus is expressed in the institution of pilgrimage. When a pilgrim goes to the southern pilgrim centre at Rameshwaram, he or she also aspires to reach the northern end of the country, at Badrinath. Most pilgrims also aspire to go to Puri in the east and to Dwarikanath in the west.

In these places of pilgrimage, there is often a fair being held during the periods pilgrims arrive in large numbers. Generally, people go to these places in large groups. Such groups are mostly formed on the basis of kin relationships. They may also include neighbours, friends and business partners.

Different sects of Hinduism have acquired pilgrim centres around the whole country over time. Besides the four centres in the four directions, the Sakta sect has more than fifty centres of pilgrimage. There are seven places of pilgrimage, dedicated to the Sun god, Surya. One of them is in Multan, in West Pakistan. Despite linguistic, racial, and cultural differences, most Hindus undertake long and arduous journeys to the many varied pilgrim places. This adds an important dimension to their social life.

4

Muslim Social Organisation

The word 'Islam' means submission to the will of Allah. The followers of Islam called Muslims believe that Quran is the true word of Allah. They believe the Quran was revealed to mankind through the medium of his Prophet and messenger, Muhammed. Islam came into being in the early seventh century in west central Arabia but its systematic formulation and establishment took place only 622 AD, when Muhammed emigrated from the city of Mecca to Medina. Thus Muslim calendar records events from the first lunar month of that year July 16th 622 AD.

Prior to the emergence of Islam in Western Central Arabia, there were only clusters of warring tribes. Prophet Muhammed brought in a number of social reforms and established a well ordered set of beliefs and practices. Islam, as a religion, became established in this region and began to spread as a political community or "ummah" with its own laws and socio-political institutions. Today Muslims form about one seventh of the world's population. They are highly concentrated in Asia and Africa. Their tiniest concentration is in Oceania (includes Polynesia, Micronesia and Melanesia).

With regard to the emergence of Islam in India, it was introduced into India by Arab traders, who gradually established settlements on the western and eastern coasts of south India. They obtained permission to practice their religion. Sind was conquered by the Arabs early in the eighth century and north west Punjab by the Turks in the eleventh century. The Delhi Sultanate was established by 1206 AD. It was about the sixteenth century that Mughals built up an extensive empire. The establishment of Muslim government at any place was usually followed by the construction of a mosque and other related socio-religious activities. As the Muslim rule strengthened in India, their numbers also increased. The large numbers of Muslims in India are mainly due to conversion.

Today numerically the Muslims comprise the largest minority community in India. According to the 1981 census Muslims constituted around twelve percent of the total population in India. In 1991 also their strength remained same as in the previous decade, around twelve percent of the total population. In 1981 Jammu and Kashmir had the highest percentage of Muslims (64.19 percent). In 1991, the Muslim population was highest in Assam. In Punjab, Himachal Pradesh and Orissa the Muslim population is low. In Kerala and in West Bengal Muslims formed nearly 21 percent of the total population of those states in 1981. Assam (28.43), Kerala (23.3), Uttar Pradesh and West Bengal were the States, which had Muslim population in 1991 above national average. Some States such as Sikkim and Meghalaya had Muslim population less than 1 per cent.

Tenets Of Islam

Islam means submission to or acceptance of the will of God. Its perfect form is found in the teachings of the Quran and the Sunnah (acts and sayings of Prophet Muhammed). Islam is a monotheistic religion, i.e. it believes in one God who is considered the Creator of the universe, of time and space whose law governs everything that exists. The Quran is the word of God, revealed to his messenger, Prophet

Muhammed, in order to lead mankind on a righteous path. The Muslims believe that there will be a 'Last Day' when God will judge all mankind. The belief is that on the judgement day, those who have led a good life will be rewarded and those who have led a bad life will be punished.

The important commands of Islam are prayer, fasting, pilgrimage to Mecca, performance of all that is enjoined and abstinence from what is forbidden and *Jihad* or striving in the way set by God with all the resources at one's disposal. The social rules of behaviour include among other things the observation of the principles of equality and brotherhood among Muslims and of earning one's livelihood through personal labour. The totality of beliefs and practices is called the *Shariah* (path) of Islam. Now let us examine the Islamic view of social equality in order to understand the link between what is believed and what is practised in relation to their social organisation.

Islam is claimed by its believers to be a religion of equality. There are a number of Quranic verses that instruct the Muslims that in evaluating an individual they should not accord much importance to such factors as race, nationality, or ancestry. What matters is the extent to which a Muslim practices the teachings of the Quran. Muslims insist that the principle of equality be upheld in day-to-day living. All Muslims irrespective of their group affiliation could say namaz together and that they need not observe restrictions on eating and drinking together whenever an occasion arises. It is also held that there are no formal restrictions on inter-group (caste) marriages, and that, in fact, Islam encourages it. The existence of an inter-group hierarchy is also denied.

Social Divisions Among Muslims

The most popularly known division among the Muslims, all over the world, is the division between Shias and Sunnis.

They hold the divergent views of and interpretations over Islamic texts and tradition. In India, a vast majority of Muslims are Sunnis. Apart from these kind of divisions there are also other kinds of social groupings among Muslims in India, which reflect the influence of Hindu beliefs and practices specially those relating to caste system.

Muslims in India are divided into two major sections, (i) those who claim to be the descendants of early Muslim immigrants and (ii) those of indigenous origin whose ancestors were converted to Islam. The former section has often been called *Ashraf* or *Shurafa* (singular *sharif*, Arabic words, meaning honourable), while the latter section does not have a specific name. In Bengal, according to Risley, it was designated as *Ajlaf* (for clean occupational castes) and *Arzal* (for unclean castes).

Here, we will first discuss the *Ashraf* category of Muslims and then Muslim converts of Indian origin.

Ashraf

In the Muslim social hierarchy, the descendants of immigrants from Persia, Afghanistan, Arabia and Turkistan are recognised as the highest category of Muslims in India. The Indian Muslim castes, known as Sayyed, Shaikh, Mughal and Pathan comprise this category.

Sayyed are considered to be descended from Fatima's line. She was the daughter of the Prophet Muhammed. As direct descendants of the Prophet, Sayyed are accorded highest social status among the Muslims. They are subdivided into two lineage sections, Hasani and Husaini. After the names of the descendants of Hasan and Husain. Further subdivisions of Sayyed are called Jafari from Jafar as Sadiq, Rizvi from Ali ibr Muras ar-Raza and so on. Some Sayyed subdivisions are named after the disciples of Sayyed saints such as Chishti, Jalali and Oadiriya.

In the second rank of social hierarchy of the Muslims come the Shaikh. They are considered to be the descendants of early Muslims migrants of Mecca and Medina. They trace their descent from either (i) The Ansar or Ansari (the helpers), meaning those who provided shelter to the Prophet and his followers, or (ii) the Muhajirum the immigrants, meaning those who were citizens of Mecca and migrated to Medina as the followers of the Prophet.

The Mughal and Pathan subdivisions of the *Ashraf* rank third in the social hierarchy of the Muslims. Both are almost equal in social status. Those who came to India with the Mughal (concept form of the word Mongol) armies and subsequently settled here were known as the Mughal. Their main subdivisions, based on different ethnic and tribal origins, are Chagtai, Uzbek, Tajik, Turkmans and Qizilbarh.

The Pathan are descendants of those who migrated to India from Afghanistan or from the Pashto-speakers of the North Western Frontier Province of Pakistan. At present, regional subdivisions of Pathan Muslims are based on their prolonged residence in one or the other parts of India, e.g., Rohila Pathan are the inhabitants of Rohilkhand region. Mostly, the Pathan have four major sub-sections namely, Yusufzai, Lodhi, Ghani and Vakar. These sub-sections are further divided into sub-sub-sections, such as, Ghilzai, Mohammed, Mohammedzai, Tarin, Durrangi.

Among the *Ashraf* groups, are also included those pseudo-*Ashraf* who claim descent from one of the Ashraf caste. Ansari has given several examples of attempts by some groups for raising their social status through their claims to Ashraf descent. Ansari has given a long list of certain castes, mentioned in the 1931 census report of Uttar Pradesh. These Muslim castes have tried to raise their social status by claiming new surnames and also corresponding high social status.

Muslim Converts

The Muslim converts of Indian origin are generally called by their caste names. In this group are placed three distinct groups, namely, converts from high caste of the Hindus, converts from clean occupational castes and converts from unclean occupational castes (Bhangi or sweeper, Chamar or tanner). We will briefly speak about each of the three groups.

Converts from High Castes

In the social hierarchy of the Muslims in India, converts from high castes of the Hindus are placed below the rank of *Ashraf*. Many of the Rajput branches of a family in north India have Muslim branches, e.g., the Bais, Bhatti, Bisen, Chandel, Bargujar, Chauhan, Pawar, Rathore, Tomar. At times some of these groups try to mix with higher-ranking groups of Muslims. By and large these converts still follow some of the Hindu practices, e.g., they do not marry first cousins, either cross or parallel. Islamic law allows the marriage of near-kin whereas among the Hindus in north India, prohibition regarding marriage extends to distant degrees of kinship relations on both father's and mother's sides.

Clean Occupational Castes

Clean castes are those, which are permitted contact with higher castes under certain rules. These are opposed to unclean castes which are not permitted any contact with higher castes. The matter of cleanliness is considered in terms of the nature of one's traditional occupation. Some occupations involve necessary contact with the persons of higher castes. People who perform such occupations belong to clean castes. For example, a barber has to necessarily come in close contact with his client. A barber belongs to a clean caste.

The castes, belonging to clean occupations rank below the *Ashraf* and Muslim Raiputs, comprise the bulk of Muslim population in India. The descendants of the converts from Hindu clean castes belong to this category. The process of conversion often involved either groups in different castes of the whole caste group. Many castes of this kind have both Hindu and Muslim sections. For example, it is common to find a carpenter, tailor, laundryman, potter, barber, and goldsmith in both the Hindu and Muslim communities.

These sections operate exclusively in matters of family, marriage and kinship while they also act as one in trade union activities. We can divide these castes in three groups, namely, (a) castes without a Hindu counterpart in existence at present, (b) castes with a larger Muslim section and a smaller Hindu section, (c) castes which are opposite of (b), i. e., with a smaller Muslim section and a larger Hindu section. Let us briefly discuss each of these groups.

Ansari (1959-60: 41-42) includes the following castes of Uttar Pradesh in this group.

a) Atishbaz (firework maker), Bhand (jester), Bhatiyara (innkeeper), Bhishti (water carrier), Gaddi (grazier), Momin Julaha (Muslim weaver), Mirasi (Musician), Qassab (butcher), and Faqir (beggar). According to Ansari, all these castes have exclusive Muslim following. Only in some cases there are Hindu castes with similar occupations. But these groups are known by different caste-labels. For example, a Bhishti (water carrier) in Hindu community is known as Kahar.

b) Castes with larger Muslim and smaller Hindu section in Uttar Pradesh, according to Ansari are known by the following names.

Darji (tailor), Dhuniya (cotton carder), Kunjra or Kabariya (green grocer), Manihar (bangle maker),

Saigalgar (metal sharpener), and Rangrez (cloth printer).

Ansari's account of these castes is based mainly on his study of the 1931 census reports. It is possible that this situation has now changed. In fact, we need fresh data on this aspect to say something with certainty.

c) Castes with larger Hindu than Muslim sections have obviously provided few followers to Islam. Speaking about Uttar Pradesh, Ansari includes Dhobi (Laundry man), Kumhar (potter), Nai or Hajjam (Barber) and Teli (oil presser) in this group.

Muslim sections of these castes are identified on account of their separate caste councils (Panchayat). These are endogamous castes, practising their own ceremonies and customs.

Unclean Castes

Lastly, we have the Muslim untouchables, occupying bottom place in the Muslim social hierarchy. These people do the menial tasks, including scavenging and sweeping. They are descendants of converts who retained their low social status along with their caste name, occupation and poverty. For example, a Bhangi (scavenger), either a Muslim or a non-Muslim, is not permitted to enter a mosque. In theory, it is possible for a Muslim Bhangi to pray in a mosque, but in practice his entry into a mosque is disapproved. On the other hand, an untouchable Muslim is permitted to learn Quran while an untouchable Hindu is not supposed to learn religious texts.

KIN RELATIONSHIPS

Having discussed social divisions among the Muslims, let us now see how these divisions reflect the operation of caste and kin relationships in Muslim social organisation. Cultural characteristics constituting caste among the Hindus may in turn be used to evaluate the situation of Muslims in India. Such a discussion will help us to follow the interrelation between caste and kinship systems. We can see how caste relationships also act as kin groups. These cultural characteristics may be put as follows.

i) caste is endogamous
ii) it involves occupational specialisation
iii) castes are hierarchically ordered
iv) there are restrictions on social intercourse and commensality.

Endogamy: Zat & Biradari

Muslims use the term *zat* (equivalent of caste) to express the purity of descent. The *zat* is, therefore, primarily an endogamous unit of society. The households belonging to each *zat* in the village conceive of themselves as a collectivity and designate themselves as *bhai-band or biradari* (literally caste-brotherhood). This solidarity among the members is not merely a fictional notion, but rests on demonstrable kinship linkages. Since all the households belonging to each caste are descendants of one common ancestor, or a few related common ancestors, who had settled in the village at the time it was established or subsequently related by ties of common descent. On account of the custom of preferential cousin marriage prevalent among some *bhai-band* or *biradaris,* there always exists a tie of descent among them.

The *biradari* resembles caste in the features of its inner structure, e.g. membership is determined only by birth and the group boundaries are maintained through endogamy. However, violations of the rules of endogamy are not dealt with in an identical manner; they range from mere disapproval to outright excommunication. Among the

Ashraf, the caste brotherhoods are subdivided again into *Biadharis* (marriage circles) to provide a restricted circle in which to choose a wife. Sometimes the endogamous circle becomes so narrow that it includes only the extended kinship group of the person's parents. Such a limited kinship group is generally termed a *kuf*. Whereas the Biradari generally functions for all ceremonial intercourse, the *biadhari* (marriage circles) within the *Biradari* is restricted to the choosing of wives. The Muslim Rajputs are very endogamous, but do not marry first cousins as the Ashrafs do.

Some of the occupational castes such as the Qasab (butcher), Manihar (bracelet maker) are almost strictly endogamous and they generally do not marry outside their castes. Certain other occupational castes, such as Julaha (weaver), Nai (barber), Kumhar (potter) may even practice isogamy (marrying equals). Finally the Bhangi (scavanger) caste is confined to itself for marriage purposes. A clean caste person would not and does not like to establish marriage relations with Bhangis.

Occupational Specialisation

The second attribute of caste or *Biradari,* which resembles the Hindu caste, is their association with a traditional occupation. An exception to this is the various *Ashraf* groups whose names are indicative of their origin or descent. But in the case of many others groups the various names are indicative of the respective traditional occupations.

Since the division of castes entails a degree of occupational specialisation amongst them, the relationship among the different castes tends toward economic interdependence. The different castes participate in this system in different capacities according to their place in the productive organisation revolving around land. The *Ashraf* groups, who are predominantly landowners and whose principal occupation in the village is cultivation, form the nucleus of the system of economic interdependence among the castes. They are referred to as the *jajmans*. Muslim castes, whose names imply a traditional occupation, render specialised and traditional economic and ritual services for their *jajmans*. Some of the Muslim castes in this respect are Barhai (carpenter), Darzi (tailor), Dhobi (laundryman) Kumhar (potter), Lohar (blacksmith), Nai or Hajjam (barber), Sunar (goldsmith) Teli (oil presser) Bhishti (water carrier), Gaddi (grazier), Julaha (weaver), Qasab (butcher) etc. Each of these occupational castes, with both Hindu and Muslim section, is sometimes united for trade-union purposes. But for social and ceremonial purposes each section is generally limited to itself.

Hierarchical Ordering

The third important attribute of caste is the hierarchical ordering of various Muslim groups. Every Muslim caste has its definite place within the total social organisation. Each caste is considered to be either high or low in relation to other castes. The *Ashraf* castes top the social ranking when compared to the other Muslim castes. Further, every Muslim belongs to a certain caste, his/her social status is, therefore, defined and often fixed according to the status of the caste to which he/she belongs. All the Muslim castes, like Hindu castes, are graded into a hierarchical scheme. The *Ashrafs,* almost by common consensus, are assigned the highest position in the ranking strata by virtue of their supposed descent from Prophet Mohammad. The Bhangis and Chamars are assigned the lowest rank. The Muslim Rajputs are ranked lower than *Ashraf* but are considered higher than the various clean occupational castes. The latter are superior to the Muslim untouchables but inferior to Muslim Rajputs.

Restrictions on Social Intercourse

Finally, one observes the presence of restrictions on social intercourse and commensalism (i.e. eating together) among the various Muslim castes. The various *Ashraf* groups observe no restriction in inter-group commensality among themselves. There are, however, several restrictions on commensal relations with the rest of the caste groupings who are considered inferior to

The various *Ashraf* groups assign low status to the non-Ashraf groups because it is maintained that the latter do not observe certain ritual cleanliness *(paki)*.

Social Control

Having described how Muslim social organisation is internally differentiated and hierarchically ranked, we shall now turn to other organisational aspects of Muslim society, specially those which restrict and control individuals and groups within the prescribed normative framework. Such an organisation takes two forms: direct control through a governing body, such as a council, and indirect control through public opinion. The Hindu social organisation operates and maintains itself through an operation of both these forms. Let us look at both of them in a little more detail. When particular acts of individuals are not approved by their caste fellows they become the victim of severe criticism. If a violation is serious, the criticism takes the form of action and the offender faces a social boycott the extent of which varies according to the nature of the offence. The other mode of control, through an authoritative body, is generally paractised among the occupational castes where such a body is known as the panchayat. membership in the caste panchayat generally includes all the adult males of the caste; the caste headman, known as *Sarpanch* is usually elected. In a situation of emergency, generally when a member of the caste has committed an offence, the whole panchayat is summoned to hear the case. The caste panchayat then gives its judgement. The most frequent punishment among them is a strict social boycott which is termed as *hugga pani band* (i.e. such a person is not welcomed or entertained by fellow caste members) or *zat biradari bahar* (expulsion from the caste brotherhood).

Among *Ashraf* and some of the higher occupational castes like higher Hindu castes, no authoritative caste council functions. Instead, the general caste opinion of approval and disapproval passes through the communicative network among caste members. Among the *Ashrafs*, joint family functions as the basic unit which controls its members in almost all social and personal matters; in the case of most occupationally related castes which have well organised caste Panchayats, the joint family remains comparatively less significant in social affairs. Among Muslims, Bhangi (Scavenger), Dhobi (washerman), Teli (oil presser), Julaha (weaver) etc. have well organised panchayats which function both as trade unions and as social organisations.

Family, Marriage and Inheritance

The regulation of the Shariah along with the traditions of the Prophet provides us with a framework for identifying practices relating to Muslim marriage, family and inheritance. The Shariah consists of regulations pertaining to marriage, family and inheritance. The traditions of the Prophet include records of the Prophet's own manner of living and pronouncements on various matters of daily life. These traditions have become a source of normative guidance for Muslim social life. Let us discuss these traditions relating to family, marriage and inheritance in Muslim society in greater detail.

Family

Muslims, like other communities in India, live in small and large households. Both types of families, i.e., joint family and nuclear family, are found among the Muslims. The size of the family varies from four to eight members or as large as twenty five in number. Vast majority of the joint families are located in the rural areas and more nuclear families are located in urban areas.

Patrilineal and Matrilineal Family: Muslim family is usually patrilocal and patrilineal. After marriage the couple establishes the family at the place of the husband. Exceptions to patrilineal family are rare but not altogether absent. For instance, with the absence of a male heir, the head of the family may invite his daughter and her conjugal family to establish residence in his house. In such a situation, son of the daughter is adopted and becomes the legal heir to property. Another example of departure from the normative type of patrilocal and patrilineal family is the matrilineal families found in Lakshadweep Islands, Malabar district (Kerala) and Ratnagiri districts (Maharashtra) in India.

Family Break-up: In Islam, celibacy is discouraged and Muslims are enjoined to marry and multiply. Although divorce is a common phenomenon among Muslims, Islam does not permit divorce to be taken lightly. This is indicated in the Prophet's words, "of all things Allah has made lawful for his servants, the most hateful to him is divorce,". Thus Islam wanted to provide both for family stability as well as divorce in situations where marital maladjustments render healthy family life impossible.

Husband and Wife: Among Muslims, it is the duty of the husband or head of the family to provide for the maintenance of the family. In Islam, the wife has a legal right to be maintained by the husband. The social life of the majority of the Muslim women is confined within the family. She spends a major portion of her time in taking care of household matters and in the upbringing of children. Her social and emotional needs are fulfilled by her family. In fact her role and function in the family determines her social position in the family.

Sons and Daughters: Within the Muslim family sons and daughters generally do not enjoy equal social position. In the past even the birth of a girl was considered as an unfortunate and unpleasant event in the Muslim family). However, these days children are given equal treatment in routine general matters. But in important matters such as education, choice of career,. choice of partner in marriage, the daughters are sometimes discriminated and sons are favoured.

Segregation of Women: Another notable practice among the Muslim families is *'purdah'* or seclusion of women. Majority of Muslims still live in joint families, where women reside in separate part of the house called *'Zanana'* . The seclusion of women from participation in certain spheres of life is enforced through the custom of *'purdah'*. In the past, this custom was considered as a symbol of higher social position of the family. Social change and education has made some dent in this custom. Yet even today this custom remains an important aspect of the Muslim family.

Marriage

Let us examine here the essential features of Muslim marriage in the context of Islamic religion, which has provided the ideological foundation for social behaviour.

Nikah: Marriage among Muslims is known by the Arabic word *'Nikah'*. It takes place in the form of contract and is not considered as sacrosanct (exceedingly sacred). It is obligatory in character. Muslim law maintains that the main objective of *'Nikah'* is procreation and legalisation of children. The essential elements of Muslim marriage are: a) marriage proposal is made by or on behalf of the concerned parties; b) acceptance of the proposal in the presence of one or two male and two female witnesses; c) settlement of Dower or *Mehr*.

The arrangement of marriage is largely the responsibility of the parents, particularly that of the father. In the past, bride or bridegroom had no say in the selection of his or her partner. This disadvantage was even more glaring in the case of female. With the passage of time male members of Muslim community have acquired some freedom in the choice of their spouse. In case of woman the situation has not much changed

Age at Marriage: Islamic law does not specify any particular age limit for marriage. The only condition is that a minor girl cannot join the husband after marriage. Although young girls may be married but the girl should join the husband only after attaining maturity. This interpretation is not related to age but to attainment of puberty. According to the latest amendment of 'Child Marriage Restraint Act' of 1929 the minimum marriageable age of male and female is 21 years and 18 years respectively. Nevertheless early marriage is still widely prevalent in the Muslim community.

Marriage Ceremony: The ceremony of Muslim marriage, i.e. *'Nikah'* is conducted by 'kazi'. It is customary to recite verses from Quran so as to seek Allah's blessings for the couple. Consent is sought from both the individuals. In order to complete the marriage ceremony, a formal document *'Nikahnama'* is prepared. Notwithstanding other aspects, *'Nikahnama'* specifies the nature of Dower or *Mehr*. *Mehr* is a particular sum of money or property, which the bride is entitled to receive from bridegroom in consideration of marriage. It's a sort of guarantee for the security of the woman. *Mehr* is an indispensable custom without which no Muslim marriage can acquire social or legal legitimacy. *Mehr* is not a fixed amount of money or property. It varies according to the social and economic status of the concerned families. The mode of payment is also flexible. It can be paid either immediately after the marriage or postponed till some mutually agreeable future date.

Mehr and Dowry: Islamic Law never mentioned about dowry. But in reality it has become a common practice. Broadly speaking, the amount of *Mehr* has been reduced to a mere symbolic value. Usually it is several times smaller than the dowry, which the parents of many girls pay at the time of marriage. Thus the ritualisation of *Mehr* and the increasing practice of dowry have adversely affected the status of Muslim women and their marriage prospects.

Polygamy: A notable practice associated with Muslim marriage is polygamy or plurality of wives. In Islam, a Muslim male may have four wives at a time. However, he must be able to treat them on equal and just bases. In India, this practice of plurality of wives became popular during the Muslim Rule. These days it is becoming less prevalent. It has considerably decreased among the urban and educated sections of Muslim population.

Islam permits marriage between both parallel and cross cousins. A notable preferential choice is whereby a male marries his father's brother's daughter. Mohammedan Law also provides for certain restrictions in marriage so far as other communities are concerned. A Muslim woman cannot marry a '*Kithabian*' or non-Muslim. But a male can marry a *'Kithabia'*. Let us make it clear that *'Kithabia'(n)* is an individual who believes in a religion revealed through a book {other than Quran) but does not engages in the practice of 'idol' or 'fire' worship, etc.

Divorce and Remarriage: Under Muslim Personal Law, husband enjoys unlimited freedom in matters of divorce. He is permitted to divorce his wife according to his own pleasure or without assigning any reason or cause. On the other hand, a woman does not enjoy such a freedom. This custom has resulted in man's domination arid power over the woman. Although the Prophet gave to the women, the right of obtaining separation on reasonable grounds but in practice this is not so. In general there are two types of divorce, i.e *'talaq'* and *'khol'*. *Talaq* is exjudicial divorce and it becomes effective when the husband unilaterally pronounces the word *'Talaq'* thrice. In *'Khol'*, divorce takes place by mutual consent.

After divorce a woman is not free to remarry immediately. She is supposed to wait for a specified period before seeking remarriage. This period is called *'iddat'*. On the whole *'talaq'* is considered the most detestable custom in Islam. In India, with the 'Dissolution of Muslim Marriage Act', 1939, Muslim woman got the right to divorce her husband on certain specified grounds but men still enjoy much greater freedom as compared to women in matters of divorce. The Quran and Islamic tradition favour widow marriage. The responsibility for marrying a widow lies with her parents. Although the provision for widow marriage is clearly stated yet until recent times such marriages were presented because of socio-cultural considerations.

Inheritance: Though Islamic society is patrilineal, women in Islam enjoy the right to inherit property. Islamic jurisprudence defines not only the scope of the property a woman may own-by inheritance, by gift and by the fruits of her own labour but also recognises the absolute ownership of it. Both daughters and widows inherit property, including land and houses, from their parents and husbands. Islamic law grants women, even if childless, remarried or divorced complete rights over their inherited property. However, women inherit smaller shares of wealth than men do, a son's share is twice that of a daughter.

Life Cycle Rituals and Festivals

Life cycle rituals and festivals constitute important elements of every religious community. They serve, apart from other things, the purpose of reaffirming one's faith in one's religion. Some of the (important Muslim ceremonies include life-cycle rituals around birth, marriage and death. A few important ones are (i) the naming of the child (ii) circumcision which is done by a barber or in a hospital (iii) the *Bismillah* ceremony, which initiates a child into reading Quran. Feasts and celebrations associated with these ceremonies and festivals not only make for social solidarity among the believers but also allow people from different socio-religious backgrounds to meet and know each other. Let us now look at some important festivals among Muslims. They have two main festivals, namely, *Id-ul-Fitr and Id-ul-Azha.*

On the last day of *Ramzan* and on the sighting of the moon, we have *Id-ul-Fitr*. A prayer service is held. Muslims exchange embraces and greetings after prayers and participate in feasting and merriment. As is clear, these major religious activities and festivals make for social solidarity among Muslims and strengthen their social organisation

Ramzan occurs in the ninth month of the calendar. It is the month of self-purification, and commiseration with the poor. Quran is recited regularly.

Another important festival is *Id-Ul-Adha* or *Bakr-Id.* It is celebrated on the tenth day of the month *Dhul Hijja*. This involves a sacrifice made by pilgrims and performed as part of the ceremonies of *Hajj* in Arabia. The ceremony is observed simultaneously by all Muslims the world over. The Muslims offer food among household members, friends and relatives and the poor. The celebration of the Prophet's birthday, *Idi-Milad* and death anniversaries of famous saints have also been added to the list of Muslim festivals. Besides these festivals, many Muslims celebrate several Hindu festivals. For example, the Moghul converts gave official status to celebration of *Diwali* and *Holi.*

Mubartam, is the first month of the Muslim calendar, commemorates the martyrdom of Imam Husain. Ta'zia processions of the Imams grave are carried out on this day. *Muharram* is not a festival in the usual sense of the term but a commemoration and a period of mourning. On the appearance of the new moon the *fatiha* (opening chapter of the Quran) is recited in the *imam bara*–and some refreshment *(sherbet)* taken. The observance lasts ten to twelve days.

5

Sikh Social Organisation

The Sikhs are those who follow the teachings of ten leaders, whom they call *Guru*. All these Gurus lived between 1469 A.D. and 1708 A.D. in Punjab. This State is the Northern part of India. Over the centuries, guided by the Gurus, the Sikh religion expanded and increased its strength in India. However, in 1947 Punjab was divided between India and Pakistan. Many Sikhs who had lived in what became Pakistan were made homeless. They had to migrate to different countries. Sikhs have settled in many parts of the world including the United Kingdom, Canada, the United States of America, Germany and Kenya. There are not more than 12 million Sikhs in the world. Most of these are settled in Punjab. They comprised a little less than 2 per cent of India's 800 million population in 1981. In 1991 their strength was 1.99 percent of the total population. The Sikhs are spread all over India. They are also in many professions including business, academics, civil service, medicine and defence of India.

The Sikh population by head of household is 1.95 per cent of the total population of India. However, there were differences in state-wise percentages. Thus in Haryana they constituted 6.21 percent, while in Punjab they constituted 60.75 percent of the population of the two states respectively. These were the two states where Sikh percentage was higher than the national average. However, there were states where this average was much lower. These states included Andhra Pradesh (0.03), Bihar (0.11), Gujarat (0.07), Rajasthan(1.44) and so on. In terms of percentage increase over 1971-81 this had been most in Sikkim (242.5) which had 0.10 percentage of Sikhs. In Orissa (39.85) and in M. P. (44.5) the percentage increase in Sikh population over 1971-81 had been 26.15. In 1991, Punjab (63 per cent) and Haryana (5.81 per cent) were the only two states, which had Sikh population higher than the national average. There were only a handful of people who follow Sikkism in States such as Nagaland, Sikkim, Tripura etc.

Over 80 percentage of the Sikhs are farmers. Next to this profession, army career is the next most popular vocation. They form ten per cent of the armed forces. The Sikh farmers played the leading role in the Green Revolution in the Sixties raising the wheat yield per acre by three hundred per cent! Again three of the nine Indians who climbed Mount Everest were Sikhs. They are eminent in many areas of life in India.

Ideological Basis Of Sikhism

The Sikh religion clearly represents a case of fission and fusion in the religious ideology of Indian society. Around five hundred years ago, it had its origins in the wider religious revolt, called *bhakti* movement which was primarily directed against the bigotry and caste-based narrowism in which the then Hindu religion in a specific region was steeped. In this variant of Hinduism, the caste system which was founded upon the notion of ritual purity and pollution and accorded top position to the Brahmin and lowest to the Shudra was particularly isolated for its inhuman bias. The same *Bhakti* movement also tended to define the relationship between man and the God in simple terms of 'devotion', 'supplication' and purity of conduct.

The movement thus tended to build a fraternity of the devoted ones, bound together in their common love of God. It came down with a heavy hand upon the iniquitous caste system, which imposed upon the lowly 'untouchables' a variety of indignities and restrictions. These included those concerning *commensality*, interdining, marriage and even of physical contact. It is worth mentioning here that the untouchables under the caste system were denied any social status or identity. The status they were accorded was that which accrues to a slave and one, which reduces a human being to the level of a 'commodity'.

Sikhism strongly denounced this caste-sanctioned inequity and declared a fraternity of God's beings. In this there were neither any barriers nor any caste-based system of inequality. Thus a spirited affirmation of the principle of religious egalitarianism and a contemptuous rejection of the purity-pollution barrier by Sikhism became a point of fission which tore away this newly-born religion from the then practised brand of Hinduism.

Simultaneously, Sikhism also declared an open revolt against an endless array of 'inhuman' practices carried on in the name of religion, most of which were simply repugnant to human sensibility and sensitivity. But, sanctioned as they were by the Brahmans themselves, who were the ritual leaders of the Hindu society, they were hardly challenged with any degree of effectiveness. Thus, the cycle of mental and moral domination by Brahmans continued, oppressing all the castes—but most of all, the lowly untouchables. Sikhism emerged and evolved as a revolt against all this religious bigotry and irrationality.

Guru Nanak

Sikhism was founded by Guru Nanak who was born in the year 1469 in a place called Talwandi-Nankana Sahib, now in Pakistan. His father, a high caste Hindu called Kalyan

Chand (also fondly addressed as 'Kalu') of the Bedi Kshatriya clan, was a village accountant in the service of the local Muslim landlord. Nanak received an education in traditional Hindu lore and the ruiments of Islam. Early in life he began associating with holy men. For a time he worked as the accountant of the Afghan chieftain at Sultanpur. There, a Muslim family servant, Mardana who was also a musician, joined him. Nanak began to compose hymns. Mardana put them to music and together they organised community hymn singing. From the offerings made, they organised a free canteen. Even now, no payment is required to be made for eating in such a place which is maintained from voluntary donations by 'devotees' and is fondly called *guru-ka-langar*, or the free kitchen. of the spiritual master.

Here Muslims, as well as Hindus of all castes eat together. It is not just the question of different castes having the facility of eating together; rather they had to eat together in order to show c nformity to Sikhism, since denial of caste-barriers was the basic characteristic of Sikhism.

At Sultanpur, Nanak had his first vision of God, in which he was ordered to preach to mankind. One day he disappeared into the water while bathing in a stream. Reappearing from it on the third day, he proclaimed: "There is no Hindu, there is no *Mussalman*".

Many miracles and marvels are associated with the life of Guru Nanak. It is important to remember that many incidents of his life as passed down historically sharply highlight some fundamental features of Sikhism. In other words, principles of religious morality in Sikhism are not taught or preached as abstractions. Rather, they are illustrated and affirmed in the way the Sikh gurus lived their lives. This character of the Sikh norms and morals adds a touch of immediate familiarity to the religion and its fundamental precepts. It removes from them the mystique, which often shrouds principles of religious morality.

For example, Guru Nanak, in one of his spiritual sojourns to Haridwar, demonstrated the futility of propitiating the far-off and unknown gods. Nanak saw some high caste pilgrims throw water in the direction of the sun by way of propitiating their ancestors. On seeing this he began to throw water in the opposite direction. When asked to account for this 'odd' behaviour of his, he explained that he was trying to water his fields. He said that these were only a few hundred miles away while the sun and the ancestors were in any case located much further.

In another incident, Nanak demonstrated the sanctity of honestly earned bread, another central canon of Sikh faith. While stopping over in a town during one of his spiritual wanderings, he deliberately chose to dine at the house of a poor carpenter, rejecting an invitation from a rich money-lender. There he demonstrated that he was correct. He squeezed the bread of the money-lender. Drops of blood came out of it. He then squeezed the bread of the carpenter. Drops of milk came out of it. He said that the money-lender earned his livelihood by exploiting the poor while the carpenter earned his livelihood through honest means. Hence he preferred to dine with the carpenter.

The purpose here is not to lend unqualified credulity to this 'folk' version of the incident. Instead the idea is to emphasise the popular perception held of both the Gurus and Sikhism. These incidents also illustrate popular beliefs in the pragmatic and livable character of Sikh faith.

Another central canon of Sikh faith has a direct relevance on the connection between religious precept and the practical day-to-day morality. This is a positive injunction by the Gurus for a virtuous engagement in the duties of a householder rather than withdrawal from the world as idealised in Hinduism or in Buddhism. The withdrawal from the affairs of this illusion-ridden world is idealised in Hinduism. It prescribes the eventual superiority of *sanyasa*, total withdrawal from the world, as something that everyone should try to approximate in the last stage of life. In Buddhism it is idealised via the formal injunction of Buddha that eventually, one should totally cut oneself off from both the urge to act and the fruits of one's actions (*karma*).

This message is brought home by the founder of Sikhism in the way he lived his life. He interspersed his spiritual sojourns or wanderings with the life of a peasant-householder Consequently, asceticism, penance, celibacy and so on have hardly any place in Sikhism.

Nanak's Concept of God

Theologically, Nanak's concept of God is proximate to the concept of *shudha-advaita* (pure or unqualified monism) which is an important school of Hindu *vedantic* philosophy. Accordingly, Nanak holds that the only entity, which exists in the world, is that of God and what everything else, in one way or the other, partakes of that entity. So much so that even *maya* or 'illusion', which mystifies this supreme reality, is created by God.

God, according to Nanak, is a 'formless', timeless, all powerful master-creator who is not influenced by feelings of jealousy and discrimination. As such he fears none and favours none. Nanak also addresses God by some 'personal' names such as Rab, Rahim, Govinda, Murari and Hari. As it can be easily seen, these invocations of God are derived both from Muslim as well as Hindu pantheons. But, perhaps the most important reason for choosing these invocations lies in the creed that Nanak was evolving. He wanted to emphasise the centrality of one-and-the-same-God apart from his diverse manifestations, as visualised by different religions. As such, he chose them from amongst the most popular usages then current among both Hindus and Muslims.

Nanak chose *Wahi-guru* as the specific way of addressing God by the members of Sikh faith. The term literally means 'hail O Guru'. Thus, an invocative or exclamatory expression has, by way of usage, turned into a proper noun.

Sacred Scripture

Every religion or religious system centres around a sacred text or set of texts having a governing or a regulating effect upon its followers and their life. Varying from religion to religion, the sacred text or texts contain, among other things, a set of instructions to be obeyed by the followers. These instructions regulate a certain range of their temporal activities.

For example, certain religions like Islam give detailed instructions to be followed. These cover virtually all the major situations that one may encounter in one's life. These may range from the minute method of worship and prayer to the death rites. They also provide rules for distributing the property of deceased parents between the heirs. On the other hand, there are religions like Hinduism which do not go into all those details about the way temporal life should be led. Hinduism stresses all the same many do's and dont's which should be strictly pursued. These include rules regarding purity and pollution or rules regarding choice of the marriage mate. Sikh scripture represents almost an extreme case of emphasising only the central canons or ethical morals which should be followed by the Sikhs in their day-to-day life.

The sacred scripture of Sikhs-The *Adi-Granth* or as reverentially called, the *Granthsahib*, was compiled by the

5th Sikh Guru, Guru Arjan Dev. It is in the script known as *Gurumukhi*, currently recognised as Punjabi. However, the hymns included in the Granth are in several languages, such as Persian, old Punjabi, medieval Prakrit, Hindi, Marathi, Multani and several local dialects, with an abundant treasure of Sanskrit and Arabic vocabulary. The Granth is the life-blood of Sikhs and is worshipped by them as respectfully as they would respect and worship their living guru. That is why, the *Granth* is normally addressed by Sikhs as Guru *Granth Sahib*, as if it is a living guide, master or a guru.

The *Granth* is handled by the devotees more like a person than a book. It is placed on a comfortable seat, flanked by colourful silken cloth sheets, which are regularly changed. It is impossible to find these clothings unclean or unkempt. The *Granth* is opened with a fine and graceful mannerism to the chanting of specific hymns in the small hours of the day. It is put to rest once again with a punctilious religious routine. After the *Granth* is closed for the night it is draped in fine colourful sheets and placed in a secluded 'room' specifically made for the purpose. All such rituals are maintained at all religious functions or at such functions as marriage or death where the presence of the *Granth* is considered necessary. The *Granth* is placed in all places of Sikh worship-called Gurudwara (the guru's bode). Some Sikh devotees also place it in their homes and look to its upkeep with all the prescribed rituals and religious solemnity. This characteristic sanctity accorded by the Sikhs to their religious scripture, the *Granth*, is incomparable with any other known religion.

A unique feature of Sikh scripture, which is not shared by any other religious scripture, lies in that it includes religious hymns not merely of the Sikh gurus, but also of several Hindu as well as Muslim saints who were contemporaries of the Sikh gurus. Most of these Hindu saints whose hymns have been included were drawn from the lowly castes, such as cobbler, butcher, barber, etc. who normally occupy bottom rungs of the Hindu caste ladder. The daily readings and recitations from the *Granth* make no distinction whatsoever between hymns of the Sikh guru and those of other. This aspect of the Sikh scripture, even though normally viewed as a 'good' and humanistic feature, still remains a puzzle. This is because no religion makes it a part of its daily worship to recite instructions or hymns not belonging to their own founders.

This can be understood only when we appreciate the central emphasis underlying the Sikh theology, philosophy and ethics. Sikhism emerged, as emphasised above, as a critique and refinement of the then existing ideas of religion and religious morality. As such, it tended to emphasise the relevance of some of the universal human values such as brotherhood and equality. It also emphasises the irrelevance of status whether economic or caste, in one's quest for God. It explains why 'saints' and devotees from across the religious and caste boundaries found their honoured place in the *Adi Granth*. They upheld these values.

What is the spiritual status of 'gurus' vis-a-vis God? It is important to re-affirm that Sikhism is a strongly monistic religion. That is why the ten Sikh gurus, even though held in utmost reverence, are not equated with God. There is only one God or *Akalpurush* (or the 'timeless being') who alone 'deserves' to be worshipped. The injunction of the much-honoured tenth guru of Sikhs, Guru Gobindsingh to his followers is noteworthy: Anyone, who calls me "God", shall perish in the fire of hell. This, however, does not imply that in terms of their religious sentiment, the Sikhs always find it possible to keep to a clear distinction between the two. Despite this, it needs to be stated that the *Granth* emphasises the 'inevitable' and instrumental role of the 'guru' in realising God. Let us also mention how the sacred book *Granth* came to be equated with a guru.

The Granthsahib and the Guru

The line of Sikh gurus, starting from their founder-Guru Nanak, went as far as the tenth Guru, Guru Gobind Singh. He enjoined upon Sikhs to regard the sacred *Granth* as their 'Guru' and turn to it for all advice and instruction for seeking direction of life. We find that today it is worshipped and read with regard and reverence.

Another historical circumstance, which nurtured this attitude of Sikhs for their sacred scripture, is the long period of persecution and suffering undergone by them at the hands of the Muslim rulers, starting from the time of their fifth guru, Guru Arjan Dev (1581-1606), to much after the tenth guru, Guru Gobind Singh (1675-1709), in fact, till the execution of Banda Singh Bahadur (in 1716) who took over the military leadership of the Sikh community after assassination of the tenth guru. Of the ten Sikh gurus, fifth Guru, Guru Arjan Dev ('guru' between 1581-1606) and the ninth Guru, Guru TeghBahadur ('guru' between 1664-1675) were executed by the Muslim rulers, whereas the last and the tenth Guru, Guru Gobind Singh ('guru' between 1675-1708), was assassinated by British hired assassins. Banda Bahadur took over the military command of the Sikh community after the tenth guru and for eight years defied the Mughals and devastated large tracts of eastern central Punjab. He was eventually captured along with seven hundred of his followers, and was executed in Delhi in the summer of 1716. During all these long years of struggle when they were hunted for their creed and at times even pushed into the remote forests, the *Granth* continued to be the centre of their day-to-day existence and chief source of inspiration.

Institution of Khalsa and Five Emblems

The pacifist religion of Guru Nanak took to arms by the time of Guru Hargobind. Less than hundred years after Guru

Nanak's passing away in 1539, Sikhism accepted use of arms for self-defence. The fifth Guru, Guru Arjan Dev, the father of Guru Hargobind, had earlier been executed by the Muslim rulers. Fifty years later, in 1699, taking to arms was formally incorporated into the main corpus of Sikhisim by Guru Gobind Singh via the institution of *Khalsa.* This had taken place as a result of severe repression and persecution let loose by the Muslim rulers against the Sikhs. Let us discuss the institution of *Khalsa*, which restructured the religious ethos among the Sikhs.

Khalsa literally means "the pure" (from the Persian *Khales*, also meaning 'pure'). On April 13,1699, Guru Gobind Singh baptised the first batch of five Sikhs and gave them the common surname, Singh (lion). Kaur 'lioness' is the corresponding surname given to all Sikh women.

The Sikhs were baptised by Guru Gobind Singh in the famous five emblems. All start with a 'k'. All believers are to maintain these in order to keep the status of a 'sikh'.

First of the Ks is *Kesa* (hair). A *Khalsa* must keep the hair unshorn. A *Khalsa* who cuts off his hair is a renegade (*patit*). The holiness of unshorn hair is older than Guru Gobind Singh, the founder of Khalsa. Many of the earlier Gurus followed the tradition of letting the hair and beards grow. The other four are *Kangha* (comb); *Kacch* (drawers) worn by the soliders; *Kirpan* (sabre); and *Kara* (bracelet) of steel, commonly worn on the right wrist.

The baptism of Sikhs into the material qualities of valour and fearlessness meant a departure from the earlier pacifist tradition. Yet it inherited an essential continuity with the past tradition in more than one way. The first of the baptised Sikhs were drawn from five different caste groups. This underscored the essential equality between men of all castes and creeds as emphasised by the founding Guru Nanak. Yet another continuity with the past lay in the concept of *Sant Sipahi* (saint-solider). This implied that a Sikh would not wield a sword for the sake of doing so. Instead, it was to be done for a right cause and for the defence of one's just rights. In addition, a Sikh was supposed to lead a noble, virtuous and pure life.

As already mentioned above, Sikhs made a strong impact upon the Mughal rulers via Banda Bahadur but did not have a strong political organisation to displace them by their own rule. The subsequent course of the evolution of *Khalsa* political power was simple. For some years the *Khalsa* vanished into the hills. However, when Mughal power waned due to the invasion in 1738-1739 of the Persian Nader Shah, they re-emerged into the plains.

The Sikhs formed into *misls* (from Persian *mesals*, meaning both "example" and "equal"). They began to demand protection money from towns and villages. The series of invasions by Ahmad Shah Durrani, 1747-1769, completely destroyed Mughal administration. In the battle of Panipat in 1761 the Afghans crushed the rising Maratha power in the north. In the gap thus created, the Sikhs moved in as rulers of the Punjab.

This situation of political instability in Punjab eventually culminated in Ranjit Singh (1780-1839) establishing the first and the last kingdom of Sikhs in Punjab, stretching right upto the Khyber pass in the north. Ranjit Singh was an enlightened and secular king and ruled till 1839.

He respected all religions and gave liberal benefices to sacred places of all religions. This was followed by ten years of internecine warfare and palace stratagems plus clever political machinations by the British which ended finally in the annexation of Punjab by them in 1849. The annexation was followed by a period of an inexplicable intimacy between the Sikhs and the British. The Sikhs strongly sided with the British administration in quelling the mutiny of 1857 and also enlisted in large numbers in the British army at the time of First World War.

Some writers, for example, Khushwant Singh, maintain that this expression of loyalty on the part of Sikhs reflected a longing for peace and order after long years of bloodshed and disorder in Punjab.

The unprovoked massacre of four hundred innocent people by the British at the Jalianwala Bagh, Amritsar, on April 13, 1919, set the Sikh against the British. Secondly, despite the popular Sikh protest the British sided with the *mahants*, the hereditary priests controlling the *gurudwaras*. Thus Sikhs turned completely against them. These factors as well as the rising temper of the independence movement pushed the Sikhs into the national movement, now led by Mahatma Gandhi. Independence in 1947 was accompanied by partition of the country and the Sikh community suffered enormously through pillage and manslaughter. At present, there are problems of compatibility between the perceived interests and political aspirations of the Sikhs on the one hand and the national policy on the other. From this description of political history of the Sikhs, we now turn to their social institutions.

Sikh Institutions

Sikh institutions seem to emanate from the centrality of ethos, philosophy and theology of Sikhism. Quite a few of the institutions like marriage, kinship, property are, on the other hand, common between the Hindus and Sikhs. Almost all the important festivals of Hindus are celebrated by Sikhs as well.

Social ties between the Hindus and Sikhs including the marital ties continue to thrive. Many sub-caste groupings among the Punjabis underlying the main caste categories like Aroras, Khatris continue to be common between them. Even though Sikhism came up primarily as a revolt against the Hindu legacy of caste, it continues to use caste titles as a principle of social location and departure. These are, however, shorn of the purity-pollution barrier. We discuss here those institutions, which are peculiar to the Sikh community. Around these institutions can be observed much of the collective behaviour of the community.

The Gurudwara

Literally meaning the guru's abode this is the Sikh name or nomenclature for a place of worship. This is the seat of the holy *Granth* and of regular recitations from it, interspersed by singing of religious hymns. There are some *gurudwaras* associated with important happenings in the lives of the gurus. *Gurudwara* Sisganj in the Chandni Chowk of Delhi is associated with the martyrdom of the ninth Guru Tegh Bahadur. *Gurudwara Bangla Sahib* is associated with the 8th Guru Harkishan. There are over 200 historical *gurudwaras* associated with the Gurus. These are controlled by the *Shiromani Gurudwara Prabhandak* Committee (S.G.P.C.) set up by the Sikh *Gurudwara* Act of 1925-offerings are made at *gurudwara* and are used for their upkeep as well as the Khalsa schools and colleges. Golden Temple of Harmandar *Sahib gurudwara* at Amritsar is the most sacred *gurudwara* of Sikhs. It has the same sanctity for Sikhs as Kashi for Hindus, Mecca for the Muslims, Vatican for the Catholics or Jerusalem for the Jews.

It was built by the fifth guru of the Sikhs, Guru Arjan Dev (1563-1606 AD). The foundation of the temple was laid down by Sayyid Main Mir—a Muslim saint of Lahore. This fact in itself highlights religious catholicity of Sikhism. There are certain other features of this temple, which dramatise, symbolically, certain essential features of Sikhism and its philosophy.

First of all, the temple was made at the ground level lower than the rest of the city—a fact which, according to some underscores the humility of the founding gurus. Second, the temple has four main gates, which open in four different directions, which is taken to mean that the temple was thrown open equally to all the four castes. Some others, however, interpret this feature thus: the Golden

Temple has four doors in the four natural directions in order to instruct people of other religions who believe the abode of God to be in a certain direction or at a certain place. However, God is not confined to a certain direction. So, according to them, *Harmandar* means *'mandar' or temple for 'har'. This means it is for every one. In this phrase, the word 'mandar'* is a Sanskritik expression, whereas *'har'* is a Persian expression.

There is yet another feature of Golden Temple, which takes us right to the centre of the Sikh religious ethos. The complex of the Golden Temple is made up of two parts. First is the main part, called *harmandar*. It is set in the centre of a tank. The tank itself is located by a wide corridor for the pilgrims to go around as an act of religious supplication. *Gurbani* or the religious hymns from the *Granth* are sung or recited in this part of the temple for most part of day and night.

The second part of the sacred complex, which lies outside and ahead of the main gate of the *Harmandar*, is called *Akaltakht* or God's court. Since the very inception of the *Harmandar* the *Akaltakht* has been the seat of temporal authority of the Sikh gurus. They sat there, as if on the 'throne' vis-a-vis their followers and considered issues of temporal import including political issues. These two seats of 'spiritual' and 'temporal' authority were and are regarded as integral parts of the basic ethos of the Sikh community. Thus, the idea of separating 'religion' from 'polities' does not appeal to the Sikhs.

Sadh Sangat

No act of Sikh worship is complete without the holy gathering or *Sadh Sangat* which is virtually equated with God's presence. Such a gathering or *'sangat'* is supreme. It can take any decision, whether of religious or temporal import, which is binding upon the rest of the community. It can even censure reprimand, or punish a person for any impropriety committed by him. Maharaja Ranjit Singh is on record having received punishment in the form of cuts of cane upon his skin from a religious gathering at Golden Temple, Amritsar, for an act of moral impropriety committed by him. Gurus, particularly Guru Gobind Singh, have in several hymns recognised the superiority of *Sadh Sangat* over their own commands.

Guru ka Langar

The secular and equalitarian character of Sikhism was manifested through the institution of *langar* community kitchen. Here everyone, without any discrimination of caste and creed, sat together and ate in company. This is also sometimes called the principle of *pangat* or the queue. This again indicates the equal status of everyone in the presence of the Guru.

Even though initiated by the founding Guru Nanak, the institution of *langar* was formalised by the Guru Angad at a place called Goindwal. This was approximately 20 miles away from the city of Amritsar. Every *gurudwara*, big oil small, has a *langar* attached to it and is maintained from offerings made at that gurudwara.

As indicated above, there has been an inflow of a certain caste bias from Hinduism into the social life of Sikhs. This is reflected especially in the area of marital selection. But the said caste bias stayed far short of its traditional rigour and severity with which it is encountered in the Hindu social life. This has been made possible by repeatedly de-emphasising the caste inequality through the institutions of *sangat* and *langar* in the day-to-day life of the Sikhs.

These institutions, therefore, prove functional for maintaining equality, so essential for the very survival of Sikh religious ethos.

Economic Orientation

The basic orientation to engage in economic activity flows, at least partly, from one's religious norms and values. This is what has been a major idea in Max Weber's analysis of the origin and development of the spirit of capitalism in contemporary Europe. The argument presupposes that the individuals in question are religious enough to let religious values hold away over them.

Thus, it has often been argued that a majority of the Sikh families, even after they were completely uprooted at the time of the partition of the country in 1947, built themselves to both 'fame' and 'prosperity'. Sikhs have been proverbially projected as compulsive do-gooders even in the teeth of most adverse circumstances. Their long-standing history of sufferings and persecution imparted the kind of fortitude that lies tacit under a highly resilient attitude. Second, a highly 'secular' and equalitarian attitude, which is reinforced by their institutions of *langar* and *sangat*. A part of their daily religious routine also seems to import the kind of pragmatism and realism which is required in the pursuit of business.

Still another mental attribute, which is conducive towards the same and is that of demystifying reality. This is apparently encouraged by the simple way some of the basic canons of their religion have been stated and repeated. The high 'achievement' orientation of their personality is evidenced by the fact that Sikhs today are found in virtually all the western countries, specifically in large numbers in Canada, the United States of America and United Kingdom where economic opportunities are relatively greater.

6

Social Organisation among Christians

In India there is no one homogeneous Christian community, but there are many different ones, organised around regional, language and sectarian bases. There are Kerala, Goan Tamil, Anglo-Indians in North India, Naga and North East Indian Christians, who are different in their language, socio-cultural practices and economic status. It is difficult to speak about a general Christian way of life in India for these very reasons. There are many churches, many denominations or groups, many sects or brotherhoods among them.

According to the 1981 Census there were 18 million Christians in India and the percentage of Christians in India's population accounted to 2.43 per cent. The total Christian population had almost kept up with the national increase of 24.69 per cent over 1971-81. In 1991 their population was 2.32 percent of the total population. However, the distribution of Christian population has been very uneven in India. There are dense settlements of Christians in some parts of the country while in other regions there are small and scattered Christian communities. In Andhra Pradesh, in the year 1981, the Christians represented 2.68 percent of the total population. In Kerala the percentage of Christians was 20.6. So also Manipur had a 29.7 per cent Christian population.

In fact, Meghalaya with 52.6 percent and Nagaland with 80.2 percent registered the highest concentration of Christian populations. Tamil Nadu had 5.78 percent Christian which was over twice the national average. Very low percentages of the Christian population had been recorded in some central and northern states of the community. For example, Jammu and Kashmir 0.14 percent, Madhya Pradesh 0.7 percent, Rajasthan 0.12 percent and Uttar Pradesh 0.15 percent. In 1991, the highest concentration of Christians was found in Nagaland (87.46 percent) and Meghalaya (85.73 percent). In some States such as Himachal Pradesh, Rajasthan, Haryana etc. the Christian population was very low.

Christianity in India

Christianity came to Kerala through the work of St. Thomas, a disciple of Jesus in the first century and in the fourth century through the influence of traders from Syria. Accounts show that St. Thomas, a follower of Jesus, converted several Nambuthiri Brahmans to Christianity. Thomas is said to have landed in the ancient port of Muziris in 52 A.D.

The Christians of St. Thomas were very prosperous, and historians write that the local kings were very pleased with them and gave them several privileges. In 345 A.D. a Christian, Thomas of Cana set out with permission from the Bishop of his land, and came to Kerala with a number of Christians from Jerusalem, Baghdad and Nineveh.

The Indian Church of St. Thomas came into a close relationship with the Persian Church from the time of the arrival of this immigrant group. However, in the sixteenth century, Persia lost control over the Indian church for the St. Thomas Christians came under the ritual domination of the Portuguese who had arrived in India for purposes of trade. When the Portuguese arrived in India they found a well established Christian Church, where the believers spoke of themselves as being "the Christians of St. Thomas". They are also called the Syrian Christians.

This period began with the 'discovery' of a sea route to India by Vasco de Gama in 1498. Trade was not their only concern. The priests who followed the first Portuguese travellers and discoverers began the establishment of Portuguese rituals in the Churches of Kerala. The Christians of St. Thomas loved their ancient ceremonies, and they did not want to transfer their loyalty from the Patriarch of the East (who was like their Pope) to the Pope of Rome.

It was only in 1653 that the St. Thomas Christians were able to free themselves from Portuguese domination. At this time a division was created in the community of St. Thomas Christians, between those who followed the Pope, and those who followed the Patriarch of the Eastern churches. Historical events, such as the coming of the English divided the community into several more groups. Some of these are called the Anglican (now a part of the church of South India) Mar Thoma, Evangelical and the Yakoba. The Yakoba are themselves divided into two parties because of a church quarrel. Yet, all these groups or denominations share a similar culture. The church practices of each of the group is somewhat different.

In 1509 Alfonso de Albuquerque saw that if the Portuguese were to consolidate their commercial interests they must have a permanent residential interest in India. Goa became central in this interest, and along with administrators the ships of the Portuguese also carried priests. Evangelical work among the native people of Goa began with the work of Franciscan friar Antony de Loueo in 1517. In 1542, Francis Xavier arrived in Goa, and soon after he began his work amongst the Paravas, the fisher-folk in the Coromandel Coast.

The Dutch followed the Portuguese in the colonisation of India and consequently, its commercial exploitation. However. they were not zealous in spreading the Christian faith, and they did not arouse the deep hostility that the Portuguese did. The English followed the Dutch, and they spread the Gospel through missionaries.

In 1793, Carey and Thomas of the Baptist Missionary society arrived in Kolkata, where they proceeded to translate and print the Bible in the vernacular. In 1806, Rev. Caludius Buchanan was already writing about the importance of the dissemination of the Bible in Malabar, and he was aided in his plans by the British Resident in Travancore. Benjamin Bailey spent decades in the translation of the Bible in Kottayam, Kerala.

In the North East hills of India the first attempt to preach Christianity was made by William Carey, the founder of Serampore College near Calcutta. He sent one of his early converts named Krishna Chandra Pal to the Khasi hills in 1813.

Christian Missions were from a very early period interested in education. Western ideas were introduced through the schools and colleges set up by Christian missionaries, and in turn had its impact in the growth of the National movement. We know how close Mahatma Gandhi was to C.F. Andrews and how the gentleness of Jesus' life made a profound impact on the ideas on non-violence that Gandhi evolved, for liberating the country from its colonial fetters.

Tenets Of Christian Faith

However, in spite of regional variations as described above there are certain tenets, which unite Christian life and experience all over the country. The first of these is that all Christians believe that Jesus Christ of Nazareth is their saviour. They believe that Jesus was born to Mary, a virgin, and that God, the Father, sent him to redeem people of their sins. The concept of virgin birth, is accepted alike by Catholic, Protestant and Orthodox Christians in India. Christianity asserts that Jesus was the Son of God. However, Jesus' father on earth was Joseph. He was a carpenter who protected Mary and took her away to Bethlehem where the baby Jesus was born in a stable. The story of the poverty surrounding Jesus' birth is a very important one for Christians. It establishes the background of much of what Jesus taught, and the manner in which his teachings celebrated poverty, meekness and humility.

The Life of Jesus

The life of Jesus is the central principle around which Christians in India organise their ritual life. The two most important religious festivals of the Christians are Christmas and Easter. Christmas marks the anniversary of Jesus' birth, and is celebrated by attending the Church, eating festival food, wearing new clothes and greeting friends and neighbours. In India, there would be differences among Christians in the kind of festive food that is served, or the kind of clothes that are worn. These are, however, regional differences of custom. The belief that Jesus' birth must be celebrated and this celebration unites Bengali, Punjabi, Tamil, Goan, Malayali, Konkan or Naga Christians. Similarly, all Christians mourn the crucifixion of Jesus on Good Friday, and celebrate his Resurrection, or victory over death on Easter Sunday. All Christians believe that Jesus was killed by his enemies who hated what he taught; but on the third day, he arose from the tomb and convinced his followers of his divinity, for soon after he ascended to heaven. The Christian church then came into existence with the belief in the Resurrection of Jesus. The Eucharist service, which is the central part of Christian rituals, enacts the life of Jesus. It is like a sacred drama, which is performed so that the Christians may continually remember the life of Jesus, hear again his teachings, and try to live their lives in the way that he taught his disciples. Let us now briefly discuss the various elements of Christian faith.

Various Elements of Christian Faith

Christianity is a historical religion, and all Indian Christians accept that their Master, born in the Middle East, was Jesus of Nazareth. The Bible is the sacred book of the Christians. It provides the basis for Christian beliefs and the norms for Christian behaviour. The Four Gospels (a part of the Bible) of Matthew, Mark, Luke and John to be found in the Bible are often read by all Christians in the country. These are memories of Jesus' life; they affirm that Jesus is authentically human, as well as Lord, Messiah (Christos, the Son of God).

For all Christians in India as elsewhere, the reality of God is affirmed in Jesus' life on earth. All Christians accept the propriety of speaking of God in a three-fold manner, as Father, Son and Holy Spirit. This is a problem of great theological complexity, and among Christians there can be differences in the interpretation of the relationship between Father, Son and Holy Spirit. Let us, for our purposes merely say that all Christians believe in the Trinity. They believe also that the Universe has been divinely created, that people are sinful, and that Jesus was sent to earth so that people and God could become reconciled. The Christian Church was founded by Jesus and his spirit is constantly present and sustains all the Church and all believers. Finally, all Christians believe that all human life (human history) must one day close, and then will follow the day of judgement when people will either be rewarded or punished according to the kinds of life they have led.

Social Organisation in India

Christianity, like any other religion, is a way of life. Differences in the social organisation of Christianity will arise from the historical, cultural, political and geographical environment in which the community is founded. Thus the social organisation of Christians in Goa, Delhi, Punjab, Nagaland or Tamil Nadu will differ from one another depending upon the region and its culture and/or sectarian differences. The social organisation of Christians of St.

Thomas, called the Syrian Christians, has been described in order to show you the specific nature of organisation of a particular Christian community in India. It is only one example of Christian life in our country, but it may help you to understand what Christianity is about. The following sections describe Christian social organisation in terms of family, the role of Priest, Church and Christmas among Syrian Christians of Kerala. The interaction between and some common rituals of the Christians and Hindus have also been referred. In the earlier sections, the origins of Christians in India and some of their basic beliefs have been given. All this should give you some ideas regarding the social life and organisation of the Christians in India.

The Christian Family

The Syrian Christian family is a very close knit one. Let us look at Christian family relationships, and see what they say about this particular Indian Christian community.

The Husband's Mother

When a Christian bride enters her husband's home, her husband's mother would have a very important role to play in her new life. Close relations between a Syrian Christian husband and wife, specially in the early years, are thought to be unseemly. When they move into an independent household with the birth of children, that husband and wife complement each other, but a certain reserve always marks their relationship.

The closeness of family bonds, which characterises the Syrian Christian family, is a tribute in fact to the relationship between a woman and her son's wives. It is not merely cooking and the organisation of the household that a bride learns from her husband's mother. She learns the Christian virtues of charity and piety as well. However, there are often tensions between the two women, since the relationship is an unequal one.

The Husband's Father

The relation of a Syrian Christian woman to her husband's father is one of respect. He is the head of the household till the time of his death. However, by the time he is about sixty years of age, he may retire from active social life. While actual control of property may be in the hands of the sons, the father is treated with great respect, and his advice is always sought. It is he who leads the family at prayer when after dinner the family kneels together on the carefully laid out reed mats. Further, it is the father who gives formal permission, necessary economic assistance and the blessings when a couple want to set up house separately. The relationship between sons and fathers is one marked by devotion, affection, obedience and respect on the one side, and by patronage and authoritarianism on the other. This relation, full of tensions, is also reflected in the relation of the bride to her husband's father.

For many Christians, while they live in *nuclear households* (consisting of parents and their unmarried children) the ideal family that they generally desire are *three generations,* in which all the sons bring their brides into the paternal households, and live all together with their children.

However, in practice, amongst the Syrian Christians, the sons set up separate households with the birth of children.

The Grandparents

For these Christians, grandparents play a very important role because they live close by. The paternal grandmother is an important person in the life of the child, particularly as the child grows up. A teasing relationship is often evident. Even before they go to formal school, they accompany their grandmother every day to the parish church. It is to her that they recount the events of the day. She teaches them stories from the bible and songs about Jesus.

On the other hand, with the grandfather the relationship is one of great formality. This is the consequence of authoritarianism and patrilineality. The grandfather in the Christian household is the *griha nayakan* (head of the house) and this idea of domestic authority is pervasive, he leads in family prayers, gets priority in being served the best at meal times, makes all important decisions regarding property, money and the arrangement of marriages.

The Mother's Brother

The mother's brother is of great importance to the children. Gifts from the mother's brother are received on occasions of marriage and birth. The mother's brother always brings abundant quantities of fruit and sweet foods called *palaharam* when he comes to visit. Many Christmas vacations are spent at the mother's brother's house with the maternal grandparents. Here the children are honoured and beloved guests.

As they grow up, however, their father's house becomes more important. It now becomes the centre of their life, particularly when they are sons. It is to this house and property that they will be heirs. This is "their own house" as opposed to their "mother's brother's house".

Patrilocal Residence

Patrilocal residence (staying in the same locality as the father) is of great importance to these Christians. Brothers always live in neighbouring houses, food and garden products are often shared. They visit each other, celebrate rituals and ceremonies in each other's houses, share sorrows and difficulties. The link between them is that they are of the same blood and the same name.

Patrilineage

For the Syrian Christian, the patrilineage is important, and the significance of house names must be understood in this respect. A man is better known as Vazhapallil Paul or Pallivadikal Thomas, for the house name carries the ideas of property, privileges and lineage. It expresses the idea of patrilineal descent or of membership in a lineage organised around the male descendants of an ancestor.

In contrast to descent is filiation, which relates an individual to both parents, not merely to the father and his male relatives. The relation of children to their mother is in striking contrast to their relation with their father. It is to the mother that the young child turns to for every need, and she mediates between the child and the father, the latter being a distant figure. In fact, among these Christians all women should be like Mary, the mother of Jesus. They must be gentle, soft and humble like the *matav* (mother).

Women are never formally included in the affairs of the outside world, those relating to the domain of property and income for instance. Even in the question of marriage it is the fathers who meet, discuss financial and practical matters and fix the alliance. Women cook, clean, take care of children and are devoted to the religious life, spending much time in prayer and attending devotions at the Church.

Inheritance

Till 1986, women were given *stridhanam* by their fathers, which was seen to be their share in father's wealth. It was controlled not by women, but by the husband's father. After a Supreme Court ruling in 1986, a woman may inherit equally with her brothers should her father die without writing a will. Written wills, however, ensure even today that it is sons who inherit property, while daughters are given away in marriage with *stridhanam,* which is never really hers to use, since her husband's father or her husband will control it.

Inheritance customs express the dominant place of the father in the Syrian Christian household. Traditionally the concept of equal share was never of importance to the Syrians. Property was divided according to the whim of the father, or according to the need of his children. The question of manipulation and favouritism arose frequently. The writing of wills has always been very popular amongst these Christians, and the father has absolute control over his sons.

What does this brief discussion of the Christian family show? It describes patriarchal authority which is in fact the basis of Christian social organisation. The next section will discuss the church in the context of Christian social organisation.

THE CHURCH

Here we will look at the priest, the church and the celebration of a Christian festival, i.e. Christians, in order to understand more aspects of Christian social organisation.

The construction of the traditional Syrian church in Kerala follows the principles laid down by the Hindu *Shastras* on architecture. It is surrounded by a courtyard on all sides. The walls are similar to Hindu temple walls in height, width and design. Inside, the Church is whitewashed;

sometimes there are religious paintings on the wall or ceilings. These pictures tell the story of Jesus, and often have pictures of St. Thomas, who is said to have brought Christianity to Kerala. The altar is placed on a higher platform, and no one may climb the steps upto this sanctuary. It's a holy place. Only the priests and his assistants are allowed access to the altar, the holy vessels, the cross and candles that are kept there. There are no chairs or pews in the traditional Syrian Church. The floor is covered with reed mats, and on these the people kneel and pray. The men stand on the left side facing the altar; the women stand on the right side. There is an aisle between them, down which the priest's assistants will walk swinging the container of burning incense, which purifies the air. Many churches have silver or bronze oil lamps that have wicks burning in them. The devotees come and pour oil into these lamps and each will light a wick in honour of Jesus. In each of these churches there will usually be a large stone cross in the outer courtyard, which can be seen from very far away.

The church is the heart of Christian social life. People in the villages visit the church every evening for *Sandhya Namaskaram* and in the morning for *Vishudha Qurbana*, the Holy Sacrifice. The Holy Sacrifice is a symbol of the life of Jesus. The priest, through the rituals of the church, acts out of the great mystery of the life of Jesus. The mystery of religious belief lies in that moment and practical reality is kept away, while the sacred world is for that moment brought closer. Everyday, the people participate in the great mystery of the Sacrifice, and specially on Sundays the churches are full. The two greatest festivals are Christmas and Easter, which are celebrated with great joy. In fact, for many traditional Christians, the perception of time is not according to the Western calendar year, but centres around the life of Jesus. It begins with the birth of Christ.

The Priest

The Christian priest is greatly respected by his parishioners. When he conducts prayers and offers the sacrifice (as the central rite of Christianity is called) he stands in place of Jesus Christ. He has the power to reveal the sacred world to those who believe. The Christian priest is a man of God. Amongst the Yakobas, the priest is expected to grow a long beard, and wear a round black cap, loose trousers and a flowing black or white gown. These are the signs by which a priest is known. He must be always calm and disciplined.

When he goes to the Church he must not talk to anyone, all of his being must be directed to God. When people are in trouble, ill, suffering or dying he must be with them. At times of joy, feasting, marriages, births, entering a new house, he must be present to bless the occasion. No one will start a celebratory meal without the priest. If the village is having an exhibition of fire-crackers on a feast day or a function, the priest must be present. He is given the best place to sit in, the best food, and the greatest respect.

The prelates or Bishops of the Church are treated with even greater respect. It is only on festivals and other important occasions that the people meet them. At other times they live in the monastery in meditation and prayer. The Bishops are the leaders of the community. Every Christian knows them by sight and by name. To be related to a Bishop in anyway is of great value. As soon as the Christians see a Bishop, all conversation stops, every one stands at attention. Even if the Bishop is younger than many of his parishioners, they express great respect, almost awe. Those who come to him must bow their heads and receive a blessing with his handcross.

Christmas

Twenty five days before Christmas are days of Lent or

abstinence, to mark the coming of great Joy. The days before Christmas are days of hectic activity. The house is cleaned and made ready for guests. On Christmas Eve all the churches are open, decorated with green leaves and plants. The houses on the roadside look bright with lights. The streets are full of children. Each Christian house is marked by a big star, because when Jesus was born, a bright star was seen in the sky. There is usually among these Christians of Kerala, no practice of decorating a tree, buying new clothes or sending greeting cards. What is given great importance is going to Church, eating an elabourately cooked meal and spending the day together with relations and friends. Those who are wealthy have their houses white washed, while others clean, polish and wash their houses for a week.

The first part of the Christmas service begins on the twenty-four evening. The main service takes place in the early hours (3 a.m.) of the twenty-fifth of December. In the evening prayers, the priest tells the people about the birth of Christ to Virgin Mary. He tells them of the wise men who came from the East and gave Jesus gifts, and how shepherds came to see the child who was born in Bethlehem. The priest tells the people again how poor Jesus was born in a manger, wrapped in rags amongst animals. After these hymns and prayers of the evening, the people go home.

At 3 a.m. on Christmas morning all the Christians will be walking to their church. They bring with them oil, candles and incense as gifts for the church. In the Church, the priest wears very beautiful golden and green robes, the candles are all lit, and the Church is filled with the fragrance of incense. In the Christmas songs and prayers that follow an important place is given to Mary. She is *deva mata* (mother of God) *rajmakal,* a princess and David *putri* (a daughter of King David).

After the celebration of Qurbana (Holy Sacrifice) the people kiss the Cross and leave their gifts of incense and oil. They are like the shepherds and the wise men who came to Jesus at his birth and left offerings for him.

Dawn breaks as people leave the Church. The narrow roads and bylanes are full of early morning worshippers each greeting the other. No one is dressed in his or her newest or best, all come to Church in simple ordinary clothes, usually white cotton. It is enough that they have woken up at 2.30 a.m. to express their devotion and belief in the birth of Jesus.

Having described one of their rituals, we shall now try to show in the next section, how Christianity in India is to be understood in relation to its regional cultural dimensions. Here we have described the relation of Christianity to Hinduism in Kerala.

Relation with Hinduism

The Christians of Kerala are in a specific cultural relationship to their Hindu neighbours. We will take some examples here in order to understand how the Christian and the Hindu share many aspects of their social life together. Let us first look at calendar and time.

Calendar and Time

The Malayalam era follows the Christian era by 825 years. It is still used in everyday speech when referring to the past, for marking the dates of the establishment of churches, houses and gravestones. If you wish to know which year 2005 is in the Malayalam era, you only have to subtract 825 years.

The months have names different from the Western calendar months. Each month has a certain attribute or character. Thus *Karkadam* (July-August) is considered to be the worst, a time of rain and hunger. *Kanni* (September-October) is thought to be a bad and inauspicious month, and during this period house construction will not begin, nor will marriages take place. *Dhanu* is the best season, and it is the time of Christmas, which the Christians celebrate with great joy.

The calculation of time according to moments is still done by the *nazhika*. The day is divided into 60 *nazhikas,* and each *nazhika* is 60 vinazhikas (24 seconds). This precise way of calculating time is used by people in making traditional (Ayurvedic) medicines, which follow given rules, held by both Hindus and Christians to be life laws of nature.

Days have special significance in terms of auspicious and inauspicious. Wednesdays are considered so dangerous that there is a saying that even a leopard cub will not emerge from its mother's womb. Fridays and Tuesdays were considered auspicious by both Hindus and Christians for oil baths and washing the head in the most elaborate fashion. On these days men would avoid travel, as this would cause extra work on a day which belonged to the women. Let us look at another example, that of house building, now.

Building of Houses

The Hindu *asari* (craftsman) who builds for the Christian, follows the customs and rules that he would for a Hindu client. The Christian places wholehearted trust in the *thachan* or carpenter who follows the rules laid down by the *Thatchu Shastra.* These are rules of measurement, location and construction. The Christian house is in architectural style essentially like any Hindu house of similar status, A traditional house-builder said, "In this matter the Christians have full faith in the Hindu *Shastras*. They know that if we do not do as the books say then some misfortune will befall the house or the occupants."

Elements of Caste in Christianity

The Syrian Christians of Kerala believe that their ancestors were Brahmans who were converted to Christianity by St. Thomas, a follower and friend of Jesus who came to Kerala in 52 A. D. The Christians believe that when they converted from Hinduism to Christianity, they were forced to break away from their original caste group.

However, their caste status is maintained by them because they are careful to behave in certain ways, which are in keeping with caste defined behaviour. They maintain the traditional boundaries and distances between high and low castes, even though this is against the moral laws of Christian life. It was the only way in which they could survive, and survive they did for almost two thousand years. Adaptation and compromise were the two laws by which this Christian community lived for many centuries. Even today, in spite of the many changes brought about by modernisation, they sustain their daily life, many of the traditional customs of the past. Let us look at some of these.

Like the Hindus, they have faith in horoscopes; like their Hindu neighbours they too tie the *tali* or marriage locket; they observe death pollution often to fifteen days, and the rituals of bathing to remove death pollution called *pula kuli*. Like the Hindus, they celebrate *onam* and *vishu* (harvest and new year festivals). They also celebrate *annaprasanam* (first feeding of a child with rice).

7

Zoroastrian Social Organisation

Zoroastrianism is one of the oldest religions of the world. It takes its name from "Zarasthustra" (Zoroaster) who probably lived around the beginning of the first millennium B.C. His life period is dated diversely by historians as being anywhere between the fourth to ninth century B.C. Another name for Zoroastrianism is "*Mazdaism*" and is derived from the name of the religion's supreme God "Mazda" (meaning wise) or *Ahura Mazda* (meaning wise Lord). Fire is worshipped as a symbol of '*Ahura Mazda*' since it has the characteristics of purity and brightness.

The roots of Zoroastrianism can be located in an Iranian tribal and basically pastoral society. Research suggests that historically this religion originated in the eastern and south central regions of the Iranian world. It began between the great mountain ranges of the Hindukush and Seistan, an area that today is divided between Iran and Afganisthan. By 500 B.C. Zoroastrianism had become the leading faith in Persia and Medea (now modern Iran). The Iranian-Zoroaster influence faced a serious challenge with the conquest of Iran by the Islamic Arabians in the seventh century A.D. The exodus or mass migration of Zoroastrians into other regions of the world can be seen to be a direct result of the forced Islamisation of Iran.

The Zoroastrian religion was introduced in India about eighth century A.D. It is said that the first batch of Zoroastrians or Parsis reached Diu about 766 A.D. However, they abandoned it and set out for another place of residence. They took refuge in Gujarat. During their voyage to Gujarat from Diu their ship was overtaken by a storm. The voyaging Parsis took a vow that if they reached the shore in Gujarat safely they would establish the most sacred fire temple (called Atash Behram) there. The vow was duly fulfilled and a fire temple was consecrated in Sanjan (in Gujarat) where the Parsis landed safely. They took to agriculture and horticulture in and around Sanjan. As their numbers increased they spread to other parts of Gujarat. When the Muslims conquered Sanjan in the fifteenth century, the sacred fire was moved frequently and finally established at Udvada. The fire temple in Udvada is looked upon as the most sacred temple of the Parsis. Zoroastrian immigrants to India are said to have come from Pars. This is why they are known as Parsee. (Parsi also sometimes spelt as Parsee). The Parsi community has adopted Gujarati as their official language. Let us now look at their numbers.

ZOROASTRIAN POPULATION

The Zoroastrian population around the world is estimated to be roughly 1,30,000 of which 82,000 are believed to be in India. Of this 82,000, more than 78.5 percent are reported to be living in Bombay. The strength of the Parsi population in India has varied between 80,000 and 82,000 as is evident from the recorded population censuses between 1881-1981. Their strength decreased to 76,382 by the year 1991. The Parsi community in India is found mainly in Maharashtra and specially in Bombay, Gujarat and Deccan. In 1991 a majority of 79.2 percent of Zorastrians lived in Maharashtra, followed by Gujarat (16.92 percent).

Socio-Economic Life

Migrating to India over 1300 years ago, the Parsis have been an important part of the economic, political, educational and social life of India. Prior to and during the Muslim rule they lent their support to Hindu princes whenever it was needed. They played an important role in the Mughal administration. Following the arrival of the British they were among the first people to adopt to the western style of life and to English education. The Parsis began in India as a small mercantile community. They excelled themselves in trade and commerce. Two of the leading areas of economic activity in the nineteenth century, shipbuilding and the textile industry, owe their rapid growth mainly to the investment and trading initiative of the Parsis. Thus, early growth of the modern shipping industry in India is associated with the name of a Parsi family the Wadias. They were commissioned by the British for the management of the biggest shipyard in Bombay continuously for 150 years from 1735-1885. Another Parsi, D.R. Bannaji owned a personal fleet of thirty trading vessels (i.e. ships). Between 1915 and 1925, nearly 20 percent to 30 percent of the cotton mills in Bombay were owned by Parsis.

Parsis have also been contributing greatly to the steel, chemical, cement, and other heavy industries. This has been so both during the British India and post Independent India. We have all heard about the Tata family. They were pioneers of the steel industry in India. Today they also run a host of other industries such as jute, chemical, tea, textile, printing, insurance, and so on. The Tata family is not only associated with industry but also with education and social work.

Parsis eminent in the political, economic, educational and social work in India during the nineteenth and early twentieth centuries included B.M. Malabari, S.S. Bengali, N.

Fardoonji, P.M. Mazban, Sir P. Mehta, Sir D. Wacha, Maneckji, D. Petit, J. Tata, C.J. Readyymony and so many others.

The Parsis began in India as a small mercantile community. Gradually, a number of their families became successful industrial entrepreneurs, merchants, educationalists, social reformers, lawyers and pioneers in many other fields.

Proof of their open attitude with regard to occupational selection lies in that many of the Parsis derive their family names from the occupations their ancestors pursued in India. Many of their descendents still do so. Interesting family titles thus include: Unwala (wool dealer), Kapadia (cloth dealer), Jhaveri (jeweller), Motiwala (pearl dealer), Biscuitwala (biscuit dealer), Batliwala (bottle dealer), Ginwala (wine dealer), Sodawaterwala (Soda dealer), Mondalwala (wine dealer), etc.

In general, Parsis are represented in different jobs. There is evidence to indicate that they have held many types of posts. Supportive data for this is available as early as the middle of the nineteenth century.

Currently more and more Parsis are establishing themselves in the scientific and other professions. Homi J. Bhabha was the pioneer of nuclear research in India and General S.H.F.J. Manekshaw is the first Field Marshall of the Indian Army. Modern education is widely shared by all the various communities in India and the entrepreneurial skills of communities like Sindhis, Punjabis and Marwaris have come to the fore in modern India. However, Parsis continue to do well in most fields of endeavour. Socio-economic life of this community is influenced by the tenets of Zoroastrianism. We shall now describe the main features of this religion.

TENETS OF ZOROASTRIANISM

Zoroaster, the founder of Zoroastrianism preached monotheism (belief in one supreme God and a deep moral life. He was against idol worship and over emphasis of ritual sacrifice. The basic tenets of Zoroastrianism are outlined mainly in two texts. The first of these is the *Avesta* or the *Zend Avesta*—it is a collection of texts gathered in writing roughly between the fourth and sixth century A.D. The second is the *Gatha* which comprises texts which are attributed to Zarathustra. These belonged initially to the oral tradition. The *Gathas* are five in number. The first four are ethical and philosophical. They describe and emphasise the omnipotence of or all pervading nature of *"Ahura Mazda"*. They also deal with the problem of evil due to the activities of the evil spirit. The fifth *Gatha*, is a hymn on the occasion of Zoroaster's daughter's marriage. The *Gathas* are written in *Avesta* which closely resembles Vedic Sanskrit. *Ahura Mazda* is considered to be the supreme God. He is the creator of heaven and earth, day and night, light and darkness. Life is seen as a struggle between the forces of good and evil.

The evil spirit is *"Angra Mainyu"*. One has to choose between good and evil. The ethical dualism (dualism indicated in the existence of good spirits and evil spirits) that Zoroaster preached, emphasised that there are differences between

human actions motivated by goodness and those that are motivated by evil. Purity in thoughts, words and deeds implies the will to do good. Anything that is not guided by this motive is apt to turn into evil. Therefore the primary task of man is to live a righteous life. He must fight against the evil spirits along with his creator *Ahura Mazda*. They will be helped by a host of good spirits. One who lives a righteous life attains paradise. This is described as a state of immortal holiness in thought, word and deed. If one leads an impious life that person is condemned to an eternal hell of evil thoughts, deeds, and physical torment. The Parsis believe that the soul lives on after death. It meets its fate on the day of judgement, under the supervision of *Ahura Mazda*.

An important feature of Zoroastrianism is that it does not preach celibacy, asceticism, renunciation or self denial in life. It demands strict purity in thought, word and deed. This consists of abstinence from acts like adultery, rape, and the like.

Purity is essentially associated with fire. For the Parsis fire is worshipped as a symbol of purity, energy, force, light and radiance. And fire is a symbol of *Ahura Mazda*. Zoroastrian temples take the form of fire temples and are of three grades—*Atash Behrams*, *Agiaris* and *Dadgahs*, in that order of sacredness. Once the sacred fire is installed in a fire temple it must always be kept alive (always kept burning).

Many fire temples are places of pilgrimage for the Parsis. The oldest fire is known as the ''Iranshah" which is supposed to have been burning for more than 1300 years. This is in Udvada. All Parsis have sacred flames burning in their houses also. These flames are kept burning constantly. In the fire temple the priest reads portions of the sacred scripture—the *Avesta*, five times a day. In each household, a Parsi is also expected to say prayers five times each day.

The translation of the sacred texts, including the Avesta was completed in 1820, from Pahalvi (ancient language) to Gujarati. The average Parsi is thus able to have access to the sacred texts for daily use in prayers. Zoroastrianism does not advocate fasting for religious merit.

The *Gathas* of Zoroaster is another source of information about Zoroastrian belief. They present the picture of a society in which agriculture and herds of domestic animals had come to be looked upon with affection. In the sacred prayer "Behram Yesht" the reverence that is shown to the cow is evident. This aspect of Zoroastrian faith (respect to the cow) reflects the interaction with Hinduism as Hindus also look upon the cow as a sacred animal. We will now discuss some of the rites, rituals and customs observed by the Parsis relating to birth, initiation, death, marriage and family. These reflect the belief systems discussed above. They also indicate the adaptations the Parsis have made as a result of the interaction with local dominant population and their rulers at different points in time.

Zoroastrian beliefs are closely linked with the way day-to-day life is carried on by the members of Parsi community. In the next section, we will see how basic rites and religious ceremonies form an important part of Parsi social life.

Aspects Oof Social Organisation

In this section we describe important life cycle rituals relating to birth and death. The social institutions of marriage and family are also discussed here. The Parsi system of inheritance and succession, the Panchayat and Festivals also figure in our discussion of the social organisation.

Rites of Initiation and Death

Even though Zoroastianism does not emphasise ritualism especially rituals sacrifices, there are some basic rites and religious ceremonies which form an integral part of the organisation of Parsi social life.

Rites of Initiation

Initiation rites mark the birth of a child into the Parsi family. On this occasion the child's lips are steeped in *haoma* (the sacred liquor). Full membership into the community is granted only when the child (both to a boy and a girl) attains the age between seven and fifteen. He or she then receives the girdle or cord called the *Kushti* or *Kusti*. This ceremony usually takes place before a child attains puberty. This initiation rite is called *Navjot* or *Naojote* (meaning new birth) and marks the admission of a Parsi boy or a girl into Zoroastrian faith. In addition, there is a host of other purificatory rites, which are often performed by many Parsis. They include the *padyab* (meaning ablution) *nahn* (meaning bath) or washing of one's body. The *bareshnum* is a complicated ritual performed at special places with the participation of a dog. The left ear of the dog is touched by the person concerned. The gaze of this animal is believed to put the evil spirit to flight. The purification rites for the initiation of priests and corpse-bearers, involve, apart from other things *gomez* (consecrated urine), originally cow's urine following Indo-Iranian practices and ideas.

Death Rites

The Parsi custom of disposing the dead is indeed unique. Death rites are probably the most elaborate of the Parsi rites. These reflect, among other things, their attitude to life and life after death. Parsis do not burn or bury their dead lest this should pollute fire or earth and make them liable to a strict punishment. They carry the dead body, amidst elaborate rituals, to a place built high up for this purpose. This is called a dokhma or 'Tower of Silence'. The body is left there to be eaten up by vultures.

The removal of the dead body (for its final disposal) must only be done during the daytime. As for the Tower of Silence, its interior consists of three concentric circles, one each for men, women and children. The corpses are exposed without any dress. The vultures do not take long (an hour or two at the most) to remove the flesh off the bones. The bones are dried by the sun, and later swept into a central well. Formerly, the bones were kept in an ossuary, (the place where bones of the dead are deposited) or what they called *astodan,* to preserve them from rain and animals. The morning of the fourth day is marked as the most solemn observance in the death ritual. It is believed that the departed soul reaches the next world and appears before the deities who are to pass judgement over it. The souls, they believe would be judged in the presence of *Ahura Mazda* and his helping spirits.

Marriage and Family

Marriage is solemnised and sanctified by a religious ceremony but it is a contract. The prayers are recited from the Avesta. As a result of Hindu influence, prayers are recited in Sanskrit too. Marriage is, by and large monogamous. Consent of both the boy and girl is essential for finalising marriage. Zoroastrianism prescribes strict monogamy. Religious tradition does not approve of child marriage. Dissolution of marriage (divorce or separation) is allowed under certain conditions. In fact in 1936, The Parsi Marriage and Divorce Act outlined clearly conditions under which divorce can be allowed. It also stated that both parties in marriage (husband and wife) could initiate 78 divorce proceedings. This law has been based on the liberal principles of Zoroastrianism, which grants rights to both men and women.

A Zoroastrian woman is considered as an equal partner in marriage and family. Both men and women are entitled to religious and secular education. Parents of the bride and the groom contribute to the expenses involved in setting up of their new household. A woman enjoys inheritance rights both in her capacity as a daughter and as a wife. Remarriage is allowed and a widow does not have to forego inheritance rights over her husband's property if she remarries.

Thus Zoroastrianism has sanctioned liberal attitudes and practices regarding marriage and family. However, some of the less liberal attitudes and customs of the local population with which the Parsis came into contact have also made their impact on the institutions of marriage. Research has pointed out that by the seventeenth century A.D. Parsis settled in Gujarat had begun to pattern their social relationships after the Hindu society. Thus child marriage became common, some males practised bigamy or polygyny and widow remarriage was not easy. The evil practice of dowry also became prevalent. Horoscopes (birth charts) came to be prepared for Parsi children by Hindu priests.

These customs, especially dowry, bigamy, polygyny, child marriages, ban on widow remarriage, and divorce, came to be challenged by the enlightened sections of the Hindu and Parsi community including the members of Parsi Panchayat. Many members of Parsi community pointed out that these customs were not sanctioned by Zoroaster and therefore had to be stopped. Their concerted efforts indeed led to the removal of many of these practices. For instance, as a result of the vigorous campaigning by the social reformers of the nineteenth and early twentieth century, the 1929 Sarda Act was passed. This act penalised marriages of girls below 14 years of age and boys below 18 years. However, by this time there were hardly any child marriages among the Parsis. In fact, since then, the age of marriage has been rising, and since the 1960's the average age at marriage for Parsi men have been between 25-28 years. For Parsi women this is between 23-25 years.

One important aspect regarding marriage and family, in which women suffer a disability even today, has been the aspect of inter-religious marriage. The child of a Parsi father and non-Parsi mother, whether in wedlock or out of it, can be initiated into the Zoroastrian faith by the Navjote or

Naojote ceremony. However, neither by religion nor by law can a child of a Parsi mother and a non-Parsi father be admitted into Zoroastrianism. The steady decline in the size of the Parsi population can be traced, (to some extent) to the increasing number of marriages between Parsi women and non-Parsi men. Children born of such marriages are not recognised as Zoroastrians. Hence the decline in the number of members enumerated as Parsis. The Parsi community has not been able to stop such inter-religious marriages since Parsi girls enjoy the right to choose their spouses. Conservative members have their reservations and resentment against marriage between a Parsi and a non-Parsi. A Parsi boy's marriage with a non-Parsi girl is accepted with greater grace than the marriage of a Parsi girl with a non-Parsi boy. Since Zoroastrianism is not a proselytising religion (it does not preach or practise conversion) it does not easily accept non-Parsi members into its fold.

Parsi girls marrying a non-Parsi boy by the 1954 Special Marriage Act have made a claim to the Parsi Panchayat that they must be given the right to visit the fire temple and remain a Parsi. It must be pointed out that these girls (those marrying non-Parsis) do not lose their rights of inheritance or intestate succession.

Inheritance and Succession

A feature of the rules governing the Parsi intestate (without making a will) is that the share of male heir is double that of a female heir of the same degree. For example, if a male Parsi dies leaving a widow and children, the property will be divided so that the share of each son and widow will be double the share of each daughter. Further if a male Parsi dies leaving one or both parents in addition to his wife and children, the property will be divided so that the father will receive a share equal to half the share of a son. The mother will receive a share equal to half the share of the daughter. On the other hand if a female Parsi dies intestate her husband and her children, will receive an equal share of her property.

Among Parsis adoption is not recognised by custom or law for purposes of inheritance and succession. A Parsi widow without any children, can adopt a son on the 4th day of her husband's death. This is for the temporary purpose of performing certain religious rites for the dead man. This adoption is for a limited purpose and does not grant any property rights on the adopted *"palak"*.

What is clear, from these Parsi rules of inheritance and succession, is that while they recognise the woman's right to inheritance and succession, the Parsi daughter's share of her father's property remains half of that of a son. It must be pointed out that most of these provisions were enacted in 1939. At that time these rules conferred more rights to women than the then existing Hindu and Muslim laws.

Parsi Panchayat

Earlier we had mentioned that the Parsi Panchayat (also called *Anjuman*) played a role in reforming certain practices which reflected the infiltration of non-Zoroastrian elements into Parsi institutions (eg. child marriage, ban of remarriage, polygyny etc). In this section we will briefly examine the role of the Parsi Panchayat in India.

From the time Parsis landed in India, there were some members among them who negotiated with the rulers and traders on behalf of their community. Gradually the Parsi Panchayat or Council of Elders came into being. This was established in Surat and Navsari around the middle of the seventeenth century.

It consisted of both priests and laypersons. In this context, it is important to talk of the divisions, which have existed, in Parsi society in India. In India, the Parsis are divided into two sections: namely the *Mobeds* (or priests) and Behdin (or laity). Priests for a long time were exclusive and intermarriage was seldom permitted. Only the son of a priest could become a priest. In terms of the Parsi Panchayat, in the seventeenth century though priests were members of the Panchayat, the laity members played a greater role in the economic role of the Parsis in India. Towards the last quarter of the seventeenth century the British started developing Bombay into their main trading centre. The Parsi community began to make full use of this trading venture in Bombay. The Parsi Panchayat played an active role in promoting the economic interests of the community. It also provided some inner stability and order to the Parsi community.

The Bombay Panchayat was formally recognised to punish members of the community who went against the traditionally accepted Parsi norms (religious and social). Punishable acts included committing bigamy or insulting members of the priestly class. A person requiring divorce and permission to marry a second wife had to represent his case in writing to the Panchayat. When the bad conduct of a wife was established the Panchayat used to punish the guilty woman by taking her securities before granting the husband permission to remarry. Those who were given permission to marry a second time had to get their marriage ceremony performed only by the priest named by the Panchayat. This would vary depending on whether the applicant belonged to the *Shehenshah* sect or the *Kadmi* sect.

Here we need to mention another social division. The Parsis are divided into two sections on the question of pronunciation of the *Avestan* prayers and the intercalation (this word means, to insert as a day on the calendar) in the Iranian-Zoroastrian calendar. In ancient Iran the length of the year was known to be 365 days and 6 hours. This difference of 6 hours was made up once in 120 years by adding one month known as *Kabisa.* Those who followed this method called themselves *Kadmis* or *Kadims,* meaning the ancient. While the Parsis who did not follow this calendar came to be known as *Shehenshahis.* Fire temples are open to both these sections. Intermarriage among these sects is quite common. For the *Shehenshahi* Parsis the New Year falls at the end of August, while for the *Kadmis* it falls a month ahead at the beginning of August. The Parsi Panchayat kept these divisions in mind when it tried to arrive at any decision. Those who violated the rules were to be turned out of the community and punished, as the Panchayat thought proper. Besides obtaining permission from the Panchayat to marry a second time (when the first wife is alive) a man had to very often pay the Panchayat some amount of money as charity. Among the punishments which could be imposed by the Panchayat were forbidding: (i) priests to enter the house of the person punished; (ii) the person to visit the Parsi temple; and (iii) the person to go to the Tower of Silence.

Other punishments included beating the offender with a shoe, shaving a woman's head, and excommunicating the deviants from the community and so on. The Panchayat continued to wield a strong influence over the religious-social life of the community till 1830. After this the sons of the old members took over and began considering their positions in the Panchayat as personal possessions. They behaved high handedly and in a biased manner. Henceforth, the Panchayat became an institution of class discrimination. Thus serious breaches like bigamy were now glossed over by the Panchayat, so far as the richer members of the community were concerned. This made some of the 'elderly' members resign their positions on the Panchayat. It had virtually become a powerless institution. The British Government also withdrew its recognition from the Panchayat. In 1865, a Parsi Law Reform Association and later in 1961 a Government Commission worked on drafting a bill which gave the Parsi community, a written law of their own. It was entitled the Parsi Marriage and Divorce Act of 1865 and Parsi Succession Act of 1865. These Acts have been amended in subsequent years to liberalise and facilitate legal proceedings relating to marriage and succession.

FESTIVALS

So far we have discussed the emergence of Parsi community in India, their basic tenets, some of the important rites and customs of the Parsis and the role of the Parsi Panchayat. There is another area of Zoroastrian social organisation that reflects the collective entity of the Parsis. The area which rejuvenates the Zoroastrian way of life are the Parsi Festivals.

Feasting is a necessary component of Parsi worship. In other words it is not just a 'desirable' or an expected mode of behaviour but one that is religiously enjoined upon Parsis. It follows directly from their fountainhead, Zoroaster, who enjoins every Parsi to lead a happy and joyous life. The principal festivals in the Parsi year are the six seasonal festivals, *Gahnbars* and the days in the memory of the dead at the Parsi year's end. Also, each day of the month and each of the twelve months of the year is dedicated to the deity. The day named after that month is when the great feast day of that particular deity is held. The new year festival, Noruz or Navroz is the most joyous and beautiful of Zoroastrian feasts. It is a spring festival in the honour or *Rapithwin,* who is the personification (i.e. considered as person) of noonday and summer. The festival to *Mithra or Mehragan* (noble spirits) was traditionally an autumn festival. This festival was as honoured as the spring feast of *Norus.*

8

The Institution of Family

Broadly speaking, "family" refers to the group comprising parents and children. It may also refer, in some places, to a patri-or matrilineage or to a group of cognates, that is, persons descended from the same ancestor. In some other cases, it may refer to a group of relatives and their dependants forming one household. All this refers to the compositional aspect of this institution. Another aspect is that of the residence of its members. They usually share a common residence, at least for some part of their lives. Thirdly, we can also speak of the relational aspect of the family. Members have reciprocal rights and duties towards each other. Finally, the family is also an agent of socialisation. All these aspects make this institution different from other units of social structure.

Family is one of the most important social institutions. Most of the world's population lives in family units. The specific form and behaviour patterns found within a family have shown variations through time across countries of the world and even within a country. A sociologist looks at the institution both in terms of an ideal type and a reality. He/she ascertains the ideals of the family system partly because they are a guide to behaviour and also because these ideals act as values, a set of norms which are passed from one generation to another. A sociologist also studies the actual way in which a family is patterned and re-patterned within a society, in a particular group through time. She will also try to identify the forces, which have been responsible for changing certain aspects of the family units in a particular manner.

Types of Family

Normally the basic unit of social structure contains the two primary links of kinship. These are of parenthood and siblingship. In simple terms, a family usually comprises various combinations and permutations of these relationships. In the Indian context, we generally speak of the contrast between nuclear and joint family types.

A classification of families into joint and nuclear types is usually based on the way in which families are organised. For instance, the most popular definition of a nuclear family is to refer to it as a group consisting of a man, his wife and their unmarried, children. The joint family is commonly defined as the nuclear family plus all kin belonging to the side of husband, and/or wife living in one homestead.

Frequently, the term 'extended' family is used instead of the term joint family to indicate that the combination of two or more nuclear families is based on an extension of the parent-child relationship. Thus, the patrilineally extended family is based on an extension of the father-son relationship, while the matrilineally extended family is based on the mother-daughter relationship. The extended family may also be extended horizontally to include a group consisting of two or more brothers, their wives and children. This horizontally extended family is called as the fraternal or collateral family.

We say that the nuclear and the joint family systems have to be viewed as a continuum. This means that these two types of family systems have to be looked at as something interrelated in a developmental cycle. The structure of a family changes over a time period in terms of size, composition, role and status of persons, the family and societal norms and sanctions. There probably is rarely a family in India, which remains perpetually nuclear in composition. Often additional members like an aged parent or unmarried brothers and sisters may come to live with a man, his wife and unmarried children. The nuclear family then, is a stage in a cycle with other structural types of families. Even when certain forces have enjoined the establishment of nuclear household, for a relatively long period of time, the ritual, economic and sentimental link with relatives who compose a joint family are often maintained.

While discussing the nature of nuclear family in India, Pauline Kolenda has discussed additions/modifications in nuclear family structure. She gives the following compositional categories.

1. *Nuclear family* refers to a couple with or without children.
2. *Supplemented nuclear family* indicates a nuclear family plus one or more unmarried, separated, or widowed relatives of the parents, other than their unmarried children.
3. *Subnuclear family* is identified as a fragment of a former nuclear family for instance a widow/widower with her/his unmarried children or siblings (unmarried or widowed or separated or divorced) living together.
4. *Single person household*
5. *Supplemented subnuclear family* refers to a group of relatives, members of a formerly complete nuclear family along with some other unmarried, divorced or widowed relative who was not a member of the nuclear family. For instance, a widow and her unmarried

children may be living together with her widowed mother-in-law. In the Indian context, it is easy to find all these types of family. However, in terms of societal norms and values, these types relate to the joint family system.

THE HINDU JOINT FAMILY

Much has been written about the joint family system, especially the Hindu joint family system. The patrilineal, patrivirilocal (residence of the couple after marriage in the husband's father's home), property owning, co-residential and commensal joint family, comprising three or more generations has been depicted as the ideal family unit of Hindu society.

M.S. Gore points out that ideally, the joint family consists of a man and his wife and their adult sons, their wives and children, and younger children of the paternal couple. In this ideal type the oldest male is the head of the family. The rights and duties in this type of family are laid down to a great extent by the hierarchical order of power and authority. Age and sex are the main ordering principles of family hierarchy.

The frequency and the nature of contact/communication between members vary on the basis of sex. A married woman, for instance works in the kitchen with her mother-in-law and sisters-in-law. Younger members are required to show respect to the older members and can hardly question the authority or decision taken by elders even when it directly concerns them. Children of the joint family are children of all the male members in the parental generation.

Emphasis on conjugal ties (i.e. between husband and wife) is supposed to weaken the stability of the joint family. The father-son relationship (filial relationship) and the relationship between brothers (fraternal relationship) are more crucial for the joint family system than the husband-wife or conjugal relationship.

In a nuclear family the husband and wife relationship is important for the survival of the system. Hence, in M.S. Gore's view, it would be inappropriate to look at the joint family system as a collection of nuclear families. Having said that joint families are not merely a collection of nuclear families we must examine what constitutes jointness.

Nature of Joint Family

There are two aspects of joint family system in India based on

1. What constitutes jointness?
2. Who constitutes a joint family?

Both the sub-sections will show us how the seemingly nuclear families in India are actually parts of larger family groups, which share the idea of 'jointness'.

Let us look at what is jointly shared by the members of a joint family. Their jointness is reflected in the factors of commensality, common residence, joint ownership of property, cooperation and sentiment of jointness, ritual bonds like worship of common deity. We shall discuss them one by one.

1. *Commensality:* Most of the studies of joint family use commensality (eating together) as a defining criterion. The joint family is the hearth group; members cook and eat food from the same kitchen.
2. *Common Residence*: In some studies the joint family as the residential family group is stressed. Though it is possible to find a joint family having the same hearth but not sharing the same dwelling or vice versa, by and large commensality and common residence are taken as essential ingredients of jointness.

3. *Joint Ownership of Property*: Some scholars have regarded joint ownership of property or *coparcenary* as the essence of jointness, irrespective of the type of residence and commensality. In legal terms, this is the most crucial factor used for defining a joint family.
4. *Cooperation and Sentiment*: Scholars like I.P. Desai and K. M. Kapadia point out that jointness should be looked in functional terms. A functionally joint family lays stress on fulfilment of obligations towards kin.

   A patrilineal joint family may consist of a number of households headed by males related through the father. They may be located even at distant places and may not even have property in common. But what is common is that they identify themselves as members of a particular 'family', cooperate in rituals and ceremonies, render financial and other kinds of help; and they cherish a common family sentiment and abide by the norms of joint living.
5. *Ritual Bonds:* The ritual bonds of a joint family are considered to be an important component of jointness. A joint family, thus, is bound together by periodic propitiation of the dead ancestors. The members perform a *'shraddha'* ceremony in which the senior male member of the joint family propitiates his dead father's or mother's spirit, offering it the *'pinda'* (balls of cooked rice) on behalf of all the members.

Another ritual bond among joint family members can be a common deity worship. In many parts of South India, each joint family has a tradition of worshipping a particular clan or village deity. Vows are made to these deities in times of joy and trouble. The first tonsure, donning of the sacred thread, marriages etc. are celebrated in or near the deity's temple. Srinivasa of Tirupathi and Subramanya of Palani are two well-known Hindu deities who have a large number of South Indian families attached to them.

Still another important bond is pollution. Birth and death results in pollution and the group observing pollution consists of the members of the joint family, patrilineal or *matrilineal*. The bonds created by ancestor worship, family deities and observation of pollution persist even after the joint family has split into separate or smaller residential and commensal units.

From the above discussion of joint family it becomes clear that common kitchen or hearth, common residence, joint rights to property and the fulfillment of obligation towards kin and ritual bonds have been outlined as the main criteria for defining what constitutes jointness. Many scholars have pointed out that of these dimensions, co-residence and commensality, are the immediately identifiable characteristics of a joint family. Such a consideration, they feel, would also accommodate family patterns found in non-Hindu communities like the Muslims, Christians, etc. It would also accommodate families, which hardly have anything by way of ancestral or immovable property.

Kin Relationship between the Members

We can say that a joint family may consist of members related lineally or collaterally or both. There is more or less an unanimous agreement that a family is essentially defined as "joint" only if it includes two or more related married couples. Also it has been observed that these couples may be related (i) lineally (usually in a father-son relationship or occasionally in a father-daughter relationship), or, (ii) collaterally (usually in a brother-brother relationship/or/ occasionally in a brother-sister relationship). Both these types refer to the compositional aspect of the patrilineal joint family. In matrilineal systems, found in South-west and North-east India, the family is usually composed of a woman, her mother and her married and unmarried daughters. The mother's brother is also an important member of the family; he is the manager of the matrilineal joint family affairs. The husbands of the female members live with them. In Kerala, a husband used to be a frequent visitor to the wife's household and he lived in his mother's household.

Pauline Kolenda presents the following types of joint family on the basis of the relatives who are its members.

a) *Collateral joint family*: It comprises two or more married couples between whom there is a sibling bond. In this type, usually a brother and his wife and another brother and his wife live together with unmarried children.

b) *Supplemented collateral joint family:* It is a collateral joint family along with unmarried, divorced or widowed relatives. The supplemented relatives are generally the widowed mother of the married brothers or the widower father, or an unmarried sibling.

c) *Lineal joint family:* Two couples, between whom there is a lineal link, like between a parent and his married son or some times between a parent and his married daughter, live together.

d) *Supplemented lineal joint family:* It is a lineal joint family together with unmarried, divorced or widowed relatives who do not belong to either of the lineally linked nuclear families; for example, the father's widower brother or the son's wife's unmarried brother or sister.

e) *Lineal collateral joint family:* In this type three or more couples are linked lineally and collaterally. For instance we can have a family consisting of parents and their two or more married sons together with the unmarried children of the couples.

f) *Supplemented lineal—collateral joint family:* In this type are found a lineal collateral joint family plus unmarried, widowed, separated relatives who belong to one of the nuclear families (lineally and collaterally linked), for example, the father's widowed sister or brother or an unmarried nephew of the father.

Number of Generations in One Unit

A joint family is also seen in terms of generations present in it. Some researchers, like I.P. Desai and T.N. Madan emphasise that the number of generations present in a family is important for identifying a joint family. A joint family is commonly defined as a three generational family. For instance a man, his married son and his grand children constitute a joint family.

Sharing of Common Property

Researchers, like F.G. Bailey, T.N. Madan, have advocated the limitation of the term joint family to a group of relatives who form a property owning group, the coparcenary family. M.S. Gore, for instance, defines a joint family as a group consisting of adult male coparceners and their dependants. The wives and young children of these male members are the dependents.

The female members have not been included in the category of the coparcenary. They have rights of residence and maintenance only as dependents. In 1937 an attempt was made to confer the same right, i.e., the right of inheritance of property on a Hindu widow as her son would have in the estate of her deceased husband. The Act enabled her to enjoy the income only from the immovable property of her husband during her lifetime.

Until the passing of the Hindu Succession Act, 1956, two systems of inheritance dominated among patrilineal

Hindus. In one system (called the Mitakshara school, adopted in most regions) a son has a vested interest in his father's ancestral property from the moment of his birth. The father cannot give away any part of this property to the detriment of his son's interest. Under the other system (the Dayabaga school, adopted in Bengal and Assam) the father is the absolute owner of his share and has a right to alienate his property the way he wants.

Among the patrilineal Hindus, some movable property is given to the daughters at the time of marriage as *stridhana.* With the passing of the Hindu Succession Act of 1956, a uniform system of inheritance has been established. The individual property of a male Hindu, dying intestate (having made no will), passes in equal shares between his son, daughter, widow and mother. Male and female heirs have come to be treated as equal in matters of inheritance and succession. Another important feature of the Act is that any property possessed by a female Hindu is held by her as her absolute property and she has full power to deal with it the way she likes. This Act has also given a woman the right to inherit from the father as well as from the husband. However the benefit conferred on a woman is limited when compared to the rights of the male members who still have rights to coparcenary ancestral property by birth. Daughters are not part of the coparcenary and have no birthrights.

The difficulty of looking at joint family as a coparcenary family unit is that it does not take into account those joint families, which possess little in the form of immovable or moveable property.

Variability in and Prevalence of Joint Family

Variability: We identified a joint family in terms of what is shared and who shares it. We went through this exercise in this manner so that we can identify and analyse the multitude of factors that make a joint family. But we must remember that a joint family is a composite whole of both the "who and what" components. The exact composition or members and what is actually shared by these members in a particular family will vary through time and will also vary between families.

The following factors relating to the compositional aspect explain these variations within a family and between families.

a) *The culturally patterned time of break-up:* It differs across caste, community and region. The time, when a married son or brother breaks away to form a separate residential and commensal unit, may vary within a family and between families.

b) *Demographic profiles:* Based on such factors like average life expectancy, average age at marriage, average number of children born per couple, age of father at the birth of various children etc., we will again find variation in the pattern of joint family living.

c) *The influence of education, spatial mobility and diversification of occupation* also bring about variation.

ii) *Prevalence:* By comparing seventy six studies which included family types across villages, caste communities and other population, Pauline Kolendaoutlined the pattern of prevalence of joint family in India. She observed that (a) joint family both lineal and collateral was more characteristic of higher twice-born castes and least characteristic among the economically poor and the untouchables, (b) there are regional differences in the proportion of joint families. For instance, the Gangetic plains showed higher incidence of joint families than Central India, i.e., in Madhya Pradesh, Western Rajasthan, parts of Maharashtra, and (c) there seem to be differences in the customary time of break-up of the joint family in various groups and places in India.

In conclusion, we can say that there is something like a patterned cycle of rearrangement of family living through time. As mentioned before, the family in India has to be viewed as a process, in terms of a developmental cycle. Some studies have described the Indian family types as stages in a family cycle.

Developmental Process Of The Family

What is means by the developmental process? It denotes a movement, which occurs in a particular pattern. Developmental process of the family denotes that elements of family life take shape in a particular manner and direction. It relates essentially to the process of fission and/or fusion occurring in the residential and compositional aspects of family living. We now look at the ideal of joint family living and elaborate the processual view of family life.

The Ideal of Joint Family Living

The Indian patrivirilocal family can be viewed in terms of a cycle. A nuclear family develops into a joint family after the marriage of a son and coming of a daughter-in-law. After the death of the father, brothers often separate. In some places, like Andhra Pradesh, sons are expected to stay together with the parents till all the children in the family are married. After this they tend to separate. Thus, the process of fission takes place and the joint family is broken into relatively smaller family units. The parents may then choose to live with one of the sons. Some parents live alternately with all the sons. There may be other kin members who come to live with members of a nuclear family. For example a widow may come to live with her brother, his wife and children if she has no children of her own. In spite of the alterations that occur in the compositional and/or the residential aspect of family living, what holds a family together is the recognition of oneness between the father and the son's households or between the brothers' households. A son's family is in a sense an extension of the father's family. In fact they are considered as 'one family'. It is in this family that the incoming wife has to be incorporated. Formal obligations towards relations by marriage and towards the daughters of the house are expected to be shared by the members of this 'one family'. In the developmental cycle of this 'one family', the emergence of fission in the form of nuclear households can be related to many factors.

One important factor is the high bargaining power of the wife. It has been pointed out that nuclear families develop out of joint families where the wife has high bargaining power. This means that in groups where the wife has a right to legal divorce, where bride price is given and where there is economic and social support to a woman from her natal family, there are considerable possibilities for the formation of nuclear households or fission in the 'one family'.

Those who have studied the family as a process point out that a particular type of composition of a household should be looked at as a stage in the developmental cycle. The presence of nuclear households should not be taken as indicative of change in the institution of joint family. Such families should be viewed as units, which will grow up into joint families when the sons grow up and marry. This may or may not happen in reality. Rather at the level of norms and expectations, most families try to achieve this ideal. We should also look at the other side of the coin. That is the side in which the concept of joint family living is not found for several reasons.

The idea of the developmental cycle of the family does not apply universally to all groups. For instance, among artisans any kind of joint family living may be more advantageous than among very poor agricultural groups where organisation of labour or pooling of labour offers little advantage. An illustration of this point can be given from the study by Cohn of the Chamars of Senapur, who are landless labourers. Among them the achievement of a joint family is difficult because of demographic, economic factors as well as due to the role of women and mobility. Let us look at these factors.

a) *Demographic factor*: With low life expectancy there is much less chance of three generations existing at the same time.

b) *Economic factors:* With no property, contribution to the income of the family is the major asset for this group. Since old people may not have the capacity to work and contribute to the family resources, they are not considered as essential and important persons in the family.

c) *Role of women:* Due to the poor financial position of the family, women are required to take up paid employment outside the home. So the traditional division of labour in a joint family where women look after the home and children and men go out to work cannot operate. Women's economic activities make the continuity of the joint family difficult

d) *Mobility*: Movement of individuals from one place to another, in search of better economic opportunity, also makes joint family living difficult.

Having discussed the factor of non-occurrence of joint family in certain groups, now we shall also look at the areas of changes in the family,

CHANGES IN FAMILY STRUCTURE

In order to measure the overall changes taking place in the family as an institution in India, we need to identify the major forces or factors that have brought about changes in the family structure. A host of interrelated factors, economic, educational, legal, demographic, have affected the family in India. The impact has been differentially felt by different groups through time. Let us look at each factor separately keeping in mind that all these factors had a cumulative effect on different aspects of family living.

Factors of Change

Generally the factors leading to changes in the family are discussed in the context of the issue of disintegration of the joint family. In addition, we will discuss these factors also in the context of social changes occurring since the British rule in India.

Economic Factors

Monetisation (introduction of cash transactions), diversification of occupational opportunities for employment in varied spheres, technological advancements (in communication and transport) are some of the major economic factors, which have affected the joint family system in India.

The economic system established by the British encouraged monetisation i.e., cash payment for services rendered and goods sold. The British also threw open opportunities for employment in government service. Those who were attracted by the employment opportunities and facilities provided by the British, often left their traditional occupations and moved to cities or towns where these occupations were available. This meant residential separation from their ancestral home. If they were married, they sometimes took their wives and children (and even one or two relatives) along with them. Since Independence, opportunities for and diversification of occupations have increased. With a constitutional commitment to promote equality between the sexes and to integrate women into the development process, a further impetus has emerged to draw women into varied kinds of occupations. In families where both the men and women go out to work, role relationships between different members of the family are affected.

Educational Factors

Again it was during the British rule that opportunities for higher education emerged in a significant way. All castes and communities had access to the facilities provided by the British with regard to education. Some of those who were able to gain access and exposure to English-medium education (exposure specially to the individualistic, liberal and humanitarian ideas) began to question some of the Hindu customs and practices relating to child marriage, denial of rights of education to women, property rights of women and ill-treatment of widows. Educated young men not only desired to postpone their marriage to a much later age than what was prescribed by family tradition, but also wanted to marry women with some educational background. Educated women (especially college educated) were expected to have a different kind of influence on family matters than uneducated or less educated women.

Legal Factors

Legislations regarding employment, education, marriage, and property, have affected the family system in many ways. Labour laws passed for the benefit of employees like the Indian Workmen Compensation Act (1923), the Minimum Wages Act 1948, helped to reduce the economic reliance of members on the joint family for economic support. In 1930 the Hindu Gains of Learning Act was passed whereby it was declared that the property acquired by a Hindu out of his education was his personal property though his education was paid for by the joint family. The distinction between self-acquired property and joint family property was drawn. In 1937, during the British rule a law was passed by which a woman acquired a limited right to her husband's property. She could hold the property of her husband after his death as a limited owner during her lifetime. But after she died the property devolved to the heirs (usually the sons) of the husband.

With regard to marriage, the Child Marriage Restraint Act was passed in 1929, to curb infant marriages. It prescribed the minimum age (18 and 14 years respectively) at marriage for boys and girls. This Act also aimed to give women an opportunity for education. Now in India the prescribed minimum age at marriage is 21 for boys and 18 for girls.

After Independence the Hindu Succession Act (1956) was passed which gave a daughter and a son equal rights to the father's property. These legislations challenged the inheritance patterns that prevailed in joint families prior to the passing of this Act and the dependent position of women within the family.

Urbanisation

The process of urbanisation has also affected the pattern of family life in India. It denotes the movement of people from rural to urban areas and a shift from agricultural to non-agricultural occupations. It also implies the adoption of an urban way of life. Urban life reflects increased density of population, heterogeneity of population, diversification and increased specialisation of occupations, complex division of labour. It also includes increased availability of educational and health facilities. Limited availability of living space, impersonality and anonymity also characterise urban life.

Partly as a result of population pressure on land, there has been a continuous influx of people into cities seeking education, jobs, medical care etc. What impact does migration to cities have on the families in villages? Residential separation due to mobility of members from one place to another affects the size and composition of the family. A man may take his wife and children along with him to establish a nuclear family in the city. There have been many studies, which show that migration to cities from villages and small towns has contributed to the rapid disintegration of large size family units. These observations have been mainly based on census data, which show a high percentage of nuclear families in cities. In the city, with problems of finding accommodation and limited space available for living, it becomes difficult for an average urbanite to maintain and support a large family.

The other factors which have been held responsible for encouraging smaller units are i) opportunities for higher education ii) heightened ambitions iii) increased occupational mobility iv) growing sense of individuality (i.e., thinking in terms of individual needs and ambitions rather than in terms of kinship needs and larger familial requirements).

Factors Leading to Reinforcement of Joint Family

So far we have talked about the forces that were seen to negatively affect the joint family functioning as commensal, co-residential and large size unit. Sociologists while trying to measure the changes taking place in family life observe that urbanisation and industrialisation have, in fact, served to strengthen some aspects of joint family system. Here we will discuss three important studies to illustrate our point.

1. K.M. Kapadia, for instance, has drawn our attention to the fact that families, which have migrated to cities, still retain their bonds with their joint family in the village or town. Even after they residentially separate themselves from a joint family and form a nuclear family, they do not function as an isolated or completely independent unit in the city. These, families retain their kinship orientation and joint family ethic. This is evident from the physical presence of relatives at the time of certain events like birth, marriage, death, illness and so on. Sometimes members from the families living in a city go to the village to participate in such events or sometimes members from the rural family come to the city to involve themselves in functions or ceremonies or activities of their kin members.

   The joint family ethic is very much evident in the performance of certain role obligations. These may include physical and financial assistance to kin members. A family in the city has the duty to give shelter and sustenance to all subsequent immigrants from the rural family, mostly young men in pursuit of education and work or relations seeking medical treatment in urban centres. So it can happen that in the course of time, a kind of joint family is formed in the city, which is linked to the family in the village by close family ties, by a system of mutual rights, duties and obligations and also by the undivided family property.

ii) Again the thesis that the joint family is dysfunctional to the process of industrialisation has been challenged by those who point out that some of the successful industrial establishments in the country are managed by the individuals who strictly live by joint family rules. They maintain coresidence, common hearth, contribute and share economic resources. In his study *The Indian Joint Family in Modern Industry*, Milton Singer points out that the joint family continues to be the norm among industrial entrepreneurs, despite changes in their material conditions of living. He observes that changes have taken place, within three generations, in residential, occupational and educational spheres. Social mobility has increased and ritual observations have been reduced in number and/or in importance. However, these alterations, he points out, have not transformed the joint family into isolated nuclear families. On the contrary, a modified joint family organisation has emerged in the urban industrial setting where even members from the ancestral home or village move into the urban setting. Thus, according to Singer, the industrial centre has simply become a new area for the working of the joint family system.

iii) Kolenda in her study *Regional Differences in Family Structure in India* observes that industrialisation serves to strengthen the joint family because an economic base has been provided to support it or because more hands are needed in a renewed family enterprise or because kin can help one another in striving for upward mobility.

No doubt the joint family that functions today in urban settings is different in many ways from the joint family which functioned in pre-independent and non-industrial India. For instance many of the coresidential, commensal joint families in urban areas remain joint because it is the norm or due to some advantages, or because of shortage of accommodation. Yet, there may be considerable separation in the management of household expenses on entertainment, education of children etc. Certain expenses may be regarded individual, like those on clothes, education, and vacation. These internal arrangements are different not only between urban and rural families but also between families in an urban area.

Among many families, across caste, class, region and communities, it is possible to find that sons along with the members of their nuclear family unit define the household of the parents as the 'main home' or 'common home'. This distinction may be given to a) the household of the eldest brother or to b) that of the brother with whom the parents live or, to c) that of the brother who lives on the ancestral or parental property. Also presence of a parental home (where one son and a parent live) or of a joint household of two brothers helps to keep the households (of parents and sons and of brothers) closer to each other, for it provides a kind of common meeting ground for all. Married daughters or sisters also come to this home. There may also be a greater sense of economic obligation between members of this "family" distributed in more than one household, residence and hearth.

EMERGING PATTERNS OF FAMILY LIFE

Today there are varied patterns of family living. In urban areas both male and female members of the family may go for gainful employment outside the home. In some families the parents of the husband may live with his wife and children. While in some others, members of the wife's family may be living with the couple and their children. With both the husband and the wife going outside the home for gainful employment and with the absence or limited availability of child care facilities, presence of kin members to look after the home and children comes handy for the smooth functioning of the household. Those working couples who prefer to live in nuclear families and who fear or resist interference from kin members, try to organise their household with professional help from outside the family (like cooks, maid servants, crèches). Aged parents, who formerly used to look towards their eldest son or other sons for support in old age, are now adjusting themselves to the new demands of family life by making economic provisions for their old age. Even within a city parents and married sons may reside separately. Another trend in family life in India is that girls are prepared to support their parent or parents in old age, and it is not impossible to find a widowed mother or parents staying with a married daughter (mainly, in the absence of sons) to help her to manage the household. Measures have been provided at the legal level to ensure that dependant old parents are looked after by a daughter if she is self-reliant even after her marriage. Bilateral kinship relations are more and more recognised and accepted today in many nuclear households in the cities.

9

Systems of Kinship

Since India is a land of immense diversity, its different regions reflect different systems of kinship. In the limited scope of two units, it is not possible to even outline all the various types of kinship systems found in India. As the country's two major geographical divisions, the north and the south, present two distinct forms and have been described in sociological literature as such, we introduce you to the North Indian and South Indian systems of kinship. You must remember that this does not mean that there are no further varieties of kinship systems in certain pockets of both North and South India. Indeed. India's north eastern parts, as well as, other regions in its west and south provide many other types.

The kinship system refers to a set of persons recognised as relatives either by virtue of a blood relationship or by virtue of a marriage relationship. In sociology, all blood relationships are known by a technical term, consanguinity. Similarly, all relationships through marriage are given the term affinity. For example, the relationships between mother and son/daughter, sister and brother/sister, father and son/daughter are consanguinal, while relationships between father/mother-in-law and daughter-/son-in-law are affinal.

Mostly, it is the social recognition of these relationships that is more important than the actual biological ties. Networks built around kin relationships play a significant role in both rural and urban social life in India.

Approaches to Study Kinship System

Sociological studies of kinship in India cover descriptions, comparisons and analytical problems based on the findings from various regions. Approaches to the study of kinship can be broadly classified under two headings (i) the Indological approach and (ii) the Anthropological approach. Here, we will discuss these approaches one by one.

Indological Approach

As the social institutions of Indian society are rooted in literary and learned traditions, many sociological studies have made use of textual sources for explaining the ideological and jural bases of our institutions. For example, K.M. Kapadia has used classical texts to describe Hindu kinship. *Hindu Social Organisation* by P.H. Prabhu is also based on Sanskrit texts. Similarly, Irawati Karve and G.S. Ghurye have extensively worked on Indian kinship system. Both have used textual sources to explain kinship pattern in different regions of India from a socio-historical perspective. We can, therefore, say that Indological approach to the study of kinship has provided a framework to understand the elements of continuity and change in the system.

Anthropological Approach

Anthropologists have looked at kinship systems from the point of view of descent and alliance.

Descent Approach

Kinship in our society is used for establishing clear-cut

corporate social units. Each one of us is a member of such a cooperating and closely bound group of people. One can depend upon the help and support given by such people. Such cooperating local groups are always larger than elementary families of spouses and their children. When these groups are recognised or defined on the basis of shared descent, anthropologists call them descent groups. Formally speaking there are six possible avenues for the transmission of descent group membership, from parents to children. These are:

1. *patrilineal*—where descent is traced in the male line from father to son,
2. *matrilineal*—where descent is traced in the female line from mother to daughter,
3. *double (duolineal or bilineal)*—where descent is traced in both the father's line as well as mother's line for different attributes such as movable property in one line and immovable in another,
4. *cognatic (bilateral)*—where attributes are transmitted equally through both parents. Here no unilineal groups can be formed but group structure can be cognatic, that is, the group of kinpersons on the father's and mother's side. Membership can be acquired through either the father or the mother,
5. *parallel descent*—a very rare form of descent where descent lines are sex specific. Men transmit to their sons while women to their daughters, and finally
6. *cross or alternative type descent*—this is also very rare. Here men transmit to their daughters and women to their sons.

In India, we generally find the patrilineal and matrilineal descent systems. Of the two, patrilineal system is more common. The description and analysis of kin relationships in a descent group have given us a fairly comprehensive sociological understanding of certain types of kinship systems in India. For example, E.K. Gough has discussed the unity of the lineage with corporate rights on land. She has focused on roles and inter-personal relationships in the wider kinship. T.N. Madan has studied the role of kinship as an organising principle in the Kashmiri Brahmin society. He has brought out the strong patrilineal ideology that characterises kinship system of the Kashmiri Pandits.

In sociological studies the terms 'line', 'lineal', 'lineage' etc. with or without the prefix 'patri' or 'matri' have in the past been used in at least four different ways.

2. they have been used to denote corporate descent groups, i.e., lineage proper,
2. often employed to denote the chosen line of inheritance, succession etc. in a given society,
3. in the study of relationship terminologies the expression "two line prescription" has sometimes been used to refer to terminological structures which are consistent with "bilateral cross-cousin marriage",
4. regardless of which lines (matriline or patriline or both) are chosen for the above three purposes, lineal relatives refer to one's ascendants or descendants. Lineal relatives are those who belong to the same ancestral stock in a direct line of descent. Opposed to lineal relatives are collaterals who belong to the same ancestral stock but not in a direct line of descent.

All of these usages, except the fourth, are context specific. i.e., they refer to particular situations. Here, social relations and groups are emphasised and sociologists study them in terms of interaction, norms and values of a particular society. For example, some scholars, following the theory of lineages or descent groups, have discussed the relation between mother's brother and sister's son in patrilineal societies. They use the idea of 'complementary filiation', i.e., the relationship ego has with the relatives on the mother's side in a patrilineal society. In a matrilineal society it refers to the relationship ego has with the relatives on his father's side. In a patrilineal society a person's maternal group is the affinal group of that person's father. This is the group, from which the person's father has taken a wife. For this reason some sociologists like to consider the question of affinity in its own right, rather than as a complementary set of relationships. We may say that in descent approach, the emphasis is laid on social organisation of descent groups. As a result, there is little focus on the 'affinity' aspect of relationships.

Alliance Approach

Another concept that figured prominently in the study of kinship systems in India is that of alliance. Kinship includes the consideration of the patterns and rules of marriage. When a sociologist pays special attention to these aspects of kinship, we say that he/she is following the alliance approach to understand the patterns of kinship. Many studies of kinship in India have focused on marriage as an alliance between two groups and on kinship terminology, as a reflection of the nature of alliance. Because of their concentration on relationships arising out of marriage, we say that these studies follow the alliance approach. The main exponent of this approach is Louis Dumont. He has emphasised the role played by marriage in the field of kinship in South India. By showing the opposition between consanguines and affines as reflected in the Dravidian kinship terminology, Dumont has made an important contribution to our understanding of kinship system in India in general and of South India in particular. He has applied to South India a structural theory of kinship. It brings out the repetition of intermarriage through the course of generations.

This pattern highlights the classification of kinsmen into two categories of parallel and cross relatives.

The alliance approach to the study of kinship has helped sociologists to discuss and explain the distinction between bride-givers and bride-takers. In addition, it has also included the discussion on the notion of *hypergamy* (i.e., the bride-45 takers are always superior to bride-givers), practice of dowry in relation to hypergamy and ideas of exchange in marriage.

Dimensions Of Kinship System

In order to describe the features of kinship systems found in North and South India, we need to focus on certain aspects. Here, we are going to identify four aspects.

1. *Kinship Groups:* Kin relationships provide both a method of passing on status and property from one generation to the next effective social groups for purposes of cooperation and conflict. So we need to identify the form of descent or of tracing one's relationships. In other words, we speak of the social groups within which relatives cooperate and conflict. That is why, we need to describe kinship groups.

2. *Kinship Terminology:* The list of terms used by the people to refer to their kin relationships expresses the nature of kinship system. This is why by describing kinship terminology, we are able to throw light on the kinship system. Most features of the kinship system of any society are usually reflected in the way kinship terms are used in that society. Generally a person would apply the same term to those relatives who belong to the same category of kin relationships. In this case, these relatives would also occupy similar kinship roles.

3. *Marriage Rules:* Just as kinship groups describe the form of kinship system found in a society, so also rules for marriage, categories of people who may/ may not marry each other, relationships between bride-takers and bride-givers provide the context within which kin relationships operate. Talking about these issues gives us an understanding of the content of kin relationships. It is therefore necessary to speak of marriage rules for understanding any kinship system.
4. *Exchange of Gifts:* Sociologists like to describe social relationships between various categories of relatives. As there are always two terms to any relationship, kinship behaviour is described in terms of pairs. For example, the parent-child relationship would describe kinship behaviour between two generations.

In this way, we feel that by describing the above four dimensions of the kinship system in relation to North and South India, we will be able to give you a fairly general picture of the patterns of kinship in the two regions.

Kinship Diagrams

Before ending this section on dimensions of kinship systems, let us also mention that the depiction of different types of kinship groups, marriage rules and their implications is made much easier by the help of kinship diagrams. Sociologists and anthropologists invariably use them for explaining various kinship structures. For following a kinship diagram you need to simply remember the following ways of drawing kinship diagrams.

1. The symbol D refers to a male and the symbol O refers to a female. When these symbols are shown in black, i.e., ▲ or, ● it means that the particular male or female is dead.

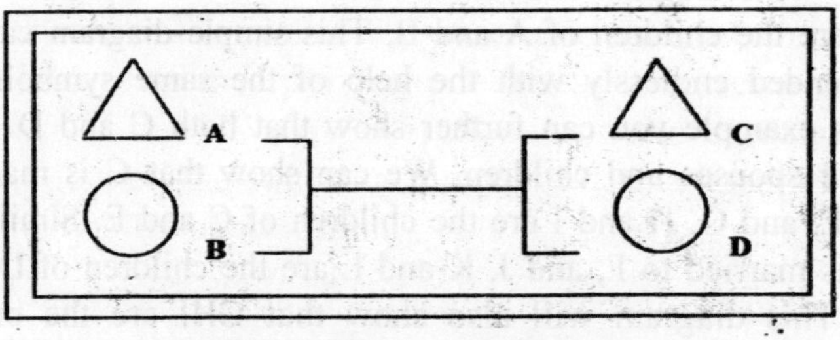

Figure 1. Basic kinship diagram

2. The symbol [refers to sibling relationship. It expresses brother/brother, sister/sister or brother/sister relationships. The symbol], on the other hand, expresses the husband-wife or the marriage relationship.
3. Thirdly, a horizontal line—connecting the symbols [and], denotes filiation or the relationship between the parent/s and child/children. Thus, with the use of above symbols, kin relationships are expressed to denote genealogical connections and to depict the structure of kinship groups. Let us take an example and see what the following diagram shows.

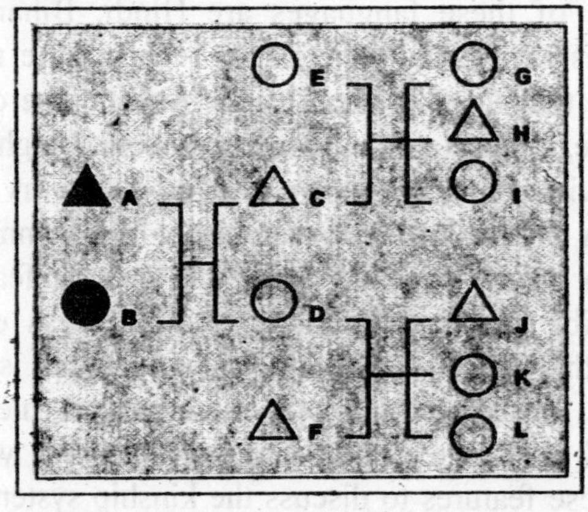

Figure 2. Elaboration of basic kinship diagram

This diagram shows that A is married to B, and C and D are the children of A and B. This simple diagram can be extended endlessly with the help of the same symbols. In this example you can further show that both C and D have their spouses and children. We can show that C is married to E, and G, H and I are the children of C and E. Similarly, D is married to F, and J, K and L are the children of D and F. This diagram will also show that GHI are the cross-cousins of JKL and that A and B are grandparents of G, H, I, J, K and L and they are now dead. Similarly, you can also locate mother's brother of J, K and L and father's sister of G, H and I. This diagram is drawn in the following manner.

KINSHIP SYSTEM IN NORTH INDIA

Let us first define what we mean by North India. For purposes of describing the kinship systems found in India, Irawati Karve identified four cultural zones the Northern, the Central, the Southern and the Eastern zones. The northern zone, according to Karve, lies between the Himalayas to the north and the Vindhya ranges to the south. In this region, the majority of the people speak languages derived from Sanskrit.

Some of these languages are Hindi, Bihari, Sindhi, Punjabi, Assamese and Bengali. In such a large region, we cannot say that there is one kinship system. The differences of language, history and culture bring about a high degree of variation within the region. We may, however, try to look at the pattern of kinship organisations of the communities in this region on the basis of broad and general features. We can describe the basic structure and process of kinship system in this area in terms of four features that is i) kinship groups, ii) kinship terminology iii) marriage rules, and iv) ceremonial exchange of gifts among kin. Now, we take up each of these features to discuss the kinship system in North India.

Kinship Groups

Sociological studies in various parts of North India show that social groups, such as patrilineage, caste, subcaste provide the basis for cooperation or conflict among the people. We now discuss these groups.

Patrilineage

We can say that broadly speaking kinship organisation in North India is based on unilineal descent groups. When the lineage membership group is traced on the basis of shared descent in one line, we call it a unilineal descent group. In North India, we have mostly patrilineal descent groups. This means that the descent is traced in the male line from father to son. Members of patrilineages cooperate as well as show antagonism in various situations. Let us see how this takes place in terms of a) cooperation, b) conflict and c) inheritance of status and property.

Cooperation. Members of a patrilineage cooperate in ritual and economic activities. They participate together in life cycle rituals. In settlement of disputes, the senior men of the lineage try to sort out the matter within the lineage. Cooperation among lineage members is strengthened because they live close together in the same village. As the farm-lands of lineage members are normally located in the same village, they set up their houses almost next to each other. In this situation, there is constant exchange of material resources from the household of one member to another. This pattern of cooperation is amply described in the studies of kinship patterns in North India by Lewis, Minturn and Hitchcock, Beremen, Nicholas. In terms of theoretical approach to the study of kinship we can say that these studies follow the descent approach because they examine the pattern of cooperation and conflict in descent groups.

Conflict. Lineage members help each other, but conflict also characterises kinship relations among them. For example, T.N. Madan shows how in a Kashmir village, rivalry among brothers leads to partition of the joint family. Later, this rivalry takes more intense form in the relationships between the children of brothers.

Inheritance of Status and Property. From one generation to the next, transmission of status and property takes place according to certain rules. In North India, these generally pass in the male line. In other words, we have a predominantly patrilineal mode of inheritance in North India. For this reason, composition of patrilineage becomes very important. Thus, the lineage fellows cooperate for economic and jural reasons. They share jural rights and therefore they cooperate in order to keep the rights. However, they also fight among themselves about who is to get more benefits from those rights. Pradhan has described how the Jats and other landowners of Meerut and other districts around Delhi have a certain portion of the village lands and how it cannot be transferred out of the lineage. To keep the land within the lineage, its male members have to remain united. Thus, it becomes a main principle of their social organisation. Let us now discuss the second kinship group.

Clan

A lineage is an exogamous unit, i.e., a boy and a girl of the same lineage cannot marry. A larger exogamous category is called the clan. Among the Hindus, this category is known as *gotra*. Each person belongs to the clan of his/her father and cannot marry within the clan or *gotra*. One usually knows about the common ancestor of lineage members as an actual person. But the common ancestor of a clan is generally a mythical figure. The members of a lineage live in close proximity and therefore have greater occasions for cooperation or conflict. Common interests or action do not characterise the relationships among clan members because they are usually scattered over a larger territory and their relationships are often quite remote. These relationships do become significant only in the context of marriage.

Caste and Subcaste

Besides lineages and clans, the kinship system operates within the families of the caste groups, living in one village or a nearby cluster of villages. As castes are endogamous, i.e., one marries within one's caste, people belonging to one caste group are kinspersons in the sense that they are already related or can be potentially related to each other. Caste-fellows generally come forward to help each other when others challenge their honour and status. They may also hold rituals together and help each other economically.

Subcaste is the largest segment of caste and it performs nearly all the functions of caste, such as endogamy and social control. In this respect, we can say that the internal structure of the subcaste would provide us the framework within which we can see the operation of kinship system. The members of a subcaste cooperate as kinspersons. They, depending on the context, work together as equals in the sphere of ritual activities and political allies in socio-economic activities.

As Vidyarthi has shown in the case of a very small subcaste, one may trace one's relationship with most members of the subcaste. On the other hand, in the case of a subcaste spreading over many villages, one may be limited to maintaining relations with only a part of the total number of kin. Klass in his study of marriage rules in Bengal calls this part of the total as one's 'effective jati' i.e., those people of the sub-caste with whom one actually has relationships of cooperation or conflict.

Among the subcaste kin, we should also include those related to a person through marriage. Here, generally a person's kin through mother are called uterine kin and those through spouse are known as affinal kin. These relatives are not members of one's family or lineage or clan. They are expected to help and support each other and, actually do so when an occasion arises for such an action. While a person belongs to only one lineage, one clan or one subcaste, he would always have a string of relatives who do not belong to his lineage/clan/subcaste.

Here we should mention how sociologists, following the descent approach to study kinship systems, try to explain the fact of special place of the relationship between a person and his/her mother's brother. For example, A.R. Radcliffe-Brown went to the extent of coining a new term to express this relationship. Following the principle of filiation (i.e., the relationship between a father and son in the case of a patrilineal society), a person's relationship with his mother's brother is to be understood by the idea of filiation on mother's side or the principle of 'complementary filiation'. Without going into further details about this theoretical issue, we would like to tell you that those following the alliance approach like to explain the same fact in terms of repetition of intermarriage through generations.

Fictive Kin

We should also mention, in passing, the recognition of fictive kinship among villagers. Often, people, who are not related either by descent or marriage, form the bonds of fictive kinship with each other. We find the evidence of such a practice in many tribal and village studies.

Mahapatra points out that fictive kinship is a mechanism to provide even such kin who are not ordinarily found in a particular situation. For example, in North India where village exogamy is a normal practice, it is rare to find a brother to a daughter-in-law living in the same locality. She can get a brother only through a fictive relationship. In urban context, you must have frequently come across small children who call any older man 'uncle' and an older woman 'aunty'. This shows how easily we make use of kinship idiom in our day-to-day behaviour towards total strangers. These transitory relationships do not however assume much importance in terms of actual kin ties and behaviour associated with them.

KINSHIP TERMS

A comparison and analysis of the various kinship terms helps us to understand the kinship structure, its make-up and the behaviour associated with each term. In other words, kinship terms provide the context and the idiom for our social relationships. In this sense, kinship terms do not just tell us about biological and social relationship. They help us to look at the whole way of social life. Only after studying the language, values and behaviour of the particular people can we fully appreciate the significance of their kinship terms. Many times the same kinship term is used to denote different meanings in different contexts. This is the reason why the study of kinship terms is closely associated with the study of language and culture. Here, we discuss how this is the case in relation to the kinship terms used in the linguistic regions of the northern zone.

The kinship terminology is the expression of kinship relations in linguistic terms. In the case of North India, we can call the system of terminology as descriptive. This is because the kinship terms generally describe the relationship from the point of view of the speaker. In a few words, even the most distant kin relationships can be accurately described. Unlike the English terms, uncle, aunty, cousin, which do not reveal age, patrilateral/matrilateral ties, the North Indian kinship terms are very clear. For example, when we say *chachera bhai,* it can be easily translated as father's younger brother's *(chacha's)* son, who stands in the relationship of a brother *(bhai)* to the speaker. Similarly, *mamera bhai* means mother's brother's *(mama's)* son. According to L. Dumont, the North Indian kinship terminology is descriptive in the sense that it describes elementary relationships starting from Ego. The elementary relationships of filiation upwards and downwards, siblingship (sister/brother) and marriage comprise the first set of terms. Then we have the relationships of the second order. These are formed by combining two elementary relationships, i.e., filiation + filiation, filiation + siblingship, siblingship + filiation, marriage + filiation, marriage + siblingship. The third order of relationships is represented by filiation + marriage + filiation. Further, for Dumont, the North Indian kinship terminology is not a classificatory type of terminology because it does not classify the kinship terms according to the number of principles of opposition. However, to emphasise the patrilineal descent, we find a clear-cut distinctionmade between parallel and cross-cousins. The children of one's brother are *bhatija* (for male child) and *bhatiji* (for female child). The children of one's sister are *bhanja* (for male child) and *bhanji* (for female child). A person's parallel relatives are members of his/her descent group and therefore they also live nearby in the same village. In contrast, a person's sister's children or cross relatives are members of a different descent group. They are also residents of a different place.

Social Behaviour

Irawati Karve has given a list of kinship terms in North Indian languages. She makes use of kinship terminologies to describe and compare kinship systems in various parts of India. She studies the terms and also uses the findings for understanding the influences which have played a part in shaping them. Besides Iravati Karve, we can also give another example of the analysis of Indo-Aryan kinship terms, made by G.S. Ghurye. He has highlighted the jural and ideological aspects of kinship systems through a comparison of kinship terms in North Indian languages. For example, among the Sarjupari Brahmins the term *'maan'* refers to the bride-taker. In ideological terms, *'maan'* reflects the high status of the bride-taker as compared to the bride-giver. In jural terms it denotes the fact that bride-takers do not share property with the bride-givers.

The very usage of kinship term also makes clear the kind of behaviour expected from a kin. For example, Oscar Lewis , in his study of a North Indian village, has described the pattern and relationship between a person and his elder brother's wife. This is popularly known as *Devar-Bhabhi* relationship, which is characteristically a joking relationship.

As a contrast to the joking relationship is the behaviour of avoidance between a woman and her husband's father. Similarly, she has to avoid her husband's elder brother. The term for husband's father is *shvasur* and for husband's elder brother is *bhasur*. *Bhasur* is a combination of the Sanskrit word *bhratr* (brother) and *shvasur* (father-in-law), and is, therefore, like father-in-law.

Marriage Rules

Because every time a marriage is contracted, new kinship bonds come into being, we can clearly see the relevance of marriage rules for discussing the patterns of kinship organisation. In the context of North India, we find that people know whom not to marry. In sociological terms, the same thing can be expressed by saying that there are negative rules of marriage in North India. We can also say that marriage is allowed only outside a defined limit. Let us see what this limit or the rule of exogamy is in North India.

Clan Exogamy

Belonging to one's natal descent line is best expressed in matters of marriage. No man is allowed to marry a daughter of his patriline. In North India lineage ties upto five or six generations are generally remembered and marriage alliances are not allowed within this range. In such a situation the lineage turns into the clan and we speak of *gotra* (clan) and *gotra bhai* (clan mates). Widely used Sanskrit term *gotra* is an exogamous category within a subcaste. Its main use is to regulate marriages within a subcaste.

The Four Clan Rule

In this connection, you may refer to the four-*gotra* or four-clan rule. In Irawati Karve's words, according to this rule, a man must not marry a woman from (i) his father's *gotra,* (ii) his mother's *gotra,* (iii) his father's mother's *gotra,* and (iv) his mother's mother's *gotra.* In other words, this rule prohibits marriage between two persons who share any two of their eight *gotra* links. This means that the rule of exogamy goes beyond one's own lineage. Another related kind of exogamy, which exists in North India, is village exogamy. A village usually has members of one or two lineages living in it. Members belonging to the same lineage are not permitted to intermarry. This principle extends even to the villages, which have more than two lineages. In other words, a boy and a girl in a village in North India are like a brother and sister and hence cannot intermarry.

It is important here to give you a word of caution. We have spoken about lineage, clan and subcaste in relation to organisation of kinship patterns. But we have not mentioned terms like *kutumb, biradari, khandan, bhai bandh* etc. These denote various colloquial meanings of the general terms (lineage, clan and subcaste) in local languages. The local terms are used in various contexts to signify different levels of kinship arrangements. In our discussion, we have limited ourselves to social structure and function in broad terms and avoided conflicting usages of local terms. Now we look at the groups within which marriage is preferred/ prescribed, in the context of North India.

Marriages within the Subcaste

Associated with local terms is the idea of the status of various units within the subcaste. Taking the example of the Sarjupari Brahmin of Mirzapur district in Uttar Pradesh, studied by Louis Dumont, we find that each of the three subcastes of Sarjupari Brahmins of this area is divided into three houses (kin groups or lineages) which range hierarchically in status. The marriages are always arranged from lower to higher house. This means that women are always given to the family, which is placed in the house above her own. In this context, we can also refer to the popular saying in North India that 'the creeper must not go back'. The same idea is reflected by another North Indian saying that *'pao pujke, ladki nahin le jainge'* (i.e., once we have washed the feet of the bridegroom during the wedding ceremony, we cannot accept a girl from his family, because this will mean that we allow that side to wash our feet or allow the reversal of relationships). This shows clearly that marriage rules in North India maintain a hierarchic relationship between the bride-givers and bride-takers. In terms of negative rules of marriage in North India, the above description reflects the rule that a man cannot marry his father's sister's daughter or his patrilateral cross-cousin. This is called the rule of no reversal.

As shown in Figure 3, Lineage B has given the woman (M) in marriage to the man (P) of lineage A. P is given the high ritual status of 'pao puj' in marriage ceremonies. If P's daughter is married to the man of lineage B, then P will have to give the same high ritual status to the man of lineage B. But lineage B is, according to the rule of hypergamy, lower to lineage A and therefore, this marriage will be a reversal of roles. In North India, such a reversal is not allowed and thus, we find the rule of prohibition on marriage with patrilateral cross-cousins.

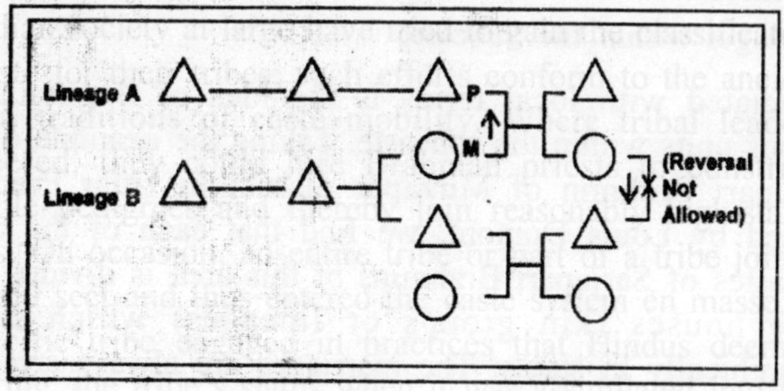

Figure 3. The rule of no reversal

Another principle should also be mentioned here. It is rule of no repetition. This means that if the father's sister has been married in a family *(khandan)*, one's own sister cannot be given in marriage to that same family . The term family or *khandan* is used here as a smaller unit of a lineage. This rule of no repetition implies the negative rule of prohibition on the marriage with matrilateral cross-cousins. In other words, a man cannot marry his mother's brother's daughter. This can be depicted in a simple kinship diagram.

As depicted in Figure 4, lineage B has given women D in marriage to the man E of lineage A. In the next generation, if a woman is again given in marriage to a man of lineage A, then a repetition will occur. A prohibition on repetition shows that matrilateral cross-cousin marriage is barred in North India. Thus, we find that both patrilateral and matrilateral cross-cousin marriages are not allowed in North India. In other words, the two rules, the rule of no reversal and the rule of no repetition, put together define the negative rules of marriage in North India.

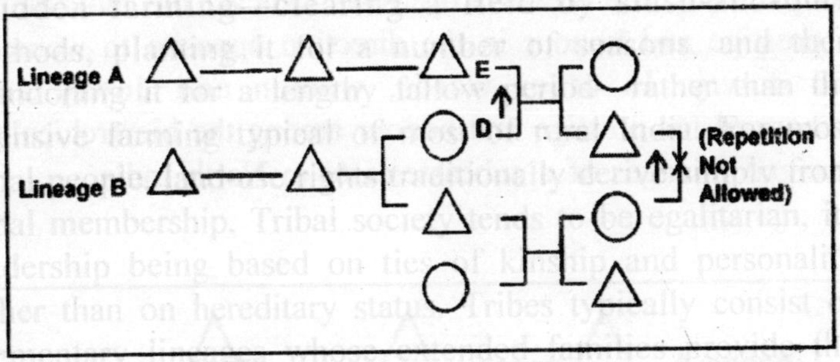

Figure 4. The rule of no repetition

Highlighting the structural implications of marriage rules in North India, T.N. Madan in his study of the Kashmiri Pandits distinguishes three classes of wife-givers and wife-takers from the perspective of the household (i) those who give it wives and those who take wives from it, (ii) those who give wives to those in class (i) and (iii) those who take wives from class (i). These three classes have unequal relationships. However honour and prestige go in the opposite direction to women in marriage. This means that wife-takers are superior to wife-givers and by the fact of giving a wife to a group, one receives honour and prestige within one's own group. Figure 5 shows how the rule of hypergamy in North India acts as a form of exchange between women and dowry on the one hand and prestige and honour on the other.

In figure 5, A, B and C are patrilineages which are ranked by high to low status. The upward arrows indicate that lineage C has given the woman and dowry to the man of lineage B. As bride-givers, the lineage C is lower to B and the lineage B is lower to A. The rule of hypergamy accords lower status to bride-givers. At the same time by giving the women and dowry to high-status lineages, the lower status lineages gain prestige and power within their groups. Thus, the downward arrows indicate the movement of prestige and honour in the direction opposite to women and dowry. In other words, women and dowry are exchanged for prestige and honour among the hierarchically arranged lineages of a subcaste/caste in North India.

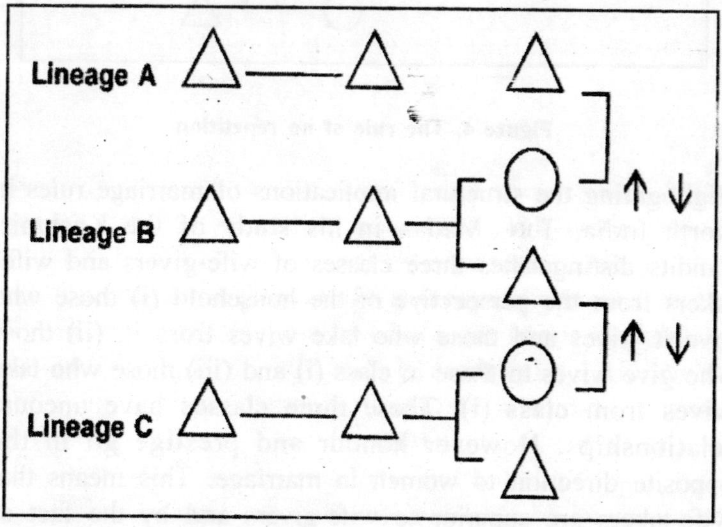

Figure 5. Hypergamy in north India as an exchange

Ceremonial Exchange of Gifts among Kin

Ceremonial exchange of gifts on the occasions of life cycle rituals provides us with the understanding of a patterned behaviour among various categories of kin. Generally, the bride-givers, in correspondence with their inferior status vis-a-vis bride-takers, initiate the process of gift-giving during marriage and continue to give greater amounts of gifts. In other words, you can say that gift-giving and receiving is a well-defined social activity. Let us take two examples of this behaviour.

L. Dumont has pointed out that mother's brother (uterine kin) and wife's brother (affinal kin) have similar ceremonial functions. Not only this, as wife's brother becomes, after a few years, mother's brother to the children, there is little difference between the two. A.C. Mayer has described in his study of kinship in a village in Malwa that all gifts given by one's mother's brother are called *mamere*. In contrast to the gifts given by the mother's brother, there are gifts known as *ban,* given by one's agnates. *Ban* is the term used also for the gift, which is given by other relatives such as the groom's sister's husband to the groom's wife's brother. This shows that the groom's sister's husband (or father's sister's husband in the context of the ascending generation) is viewed to be a part of agnatic kin vis-a-vis the groom's wife's brother (or mother's brother for the ascending generation).

In sociological vocabulary we can put the same thing in this way. We look at the groom's sister's husband (zh) or father's sister's husband (fzh) as a wife-taker. Similarly, we look at the groom's wife's brother (wb) or his mother's brother (mb) as a wife-giver. Now if the gift to A's wife-givers (i.e., mother's brother or wife's brother) by A's wife-taker (sister's husband or father's sister's husband) and by A's agnates are known by the same term *'ban'* then we can say that in opposition to A's wife-givers, his agnates and wife-takers have been merged into one category. This is so because for the groom's wife's brother (or mother's brother) the groom is a wife-taker and groom's wife-taker is his sister's husband or father's sister's husband. These two sets of wife-takers are on one side and the wife-givers are on the other.

To this example of ceremonial gift-giving at wedding we can add one more, given by L. Dumont. He has shown a similar distinction being made between wife-givers and wife-takers (the terms used by L. Dumont) in the context of gift-giving at the end of mourning in a village of Gorakhpur district in Eastern Uttar Pradesh. Here, the main mourner is generally a son or an agnate of the deceased. The ceremony of tying a turban on the head of the main mourner is done by an affine who has taken a wife. In other words, the turban is preferably tied by sister's husband (zh) or father's sister's husband (fzh). Then again for the ceremony of *shaiyyadan* (gift of a bed), a sister's husband (zh) or father's sister's husband (fzh) is asked **prohibition** the gift. This ceremony emphasises their status **within** takers. The priest clearly asks for those who have **rother and** daughters to come forward for receiving the *shaiyya* (bed). Thus, of the two kinds of affines (the wife's-taker and wife-giver) the affines of the wife-taking type are preferred over the affines of wife-giving type. In the hypergamous situation wife-takers are higher than the wife-givers and therefore in ceremonial gift-giving they remain at the receiving end while the wife-givers remain at the giving end.

Flow of gifts from affinal kin (wife's relatives) and uterine kin (mother's relatives) have also been recorded in the studies made by F.G. Bailey in Orissa and Oscar Lewis in Rampur. According to A.C. Mayer, the function of the gifts made by uterine and affinal kin is similar, i.e. to enhance the status of wife-takers. In sociological terms, we say that this type of exchange of gifts shows the hypergamous nature of marriage in North India. In other words, the woman is always given into the group, which is higher in status, and the flow of gifts from the family maintains this distinction forever. This, in turn, explains the nature of kin relationships in North India.

10

Marriage: Changing Patterns

Marriage is an important social institution. It is a relationship, which is socially approved. The relationship is defined and sanctioned by custom and law. The definition of the relationship includes not only guidelines for behaviour relating to sex but also regarding things like the particular way labour is to be divided and other duties and privileges. Children born of marriage are considered the legitimate offspring of the married couple. This legitimacy is important in the matter of inheritance and succession. Thus marriage is not only a means of sexual gratification but also a set of cultural mechanisms to ensure the continuation of the family. It is more or less a universal social institution in India.

The religious texts of many communities in India have outlined the purpose, rights and duties involved in marriage. Among the Hindus, for instance, marriage is regarded as a socio-religious duty. Ancient Hindu texts point out three main aims of marriage. These are *dharma* (duty), *praja* (progeny) and *rati* (sensual pleasure). That is to say that marriage is significant from both the societal as well as the individual's point of view. Marriage is significant in that it provides children especially sons who would not only carry on the family name but also perform periodic rituals including the annual *"shraddha"* to propitiate the dead ancestors. Majority of the Hindus look upon son(s) as a support in old age to parents and as the most important source of economic enrichment to the family. Marriage, in the Hindu system, enables a man to enter into the stage of a householder. Both a man and a woman are regarded incomplete without marriage.

Even among other communities in India, marriage is regarded as an essential obligation. Islam looks upon marriage as *"sunnah"* (an obligation) which must be fulfilled by every Muslim. Christianity holds marriage as crucial to life and lays emphasis on the establishment of a mutual relationship between husband and wife and on their duty to each other.

The significance attached to marriage is reflected in the fact that only a very small percentage of men and women remain unmarried. The Report of the Committee on the Status of Women in India has indicated that only 0.5 percent of women never marry in India. By and large girls are brought up to believe that marriage is a woman's destiny; married state is desirable and motherhood is a cherished achievement. Only a very small percentage of men and women remain unmarried by choice. Today, marriage is still considered important and necessary, and only few individuals remain unmarried by choice. Goals of marriage are, however, undergoing changes especially for the urban and educated sections of the population. The older notions regarding large size family, (i.e., large number of children especially sons being the source of status for parents) are being replaced by preference for small size family. Marriage for self-fulfillment rather than primarily for procreation or societal welfare is also becoming prevalent.

Age of Marriage

Apart from marriage being universal, early marriage is also common in India. Though there are differences between various religious groups, classes and castes in the matter of age at marriage, the median age at marriage is low in India. As early as the 18th and nineteenth century, efforts have been made to curb infant or child marriage. Reformers like Raja Rammohun Roy, Ishwar Chandra Vidyasagar, Jyotiba Phule and others in the nineteenth and early twentieth century opposed child marriage. In 1929, the Child Marriage Restraint Act was passed (popularly known as the Sarda Act) and the minimum age for marriage for girls and boys was fixed at 14 years and 17 years respectively. The Act was made applicable to all Indians. The latest amendment has raised the minimum age for marriage for boys and girls to 18 years and 21 years, respectively. Though the age at marriage of females in India has been rising slowly since around the middle of the twentieth century; the level at the end of the twentieth century was low in comparison to the most of the low fertility countries.

Low Age at Marriage

In spite of legislations, and governmental and non-governmental efforts to educate the people about the dangers of early marriage, age at marriage is low in India. The 1971 Census data on marital status of women indicate that the average age of marriage for girls in more than one-third of the total number of districts in our country was below 15 years. The mean age at marriage for females for the year 1991 was 18.3. The female age at marriage was lowest in Rajasthan (17.5) followed by states of Madhya Pradesh and Bihar (17.6 and 17.8 respectively) and it was highest in Kerala (22.3) followed by Assam and Punjab (21.1 and 21.0 respectively. In newspapers and journals we read about marriage melas, specially in rural areas, in which the average age of the bride is reported to be below fifteen years. In some states like Orissa, Madhya Pradesh, Uttar Pradesh and Rajasthan, child marriages continue.

Low age at marriage is related with the near universality of marriage in India. Marriage is regarded essential and thought of a girl's marriage is entertained right from her childhood. In some regions, the existence of clear-cut expectations, preferences, and rules regarding choice of a marriage partner also lead to early marriage. The desire and concern to preserve the chastity or purity of women is yet another factor. In fact, till the 1920's among certain upper castes, pre-puberty marriages were not only popular but also mandatory. There is the belief that the onset of puberty is the right age for marriage for a girl as she is then ready for maternity. This is also another important factor leading to early marriage .

Rise in the Age at Marriage

Female age at marriage rose from 16.1 years in 1961 to 19.3 in 1991. The rural urban gap in female age at marriage for 1991 is 2 years and this indicates that in spite of rise in age at marriage a wide gap persists between the rural and urban areas of the country. It is important to point out on the basis of growing evidence that age at marriage has not been low for all communities in India. For instance, among many of the hill tribes in India the average age at marriage has been above 15 years for girls. Also among the Christians, Parsis and some educated sections living in urban areas, the age at marriage has been above the minimum age prescribed by law.

You may ask what have been some of the factors that have helped in raising the age at marriage among certain sections of the population. Research suggests that in urban areas and for the well to do in rural areas education and the need for employment of boys have raised the age of marriage. In states where the literacy rate is high, age at marriage is also much higher than in those states where literacy level is low.

While, it is encouraging to note that education has helped in raising the age at marriage, it has however led to some unintended consequences. Education combined with increasing demands for dowry have led to a rise in the age at marriage. Educated girls seek educated boys and the price (dowry) of an educated groom in the 'marriage market' is high. Since most marriages in India are arranged, parents arrange a marriage only when they meet the dowry demands. Thus, necessarily the marriages of the girls are postponed and age at marriage increases.

Forms Of Marriage

All the commonly listed forms of marriage, namely, *monogamy* (marriage of a man to a woman at a time), and polygamy (marriage of a man or woman to more than one spouse) are found in India. The latter, that is polygamy, has two forms, namely, polygyny (marriage of a man to several women at a time) and polyandry (marriage of a woman to several men at a time). In ancient texts of the Hindus we find references to eight forms of marriage.

Monogamy, Polygyny, Polyandry

In this section, we shall focus only on monogamy, and both forms of polygamy. With regard to the prevalence of these three forms, one has to distinguish between what is permitted and what is practised by different sections of the population through time.

Monogamy

Among the Hindus, until the passing of the Hindu Marriage Act of 1955, a Hindu man was permitted to marry more than one woman at a time. Although permitted, polygyny has not been common among the Hindus. Only limited sections of the population like kings, chieftains, headmen of villages, members of the landed aristocracy actually practised polygyny.

We may say that those who had the means and the power to acquire more than one wife at a time were polygynous. The other important reasons for polygyny were the barrenness of the wife and or her prolonged sickness. Among some occupational groups like the agriculturists and artisans, polygyny prevailed because of an economic gain involved in it. Where women are self-supporting and contribute substantially to the productive activity a man can gain by having more than one wife.

Concerted efforts to remove this practice were made in the nineteenth century and early twentieth century by social reformers like Raja Rammohun Roy, Ishwar Chandra Vidyasagar, Dayanand Saraswati and others. After Independence, the Hindu Marriage Act of 1955 established monogamy for all Hindus and others who came to be governed by this Act. Some of the 'other' communities covered by this Act are the Sikhs, Jains and Buddhists. Strict monogamy is prescribed in Christian and Parsi communities.

Polygyny

Islam, on the other hand, has allowed polygyny. A Muslim man can have as many as four wives at a time, provided all are treated as equals. However, it seems that polygynous unions have been restricted to a small percentage of Muslims, namely the rich and the powerful. With regard to the tribal population, we find that the customary law of the tribals in general has not forbidden polygyny. Polygyny is more widespread among the tribes of north and central India.

Polyandry

Polyandry is even less common than polygyny. A few

Kerala castes practised polyandry until recently. The Toda of the Nilgiris in Tamilnadu, the Khasa of Jaunsar Bawar in Dehradun district of Uttaranchal and some North Indian castes practise polyandry. In the fraternal form of polyandry, the husbands are brothers. In 1958, C.M. Abraham has reported that in Central Travancore fraternal polyandry was practised by large number of groups like the Irava, Kaniyan, the Vellan and the Asari.

The factors that are related to the prevalence of polyandry are

a) desire to prevent division of property within a family (especially in fraternal polyandry)

b) desire to preserve the unity and solidarity of the sibling group (in fraternal polyandry)

c) the need for more than one husband in a society where men are away on a commercial or military journey

d a difficult economy, especially an unfertile soil, which does not favour division of land and belongings (Peter 1968).

Prevailing Patterns

Monogamy is the most prevalent form of marriage in India. However, bigamous (having two spouses at a time) marriages have been reported among the Hindus in many parts of India. It is the man who very often commits bigamy and escapes punishment by turning the loopholes of the law to his advantage. It is the wife who is often unaware of his second marriage, and even if she is aware of it, is unaware of her legal rights and accepts her fate. Social and economic dependence on husband and inadequate social condemnation of the man's actions are some of the reasons for the wife's acceptance of the husband's second marriage.

Among the Muslims it is the man who is allowed to have four wives. Among them men enjoy greater privileges than women. A Muslim woman cannot marry a second time when her first husband is alive or if she has not been divorced by him.

Selection Of Spouse

There are three striking features regarding selection of spouse in India. Firstly the rules of endogamy, including those of hypergamy, indicate the groups into which a person is expected to find a spouse. Secondly, rules of exogamy, on the other hand, prohibit a person form marrying into certain groups. Both the rules of endogamy and exogamy are linked mainly to the caste and kinship structure. Thirdly, marriages in India are mostly arranged by the parents or elders.

Rule of Endogamy

The rule of endogamy requires an individual to marry within a specified or defined group of which he or she is a member. The group may be a caste, clan, racial, ethnic or religious group.

Religious and caste endogamy are two of the most pervasive forms of endogamy in India. Though legally permitted, inter-religious marriages are not commonly arranged or popular. In India there are innumerable castes which are divided into innumerable sub-castes which are further divided into subsections and each one of them is endogamous. The endogamous unit, for many Hindu sub-castes, consists of a series of kin clusters living in a fairly restricted geographical area. The operation of the rule of endogamy shows interesting variation by region and religion.

In South India, for instance, among many castes marriage with some relatives is preferred. In the Marathi, Telugu, Tamil and Kannada speaking areas, marriages with the cross-cousins (children of father's sisters or mother's brothers) are preferred. In North India, neither the parallel nor the cross-cousins can intermarry. In North India, on the other hand, there is a tendency to marry into villages that are not farther than twelve or thirteen kilometres from one's village. Social and economic links are restricted to a few kin groups residing in certain areas. There are spatial as well as social boundaries which limit the field of marriage and these boundaries vary from region to region.

Endogamous rules are operative in non-Hindu sections of the population too. Among the Muslims, the 'Syeds', recognised as an aristocratic class, are divided into various endogamous groups. Sometimes the endogamous group is so small that it includes only the extended families of a man's parents.

Muslims permit marriages between both cross (mother's brother's children and father's sister's children) and parallel (mother's sister's children and father's brother's children) cousins. In fact, the father's brother's daughter is a preferred mate. Among Muslims the concept of purity of blood seems to be mainly responsible for preference of marriage between close relatives particularly between children of siblings. Many Muslim groups in North and Western India consider marriage between children of two brothers as most desirable. It is held that the desire to keep the family property within the family has been another important reason for close kin marriages. It is generally believed that marriage of the near kin helps to mitigate the conflict between a mother-in-law and daughter-in-law and this helps to strengthen the intra-as well as inter-familial ties.

Rule of Hypergamy

According to the rule of hypergamy, the status of the husband is always higher than that of the wife. Those who follow this rule always seek for their daughters those men who have social status higher than their own. It is a rule whereby marriage takes place or is generally arranged within a sub caste between a girl of a lower social status and a boy of a higher social status. This practice has occurred mainly among different subsections of a caste or sub caste rather than between castes. It is found that the tendency towards hypergamous stratification is available among all castes. Each caste is divided into several sub-castes, which are again divided into hierarchically ordered groups. It is quite clear that the rule of hypergamy operates within the confines of each endogamous group.

In ancient scriptures, it is given that *anuloma* marriages, based on the rule of hypergamy whereby a girl is married to a boy from upper caste sub-caste, were permitted. It is also given that *pratiloma* marriages, based on the rule of hypogamy, whereby a girl is married to a boy from a lower caste sub-caste, were not permitted. It would seem that in ancient times hypergamy *(anuloma)* across the four fold *varna* order was acceptable while hypogamy *(pratiloma)* was not permitted.

Practice of hypergamy has been found among such groups as the Rajput and the Jat of North India, Anavil Brahmin and Patidar of Gujarat, Maithil Brahmin of Bihar, Rarhi Brahmin of Bengal and among the Kanyakubja and Saryupari Brahmin of Uttar Pradesh to some extent. It has also been found among the Nayar, Kshatriya and Ambalavasi of Kerala.

The practice has shown a regional pattern. For instance, among the Rajput of Uttar Pradesh, traditionally girls were given in marriage from east to the west direction within a sub-caste. This is so because the Rajput clans were associated with a geographic region and a corresponding rating by region. Prestige of regions increased towards the westerly direction.

In the areas where hypergamy is practised, clans and lineages are of unequal status. Research has indicated that female infanticide among the Jat and Rajput was mainly a consequence of hypergamy. This was so because the girls of the highest groups had very little choice for marriage. Boys of their group could marry lower down while they had only the boys in groups which were at least equal to their own. Dowry has been generally high in hypergamous communities. Men from the Kulin subcaste of Bengal (belonging to the Rarhi Brahmin caste) often married many women at a time and demanded huge dowries.

This is so because they are ranked as the highest subcaste and women of this group have to be married within the group.

Exogamy

Exogamous rules are complementary to endogamous rules. These rules prohibit marriage between members of certain groups. The prohibition may be so narrow as to include those members within the elementary family (i.e. marriage between a brother and sister or parent and child) or so wide to include all those with whom genealogical kinship can be traced. The prohibition placed, on sexual intercourse between persons related in certain prohibited degrees of kinship is called incest, e.g., sexual relations or marriage between a brother and sister are defined as incestuous in most groups. The definitions of these groups, however, show variations mainly by region and religion. In North India, a girl born within a village is considered the daughter of the village and hence cannot marry a boy from her own village. Thus, the village becomes the exogamous unit here. In South India, the exogamous unit in one's own generation is defined by one's own sisters/brothers and real and classificatory parallel cousins.

Two other kinds of exogamy, which have been prevalent among several Hindu communities in North and South India, are sagotra and *sapinda* exogamy.

Sagotra exogamy: In the context of the 'twice born' castes (belonging to the Brahmin, Kshatriya and Vaishya *varna* across) India *sagotra* exogamy applies to those who trace descent from a common ancestor, usually a *rishi* or a sage. All these people cannot intermarry. The term *gotra* is commonly used to mean an exogamous category within a *jati.* One of its principal uses is to regulate marriage alliance. All members of a *gotra* are supposed to be descendants of or associated with the same ancestral figure.

A four-clan rule or four *gotra* exogamous rule prevails among Hindu castes in North India. In accordance with this four clan *(gotra)* rule, a man cannot marry a girl from (i) his father's *gotra* or clan, (ii) his mother's *gotra* or clan, (iii) his *dadi*'s, i.e. his father's mother's *gotra* or clan, and (iv) his *nani*'s, i.e., his mother's mother's gotra or clan. In almost all castes in the northern zone, according to Karve , the marriage between cousins is prohibited.

Sapinda: Sapinda exogamy indicates the prohibition placed on the inter-marriage between certain sets of relatives. *Sapinda* represents the relationship between the living member and their dead ancestors. The term *sapinda* means (i) those who share the particles of the same body (ii) people who are united by offering *'pinda'* or balls of cooked rice to the same dead ancestor. Hindu lawgivers do not give a uniform definition regarding the kinship groups within which marriage cannot take place. Some prohibit marriage of members within seven generations on the father's side and five generations of members from Mother —' the mother's side. Some others have restricted the prohibited generations to five on the father' and three on the mother's side. Several others have permitted the marriage of cross-cousins (marriage of a person with his father's sister's children or mother's brother's children).

The Hindu Marriage Act of 1955 does not allow marriage within five generations on the father's side and three on the mother's side. However, it permits the marriage of cross- cousins where this is customary. The patrilineal joint family is an important exogamous unit among Hindus. This much is quite clear from the fact that marriage is prohibited within five generations on the father's side.

Among Christians and Muslims, the elementary or nuclear family is the exogamous unit. Moplah Muslims of North Malabar in Kerala live in matrilineal units and among them matrilineage is the exogamous unit. Lineage exogamy also exists among the Muslim Gujjars of Jammu and Kashmir. Among the Nayars, who are a matrilineal group, a girl can never marry her mother's brother.

Arranged Marriages

Majority of the marriages in India are fixed or arranged by parents or elders on behalf of and/or with the consent of the boy or the girl involved in marriage. When marriage is fixed by parents or elders it is called an arranged marriage. This is in contrast to marriage by self choice (popular example of marriage by self choice is the so called "love marriage"). In some instances both these types of selection of one's spouse can be found together.

The prevalence of arranged marriages in India can be traced in relation to what has been said before, that is (i) existence of the rules of endogamy which limit marriage alliance within certain groups, (ii) the rules of exogamy which disallow marriage within *gotra,* (iii) regulations about prescriptive (allowing) and proscriptive (prohibiting) rules about marriage with parallel and cross-cousins and (iv) customs which indicate a specific preference for marriage between certain types of relatives or groups. All these factors make arranged marriages the most desirable form of selection of spouse. Choice of spouse cannot be left to the decision of the young if these restrictions and preferences are to be effectively carried out. The restrictions placed on free interaction between a boy and a girl in India is yet another factor which does not allow marriage by self choice. Though the measure of participation in choosing one's life partner has shown

variations between different groups, by and large, marriage arranged by parents/ elders is the most prevalent form of selection of spouse. For majority of the high caste Hindus, matching of horoscope (charts relating to one's birth under certain astrological calculations) constitutes an important element in the final choice of the marriage partner. Today apart from astrologers matching the horoscopes of a boy and a girl, computers are also used to match horoscopes. Among the Muslims, the parents, elders or *wali* (guardian) arrange a marriage.

Recent Trends

To what extent are the rules of endogamy, hypergamy, exogamy and arranged marriages operative today? Intercaste marriages are now recognised by law and take place on a larger scale than before. These intercaste marriages constitute only a very small proportion of the total number of marriages taking place. They are increasing at a slow rate. Caste endogamy is still highly relevant in the context of the patterns of selection of spouse. Many caste organisations devise all kinds of strategies to confine marriages within their castes and subcastes. There are even marriage *"melas"* (fairs) to ensure that the choice of the spouse is made within the particular subcaste.

Though majority of marriages continue to be arranged by parents/elders/*wali*, the pattern of choosing one's spouse has undergone some modifications today. We find the following patterns i) marriage by parents'/elders' choice without consulting either the boy or girl, ii) marriage by self-choice, iii) marriage by self-choice but with parents' consent, iv) marriage by parents' choice but with the consent of both the boy and the girl involved in the marriage, v) marriage by parents' choice but with the consent of only one of the two partners involved. Very often, the boy is consulted and his consent is taken. Parents/elders do not think it is important to ask the girl whether she approves the match. Among urban educated classes arranged marriage with the consent of the boy and the girl is often the most preferred pattern. Marriages are even arranged through newspaper advertisement for both the boy and the girl.

Marriage Rites

Rites constitute an important part of marriage in India. We find variations in rites not only in terms of religion but also in terms of caste, sect and rural or urban residence. Let us look at some of the basic rites in a few communities in India.

Basic Rites of Marriage in Different Communities

For the Hindus, marriage is a sacrament. This means that a Hindu marriage cannot be dissolved. It is a union for life. This is also reflected in the marital rites. Some of the essential rites are *kanyadan* (the giving off of the bride to the groom by the father), *panigrahana* (the clasping of the bride's hand by the groom), *agniparinaya* (going around the sacred fire by the bride and the groom), *lajahoma* (offering of the parched grain to the sacrificial fire) and *saptapadi* (walking seven steps by the bride and the groom). These basic rituals are not confined to the twice born castes (the Brahmin, Kshatriya and Vaishya) only, but these are also performed with some variations among other castes too. Some invite a Brahmin priest to recite the *mantra* which are religious invocations. The ritual of *kanyadan* is the most popular of all the basic rituals.

If we analyse the significance of the rituals of Hindu marriage we find that they stress male primacy and superiority and reflect the notion of transfer of the bride from her father's side to her husband's side. While emphasising life partnership for the two people involved in marriage, the basic rituals exhort the bride to follow the husband, to act according to his wishes and to remain steadfast in loyalty and love. In fact, marriage is the first major *samskara* (life cycle ritual) for a Hindu woman.

In some regions, among certain castes, the pre-marriage ritual is more elaborate than the actual wedding ceremony. For instance, among certain sections of the Nayar castes in Kerala, the actual marriage constitutes only the exchange of cloth between the bride and the groom, mutual garlanding and going around the lighted lamps. The pre-marital ritual of "*talikettu kalyanam*" is more elaborate than the actual marriage ceremony.

Certain sections of the Jain community (like the Digambara and Svetambara) and the Sikh community have marriage customs and rituals which are similar to those of the Hindus. The core ceremony of the Sikhs however is different. It is called "*anand karaj*" and is solemnised in the presence of the Guru Granth Sahib, the holy book of the Sikhs. The main ceremony consists of the bridal couple going four times around the holy book. Appropriate verses, known as '*shabad*' are recited by the officiating priest. Unlike Hindus, Sikhs do not have any particular period or season for marriages.

Muslim marriage is not a sacrament. Rather, it is a contract, which can be terminated. Among the Muslims, the marriage rituals show variation by sect and region. Some rites of the Shia sect of the Muslims differ from the Sunni, a sect among the Muslims. However, the essential ceremony of Muslim marriage is known as the *nikah*. The ceremony is performed by the priest or the *kazi*. The *nikah* is considered to be complete only when the consent of both the groom and the bride has been obtained. A formal document known as *nikahnama* bears the signatures of the couple. Among certain sections, the signatures of two witnesses are also included in the document and the document may also contain details of the payment to be made to the bride by the groom. This payment is called the *mehr* which is a stipulated sum of money or other assets paid to the wife either immediately after the wedding or postponed till some future date.

Many of the marriage customs and rituals of the Muslims are similar to those of the Hindus. Thus, customs like smearing of turmeric, applying *mehndi,* mock testing of the bride's proficiency at domestic work are as much a part of the Muslim marriage as Hindu marriage. In fact, among the Moplah Muslims of Kerala, the *nikah* ceremony is performed as laid down by Islam but their marriage is not regarded complete without the Hindu function *'kalyanam'*.

What is most significant to note in the rituals of Muslim marriage is that the custom of paying a *mehr* to the wife provides some sort of guarantee of security to the woman.

Among the Christians, the wedding takes place in a church. The exchange of the ring is an important ritual among them. Some sections of the Christians, like the Syrian Christians of Kerala, have the Hindu rite of the groom tying a *'tali'* on the bride's neck. *Tali* is a symbol of the married state of Hindu women in South India.

Among Christians, the following pronouncement, which forms a part of the marriage rites, reflects the importance assigned to the relationship of the husband and wife, rather than the relationship between the families of the husband and the wife. "Man shall leave his father and mother and shall cleave to his wife and they shall be one flesh." This outlook emphasises the fact that marriage is a bond between two individuals and not between two families. It does not focus on the transfer of the girl from one family to another. As a part of marriage celebrations all communities hold wedding processions and feasts. Their scale may vary according to the socio-economic status of the bride and bridegroom's families.

Customary Marriages

While rites constitute an important component of marriage among many communities, there are sections or groups of people who do not have religious rites in marriage. Marriages with no rites are referred as customary marriages. These marriages are based on simple practices. For instance, in some groups living in the Himalayan tract, putting a ring in the bride's nose is a customary form of marriage. Customary forms of marriage are generally found among those groups where divorce and secondary marriages are permitted and practised. Secondary marriage of a widow or a separated or divorced woman is usually celebrated in a simple way, which indicates essentially the renewal of her married state.

Today marriage rites have been condensed to a great extent. The Special Marriage Act of 1954 provides for secular and civil marriage before a registrar. This Act applies to all Indian citizens who chose to make use of its provisions, irrespective of religious affiliations. Civil marriage enables persons to avoid the expense of traditional weddings. However, weddings continue to be an expensive affair for a large majority of people. Large sums of money, gifts of jewellery, furniture, vessels, clothes have to be bought and generally the expenses are more for the bride's side than the groom's side.

Transfer Of Wealth in Marriage

Marriage, in most cases, involves material as well as non-material transactions between the bride-giver and the bride-taker. It involves, with a few exceptions, the transfer of the wife to the husband's family. Two major types of transfers of material wealth accompany marriage. In one, wealth travels in the opposite direction of the bride and in another it travels along with the bride in the same direction. The former is identified as bride price while the latter as dowry.

Bride-Price

The tradition of bride-price is found among certain patrilineal tribes and some castes in the middle and lower rung of the caste ladder. The form and amount of bride-price vary from region to region, from tribe to tribe and within a tribe from time to time. Some pay only cash, some others only in kind while some pay both in kind and cash. Payment in kind includes a wide variety of things like clothes, ornaments, tools and implements, liquor, grain, cattle, goats and other forms of livestock. For instance, among the Uraon tribe of Chotanagpur a man takes sets of clothes for the bride's relatives. Bhumias of Orissa give cash, five or six sarees and three goats as bride-price. Bargaining for bride-price is also common. In some tribes, the groom offers his services to the bride's father as a form of bride-price.

Under the local influence of high caste values and practices, some groups have given up their custom of bride-price and have adopted the custom of dowry. For example, the peasants of the villages of Karnataka and the Godia (or the cowherds) caste in Andhra Pradesh have given up their custom of bride-price and adopted the custom of dowry.

Bride-price or the payment in cash and/or kind to the bride's father by the groom's father reflects the transfer of authority over the bride from her father to the groom and his family. The idea of compensation for the loss of a productive worker is also implicit in it. The bride's family loses a productive worker when the girl gets married and leaves her parental home. So, the bride's family is paid a compensation for this loss. The girl is a source of wealth and prestige to her natal family, that is the family in which she is born. In this sense, the transaction implies the transfor of all that the girl stands for.

Practice of Dowry

Broadly speaking, dowry refers to a specific category of gifts given by the bride's side to the groom's side. This set of gifts symbolises the transfer of wealth from the bride's side to the groom's side. This act confers prestige and honour to both the sides. The bride-giver gains prestige within his community by giving dowry while the bride-taker receives both wealth and prestige in his own and other communities. Of late it has become groom-price.

Today, in legal terms, dowry constitutes what is given to the son-in-law and or to his parents on demand either in cash or in kind by the bride's side. There are, of course, regional variations in the practice and people's understanding of the term 'dowry'. Some view it mainly as 'groom-price' and often the price paid to the groom depends on the groom's qualifications, job, social status regardless of the bride's parents' ability to pay the price demanded by the groom's side. Some include in the custom of dowry i) what is given to the bride during and after the wedding, during occasions like festivals, child birth, initiation etc. in the first few years of marriage ii) what is given to the bridegroom before or after marriage and iii) what is presented to the in-laws of the girl.

Here, we need to note that (a) dowry constitutes an array of gifts given to the groom's side over time and (b) what is given at the time of the wedding is substantial and conspicuous. Goods that constitute dowry are i) movable property like sarees, jewels, silver vessels, cash, vehicles like car, tractor and ii) immovable property such as land, house, factories, jobs etc.

The form and amount of dowry and purpose to which dowry is put have shown variations based on caste, class, region and socio-economic status. Among the landowning castes of Andhra Pradesh (like Reddy, Kamma) a father may give to his daughter land and jewellery. The cash may be handed over to the groom or his parents but the land is registered in the name of the daughter. Money also is deposited in the name of the bride or put in trust for her. In North India, where there has been a tradition of giving large utensils to the girl, the utensils generally come under the use and control of the in-laws. The amount of cash involved in dowry varies mainly according to the socio-economic status and expectations of the groom's community as well as the socio-economic status of the bride's family. Again, the gift in cash or in kind involved in dowry may be put to productive purposes or just hoarded as wealth by the bride, the groom and/or his family.

The practice of giving gift to the girl at the time of and after the wedding has been viewed as *streedhana.* This means that the gifts given to the daughter are a kind of property given to the daughter of the house who has to leave her natal home to join her husband. *Streedhana* reflects the notion of female right to property. It is looked as a source of wealth for the married daughter to fall back in times of crisis and need. In many regions of South India, the gifts (ornaments, vessels) given to the daughter belong to her exclusively and she has the right to use them the way she wants. Her in-laws generally do not claim possession over them.

Today, the practice of dowry has taken a very ugly turn. In many instances, the practice of dowry has worsened. Educated girls look out for boys who are more qualified than them. Highly qualified boys demand a high dowry. As a result of increase in dowry demand, parents often are unable to get their daughters married. If they do, they get them married beyond their means and are subject to different kinds of continuing pressures in the form of dowry demands from the groom's side. We often hear of dowry deaths or the girl being sent back to her parents' home for not fulfilling the dowry demands. Today, we even hear cases of unmarried girls committing suicide in order to ease the burden of their anxious, guilt-ridden parents, who have not been able to settle a marriage for them.

In 1961, the Government of India passed the Dowry Prohibition Act. In 1984 and again in 1986, the Act was amended to make the law more stringent and effective. For instance, today, the husband and his family can be penalised for demanding dowry if his bride dies within seven years of the marriage in other than normal circumstance. We even have a Dowry Prohibition Cell to look into complaints about dowry.

All this does not mean that there are no marriages taking place without dowry. There are progressive young people who voice their strong opinion against dowry and marry without it. There are at the same time, young, educated people who accept this practice and say they see no harm in it. Some get away by saying that it is their parents (whose wishes they never want to disobey) who perpetuate this practice. Even among other communities, like the Muslim and Christian, some people demand dowry. Often, discord in family is caused because of the continuous demand for dowry even after marriage. This may lead to divorce.

Divorce And Widow Remarriage

No discussion of marriage is complete without considering the issues of divorce and remarriage. Here, we look first at the possibilities and mechanism of dissolving a marriage and then discuss briefly the question of widow remarriage in India.

Divorce

The possibilities and mechanisms of dissolving a marital union have varied through time, between and within communities. Hindu marriage is in theory a sacrament and irrevocable. However, among many *non-dwija* (or non-twice born) castes, divorce is customarily allowed. When we say non-twice born castes, we mean those castes, which do not observe the practice of performing the life-cycle rituals or Hindu *Samskara.* Their performance symbolises the second birth or social birth of a biological person and hence the term twice-born for the first three categories of Hindu castes—the Brahmin, Kshatriya and Vaishya, which must and do perform these rituals. The notion that marriage is indissoluble has gradually been eroded and through legislation, the right of divorce has been introduced in all legal systems in India.

The grounds for divorce have been spelt out both by custom and by law in different communities. During 1940-48, several provinces and states passed laws permitting divorce for Hindus. The Special Marriage Act of 1954 introduced and 'clarified the grounds for divorce'. It has been available to all Indians who have chosen to register their marriages under this Act. The Hindu Marriage Act of 1955 was amended several times since 1955 (the next one being in 1976) to incorporate a wide range of grounds for divorce available to both men and women coming under the purview of this Act. Some of the important grounds for divorce outlined by law are i) impotency, ii) lunacy (for a specified time period), iii) disappearance for seven years, iv) contagious disease, v) rape, vi) homo-sexuality, and vii) bestiality (sexual relationship between a human being and a lower animal). Now adultery and cruelty have also become the grounds on which divorce may be sought. The condition that one can apply for divorce after three years of marriage has been reduced to one year. The waiting period of divorce by mutual consent is now only 6 months.

Among the Muslims, marriage is a contract and divorce is allowed. Muslim law provides for different types of divorce of which *talaq* and *khol* need special mention. *Talaq* is an exjudicial divorce. It becomes effective if pronounced thrice unilaterally by the husband. It signifies the power the husband has to divorce his wife at will. The other form of divorce *khol* takes place by mutual consent.

Public attitude to divorce in a Hindu dominated culture is not yet very liberal in spite of the legal permission for divorce. In many communities of the Indian population, divorce even when it is required is not sought, despite legal provisions. Even in cases where women have turned to the legal system for help, law is not very clear about the rights of a woman in her marriage. For instance, the respective judgments of Andhra Pradesh High Court and Punjab High Court in two cases relating to the Hindu woman's right in the matter of being a wife or a mother reflect the ambiguity. In one case in Andhra Pradesh the judgment favoured the woman. Her right to decide whether she wanted to bear the child of the husband whom she did not find compatible was upheld. In the other case in Punjab, the wife was held guilty for refusing to bear a child by her spouse whom she did not find compatible. Women activists point out that though our constitution supports the notion of equality between sexes, the laws passed to promote such a notion have not been able to end the discrimination shown toward women. Even among the Muslims, where divorce has been permitted for a long time, laws favour men more than the women.

Widow Remarriage

Certain sections of the Indian population have a tradition of widow remarriage. Levirate alliances have been reported among the Ahirs of Haryana, some Jats and Girjans and several castes in U.P. and among the Kodagu of Mysore. In a levirate marriage, a man is obliged to marry the widow of a brother.

In many castes of the Hindu fold, widow remarriage has been customarily sanctioned and practised. Only those castes which imitate the life-style and values of the high castes adopt the practice of banning widow remarriage. Widow remarriage is permitted among the Muslims, Christians and Parsis. Among the Jains local and caste customs determine the issue.

Generally, everywhere the widower has the right to remarry. The 1971 census of India showed that there were 8 million widowers as against 23 million widows. In the year 1991, among the elderly (60+ age group) the percentage of widows was 60.7 and that of widowers was 19 (Census of India 1991). It is often said that the problem of widow remarriage is the problem only of a section of society because only the high castes put a strict ban on widow remarriage. Not only this, in the past, widows of some priestly castes, royal families were also expected to commit the practice of sati orwidow burning. The practice of widow burning comprises self-immolation of the widow on the funeral pyre of her husband. Respect is paid to such women who end their lives as a mark of devotion to their husbands.

As early as in the nineteenth century, reformers like Vidyasagar, fought against the practice of sati and exploitation of widows. In 1856, the Hindu Widows Remarriage Act legalised the marriage of widows of all castes. Traditional notions about widow remarriage and the treatment of widows still seem to be prevalent. Widows are still regarded as inauspicious; they are not expected or permitted to participate in certain religious and social functions. It is shocking to hear that widows are still burnt alive on their husband's pyre and there is a section of the population, which glorifies such act. The most recent case of law being enacted to protect the woman victim is the law against the practice of widow burning or sati. This was passed by the Parliament in response to a national demand

and reaction following the burning of a young educated woman, Roop Kanwar, on the funeral pyre of her husband in Deorala, a village in Rajasthan. The Act is called Commission of Sati (Prevention) Act, 1987.

11

Language, Ethnicity, and Regionalism in Indian Society

India's ethnic, linguistic, and regional complexity sets it apart from other nations. To gain even a superficial understanding of the relationships governing the huge number of ethnic, linguistic, and regional groups, the country should be visualised not as a nation-state but as the seat of a major world civilisation on the scale of Europe. The population—estimated at 936.5 million in 1995—is not only immense but also has been highly varied throughout recorded history; its systems of values have always encouraged diversity. The linguistic requirements of numerous former empires, an independent nation, and modern communication are superimposed on a heterogeneous sociocultural base. Almost 8 percent of the population, approaching 65 million people at the time of the 1991 census, belongs to social groups recognised by the government as Scheduled Tribes, with social structures somewhat different from the mainstream of society. Powerful trends of "regionalism"—both in the sense of an increasing attachment to the states as opposed to the central government, and in the sense of movements for separation from the present states or greater autonomy for regions within them—threaten the current distribution of power and delineation of political divisions of territory.

LINGUISTIC RELATIONS

The languages of India belong to four major families: Indo-Aryan (a branch of the Indo-European family), Dravidian, Austroasiatic (Austric), and Sino-Tibetan, with the overwhelming majority of the population speaking languages belonging to the first two families. (A fifth family, Andamanese, is spoken by at most a few hundred among the indigenous tribal peoples in the Andaman Islands, and has no agreed upon connections with families outside them.) The four major families are as different in their form and construction as are, for example, the Indo-European and Semitic families. A variety of scripts are employed in writing the different languages. Furthermore, most of the more widely used Indian languages exist in a number of different forms or dialects influenced by complex geographic and social patterns.

Sir George Grierson's twelve-volume *Linguistic Survey of India*, published between 1903 and 1923, identified 179 languages and 544 dialects. The 1921 census listed 188 languages and forty-nine dialects. The 1961 census listed 184 "mother tongues," including those with fewer than 10,000 speakers. This census also gave a list of all the names of mother tongues provided by the respondents themselves; the list totals 1,652 names. The 1981 census—the last census to tabulate languages—reported 112 mother tongues with more than 10,000 speakers and almost 1 million people speaking other languages. The encyclopedic *People of India* series, published by the government's Anthropological Survey of India in the 1980s and early 1990s, identified seventy-five "major languages" within a total of 325 languages used in Indian households. In the early 1990s, there were thirty-two languages with 1 million or more speakers.

The Indian constitution recognizes official languages. Articles 343 through 351 address the use of Hindi, English, and regional languages for official purposes, with the aim of a nationwide use of Hindi while guaranteeing the use of minority languages at the state and local levels. Hindi has been designated India's official language, although many impediments to its official use exist.

The constitution's Eighth Schedule, as amended by Parliament in 1992, lists eighteen official or Scheduled Languages. They are Assamese, Bengali, Gujarati, Hindi, Kannada, Kashmiri, Konkani, Malayalam, Manipuri, Marathi, Nepali, Oriya, Punjabi, Sanskrit, Sindhi, Tamil, Telugu, and Urdu. (Precise numbers of speakers of these languages are not known. They were not reported in the 1991 census, and estimates are subject to considerable variation because of the use of multiple languages by individual speakers.) Of the official languages, approximately 403 million people, or about 43 percent of the estimated total 1995 population, speak Hindi as their mother tongue. Telugu, Bengali, Marathi, and Tamil rank next, each the mother tongue of about 4 to 5 percent (about 37 million to 47 million people); Urdu, Gujarati, Malayalam, Kannada, and Oriya are claimed by between 2 and 3 percent (roughly 19 million to 28 million people); Bhojpuri, Punjabi, and Assamese by 1 to 2 percent (9 million to 19 million people); and all other languages by less than 1 percent (less than 9 million speakers) each.

Since independence in 1947, linguistic affinity has served as a basis for organising interest groups; the "language question" itself has become an increasingly sensitive political issue. Efforts to reach a consensus on a single national language that transcends the myriad linguistic regions and is acceptable to diverse language communities have been largely unsuccessful.

Many Indian nationalists originally intended that Hindi would replace English—the language of British rule (1757-1947)—as a medium of common communication. Both

Hindi and English are extensively used, and each has its own supporters. Native speakers of Hindi, who are concentrated in North India, contend that English, as a relic from the colonial past and spoken by only a small fraction of the population, is hopelessly elitist and unsuitable as the nation's official language. Proponents of English argue, in contrast, that the use of Hindi is unfair because it is a liability for those Indians who do not speak it as their native tongue. English, they say, at least represents an equal handicap for Indians of every region.

English continues to serve as the language of prestige. Efforts to switch to Hindi or other regional tongues encounter stiff opposition both from those who know English well and whose privileged position requires proficiency in that tongue and from those who see it as a means of upward mobility. Partisans of English also maintain it is useful and indeed necessary as a link to the rest of the world, that India is lucky that the colonial period left a language that is now the world's predominant international language in the fields of culture, science, technology, and commerce. They hold, too, that widespread knowledge of English is necessary for technological and economic progress and that reducing its role would leave India a backwater in world affairs.

Linguistic diversity is apparent on a variety of levels. Major regional languages have stylised literary forms, often with an extensive body of literature, which may date back from a few centuries to two millennia ago. These literary languages differ markedly from the spoken forms and village dialects that coexist with a plethora of caste idioms and regional lingua francas. Part of the reason for such linguistic diversity lies in the complex social realities of South Asia. India's languages reflect the intricate levels of social hierarchy and caste. Individuals have in their speech repertoire a variety of styles and dialects appropriate to various social situations. In general, the higher the speaker's status, the more speech forms there are at his or her disposal. Speech is adapted in countless ways to reflect the specific social context and the relative standing of the speakers.

Determining what should be called a language or a dialect is more a political than a linguistic question. Sometimes the word *language* is applied to a standardised and prestigious form, recognised as such over a large geographic area, whereas the word *dialect* is used for the various forms of speech that lack prestige or that are restricted to certain regions or castes but are still regarded as forms of the same language. Sometimes mutual intelligibility is the criterion: if the speakers can understand each other, even though with some difficulty, they are speaking the same language, although they may speak different dialects. However, speakers of Hindi, Urdu, and Punjabi can often understand each other, yet they are regarded as speakers of different languages. Whether or not one thinks Konkani—spoken in Goa, Karnataka, and the Konkan region of Maharashtra—is a distinct language or a dialect of Marathi has tended to be linked with whether or not one thinks Goa ought to be merged with Maharashtra. The question has been settled from the central government's point of view by making Goa a state and Konkani a Scheduled Language. Moreover, the fact that the Latin script is predominantly used for Konkani separates it further from Marathi, which uses the Devanagariscript. However, Konkani is also sometimes written in Devanagari and Kannada scripts.

Regional languages are an issue in the politically charged atmosphere surrounding language policy. Throughout the 1950s and 1960s, attempts were made to redraw state boundaries to coincide with linguistic usage. Such efforts have had mixed results. Linguistic affinity has often failed to overcome other social and economic differences. In addition, most states have linguistic minorities, and questions surrounding the definition and use of the official language in those regions are fraught with controversy.

States have been accused of failure to fulfill their obligations under the national constitution to provide for the education of linguistic minorities in their mother tongues, even when the minority language is a Scheduled Language. Although the constitution requires that legal documents and petitions may be submitted in any of the Scheduled Languages to any government authority, this right is rarely exercised. Under such circumstances, members of linguistic minorities may feel they and their language are oppressed by the majority, while people who are among linguistic majorities may feel threatened by what some might consider minor concessions. Thus, attempts to make seemingly minor accommodations for social diversity may have extensive and volatile ramifications. For example, in 1994 a proposal in Bangalore to introduce an Urdu-language television news segment (aimed primarily at Muslim viewers) led to a week of urban riots that left dozens dead and millions of dollars in property damage.

Languages of India

About 80 percent of all Indians—nearly 750 million people based on 1995 population estimates—speak one of the Indo-Aryan group of languages. Persian and the languages of Afghanistan are close relatives, belonging, like the Indo-Aryan languages, to the Indo-Iranian branch of the Indo-European family. Brought into India from the northwest during the second millennium B.C., the Indo-Aryan tongues spread throughout the north, gradually displacing the earlier languages of the area.

Modern linguistic knowledge of this process of assimilation comes through the Sanskrit language employed in the sacred literature known as the Vedas. Over a period of centuries, Indo-Aryan languages came to predominate in the northern and central portions of South Asia.

As Indo-Aryan speakers spread across northern and central India, their languages experienced constant change and development. By about 500 B.C., Prakrits, or "common" forms of speech, were widespread throughout the north. By about the same time, the "sacred," "polished," or "pure" tongue—Sanskrit—used in religious rites had also developed along independent lines, changing significantly from the form used in the Vedas. However, its use in ritual settings encouraged the retention of archaic forms lost in the Prakrits. Concerns for the purity and correctness of Sanskrit gave rise to an elaborate science of grammar and phonetics and an alphabetical system seen by some scholars as superior to the Roman system. By the fourth century B.C., these trends had culminated in the work of Panini, whose Sanskrit grammar, the *Ashtadhyayi* (Eight Chapters), set the basic form of Sanskrit for subsequent generations. Panini's work is often compared to Euclid's as an intellectual feat of systematisation.

The Prakrits continued to evolve through everyday use. One of these dialects was Pali, which was spoken in the western portion of peninsular India. Pali became the language of Theravada Buddhism; eventually it came to be identified exclusively with religious contexts. By around A.D. 500, the Prakrits had changed further into Apabhramshas, or the "decayed" speech; it is from these dialects that the contemporary Indo-Aryan languages of South Asia developed. The rudiments of modern Indo-Aryan vernaculars were in place by about A.D. 1000 to 1300.

It would be misleading, however, to call Sanskrit a dead language because for many centuries huge numbers of works in all genres and on all subjects continued to be written in Sanskrit. Original works are still written in it, although in much smaller numbers than formerly. Many students still learn Sanskrit as a second or third language, classical music concerts regularly feature Sanskrit vocal compositions, and there are even television programs conducted entirely in Sanskrit.

Around 18 percent of the Indian populace (about 169 million people in 1995) speak Dravidian languages. Most Dravidian speakers reside in South India, where Indo-Aryan influence was less extensive than in the north. Only a few isolated groups of Dravidian speakers, such as the Gonds in Madhya Pradesh and Orissa, and the Kurukhs in Madhya Pradesh and Bihar, remain in the north as representatives of the Dravidian speakers who presumably once dominated much more of South Asia.

The oldest documented Dravidian language is Tamil, with a substantial body of literature, particularly the Cankam poetry, going back to the first century A.D. Kannada and Telugu developed extensive bodies of literature after the sixth century, while Malayalam split from Tamil as a literary language by the twelfth century. In spite of the profound influence of the Sanskrit language and Sanskritic culture on the Dravidian languages, a strong consciousness of the distinctness of Dravidian languages from Sanskrit remained. All four major Dravidian languages had consciously differentiated styles varying in the amount of Sanskrit they contained. In the twentieth century, as part of an anti-Brahman movement in Tamil Nadu, a strong movement arose to "purify" Tamil of its Sanskrit elements, with mixed success. The other three Dravidian languages were not much affected by this trend.

There are smaller groups, mostly tribal peoples, who speak Sino-Tibetan and Austroasiatic languages. Sino-Tibetan speakers live along the Himalayan fringe from Jammu and Kashmir to eastern Assam. They comprise about 1.3 percent, or 12 million, of India's 1995 population. The

Austroasiatic languages, composed of the Munda tongues and others thought to be related to them, are spoken by groups of tribal peoples from West Bengal through Bihar and Orissa and into Madhya Pradesh. These groups make up approximately 0.7 percent (about 6.5 million people) of the population.

Despite the extensive linguistic diversity in India, many scholars treat South Asia as a single linguistic area because the various language families share a number of features not found together outside South Asia. Languages entering South Asia were "Indianised." Scholars cite the presence of retroflex consonants, characteristic structures in verb formations, and a significant amount of vocabulary in Sanskrit with Dravidian or Austroasiatic origin as indications of mutual borrowing, influences, and counterinfluences. Retroflex consonants, for example, which are formed with the tongue curled back to the hard palate, appear to have been incorporated into Sanskrit and other Indo-Aryan languages through the medium of borrowed Dravidian words

Hindi and English

For the speakers of the country's myriad tongues to function within a single administrative unit requires some medium of common communication. The choice of this tongue, known in India as the "link" language, has been a point of significant controversy since independence. Central government policy on the question has been necessarily equivocal. The vested interests proposing a number of language policies have made a decisive resolution of the "language question" all but impossible.

The central issue in the link-language controversy has been and remains whether Hindi should replace English. Proponents of Hindi as the link language assert that English is a foreign tongue left over from the British Raj. English is used fluently only by a small, privileged segment of the population; the role of English in public life and governmental affairs constitutes an effective bar to social mobility and further democratisation. Hindi, in this view, is not only already spoken by a sizable minority of all Indians but also would be easier to spread because it would be more congenial to the cultural habits of the people. On the other hand, Dravidian-speaking southerners in particular feel that a switch to Hindi in the well-paid, nationwide bureaucracies, such as the Indian Administrative Service, the military, and other forms of national service would give northerners an unfair advantage in gov-ernment examinations. If the learning of English is burdensome, they argue, at least the burden weighs equally on Indians from all parts of the country. In the meantime, an increasing percentage of Indians send their children to private English-medium schools, to help assure their offspring a chance at high-privilege positions in business, education, the professions, and government.

Linguistic States

The constitution and various other government documents are purposely vague in defining such terms as national languages and official languages and in distinguishing either one from officially adopted regional languages. States are free to adopt their own language of administration and educational instruction from among the country's officially recognised languages, the Scheduled Languages. Further, all citizens have the right to primary education in their native tongue, although the constitution does not stipulate how this objective is to be accomplished.

As drafted, the constitution provided that Hindi and English were to be the languages of communication for the central government until 1965, when the switch to Hindi was mandated. The Official Languages Act of 1963, pursuing this mandate, said that Hindi would become the sole official national language in 1965. English, however, would continue as an "associate additional official language." After ten years, a parlia-mentary committee was to consider the situation and whether the status of English should continue if the knowledge of Hindi among peoples of other native languages had not progressed sufficiently. The act, however, was ambiguous about whether Hindi could be imposed on unwilling states by 1975. In 1964 the Ministry of Home Affairs requested all central ministries to state their progress on the switch to Hindi and their plans for the period after the transition date in 1965. The news of this directive led to massive riots and self-immolations in Tamil Nadu in late 1964 and early 1965, leading the central government, then run by the Congress, to back away from its stand. A conference of Congress leaders, cabinet ministers, and chief ministers of all the states was held in New Delhi in June 1965. Non-Hindi-speaking states were assured that Hindi would not be imposed as the sole language of communication between the central government and the states as long as even one state objected. In addition any of the Scheduled Languages could be used in taking examinations for entry into the central government services.

Before independence in 1947, the Congress was committed to redrawing state boundaries to correspond with linguistics. The States Reorganisation Commission, which was formed in 1953 to study the problems involved in redrawing state boundaries, viewed language as an important, although by no means the sole, factor. Other factors, such as economic viability and geographic realities, had to be taken into account. The commission issued its report in 1955; the government's request for comments from the populace generated a flood of petitions and letters. The final bill, passed in 1956 and amended several times in the 1960s, by no means resolved even the individual states' linguistic problems.

Even regions with a long history of agitation for a linguistic state sometimes have found the actual transition less than smooth. For example, proponents began lobbying for a Te-lugu-speaking state in the early twentieth century. In 1956 the central government formed a single state, Andhra Pradesh, composed of the predominantly Telugu-speaking parts of what in British India had been the Madras Presidency and the large polyglot princely state of Hyderabad. Although more than 80 percent of the residents (some 53 million people as of 1991) of Andhra Pradesh speak Telugu, like most linguistic states it has a sizable linguistic minority. In this case, the minority consists of Urdu speakers centered in the state's capital, Hyderabad, where nearly 40 percent (some 1.7 million people in 1991) of the population speak that language. Linguistic affinity did not form a firm basis for unity between the two regions from which the state had been formed because they were separated by cultural and economic differences. Although there were riots in the late 1960s and early 1970s in support of the formation of two separate states, the separation did not occur.

The violence that broke out in the state of Assam in the early 1980s reflected the complexities of linguistic and ethnic politics in South Asia. The state has a significant number of Bengali-speaking Muslims—immigrants and their descendants who began settling the region in the late nineteenth and early twentieth centuries. The Muslims came in response to a British-initiated colonisation plan to bring under cultivation land left fallow by the Assamese. By the 1931 census, the Assamese not only had lost a hefty portion of their land but also had become a disadvantaged minority in their traditional homeland. They represented less than 33 percent of the total population of Assam, and the Muslim immigrants (who accounted for roughly 25 percent of the population) dominated commerce and the government bureaucracy.

Assamese-Bengali rioting started in 1950, and in the 1951 census many Bengalis listed Assamese as their native tongue in an effort to placate the Assamese. Further immigration of Bengali speakers after the formation of Bangladesh in 1971 and a resurgence of pro-Bengali feeling among earlier immigrants and their descendants reawakened Assamese fears of being outnumbered. Renewed violence in the early and mid-1980s was sufficiently serious for the central government to avoid holding general elections in Assam during December 1984.

Social Context of Language

Contemporary languages and dialects, as they figure in the lives of most Indians, are a far cry from the stylised literary forms of Indo-Aryan or Dravidian languages. North India especially can be viewed as a continuum of village dialects. As a proverb has it, "Every two miles the water changes, every four miles the speech." Spoken dialects of more distant villages will be less and less mutually understandable and finally become simply mutually unintelligible outside the immediate region. In some cases, a variety of caste dialects coexist in the same village or region. In addition, there are numerous regional dialects that villagers use when doing business in nearby towns or bazaars.

Since the late eighteenth and early nineteenth centuries, regional languages, such as Bengali, Punjabi, and Marathi, have become relatively standardised and are now used throughout their respective states for most levels of administration, business, and social intercourse. Each is associated with a body of literature. British rule was an impetus for the official codification of these regional tongues. British colonial administrators and missionaries learned regional languages and often studied their literatures, and their translations of English-language materials and the Bible encouraged the development of written, standard languages. To provide teaching materials, prose compositions, grammars, and textbooks were often commissioned and, in some cases, were closer to everyday speech than was the standard literary language. Industrialisation, modernisation, and printing gave a major boost to the vocabulary and standardisation of regional tongues, especially by making possible the wide dissemination of dictionaries.

Such written forms still often differ widely from spoken vernaculars and village dialects. Diglossia—the coexistence of a highly elaborate, formal language alongside a more colloquial form of the same tongue—occurs in many instances. For example, spoken Bengali is so divergent from written Bengali as to be nearly another tongue. Similarly, Telugu scholars waged a bitter battle in the early twentieth century over proper language style. Reformers favored a simplified prose format for written Telugu, while traditional classicists wished to continue using a classical literary poetic form. In the end, the classicists won, although a more colloquial written form eventually began to appear in the mass media. Diglossia reinforces social barriers because only a fraction of the populace is sufficiently educated to master the more literary form of the language.

The standard regional language may be the household tongue of only a small group of educated inhabitants of the region's major urban center that has long exercised politico-economic hegemony in a region. Even literate villagers may have difficulty understanding it. The more socially isolated—women and Dalits —tend to be more parochial in their speech than people of higher caste, who are often able to use a colloquial form of the regional dialect, the caste patois, and the regional standard dialect. An educated person may master several different speech forms that are often so different as to be considered separate languages. Western-educated scholars may well use the regional standard language mixed with English vocabulary with their colleagues at work. At home, a man may switch to a more colloquial vernacular, particularly if his wife is uneducated. Even the highly educated frequently communicate in their village dialects at home.

Only around 3 percent of the population (about 28 million people in 1995) is truly fluent in both English and an Indian language. By necessity, a substantial minority are able to speak two Indian languages; even in the so-called linguistic states, there are minorities who do not speak the official language as their native tongue and must therefore learn it as a second language. Many tribal people are bilingual. Rural-urban migrants are frequently bilingual in the regional standard language as well as in their village dialect. In Bombay, for example, many migrants speak Hindi or Marathi in addition to their native tongue. Religious celebrations, popular festivals, and political meetings are typically carried on in the regional language, which may be unintelligible to many attendees. Bilingualism in India, however, is inextricably linked to social context. South Asia's long history of foreign rule has fostered what Clarence Maloney terms "the linguistic flight of the elite." Language—either Sanskrit, Persian, or English—has formed a barrier to advancement that only a few have been fortunate enough to overcome.

Throughout the twentieth century, radio, television, and the print media have fostered standardisation of regional dialects, if only to facilitate communication. Linguistic standardisation has contributed to ethnic or regional differentiation insofar as language has served as a cultural marker. Mass communication forces the adoption of a single standard regional tongue; typically, the choice is the dialect of the majority in the region or of the region's preeminent business or cultural center. The use of less standard forms clearly labels speakers outside their immediate home base.

To fulfill its purposes, the regional language must be standardised and taught to an increasing percentage of the population, thereby encroaching both on its own dialects and the minority languages of the region. The language of instruction and administration affects the economic and career interests and the self-respect of an ever-greater proportion of the population.

Ethnicity

Tribes

Tribal peoples constitute roughly 8 percent of the nation's total population, nearly 68 million people according to the 1991 census. One concentration lives in a belt along the Himalayas stretching through Jammu and Kashmir, Himachal Pradesh, and Uttar Pradesh in the west, to Assam, Meghalaya, Tripura, Arunachal Pradesh, Mizoram, Manipur, and Nagaland in the northeast. Another concentration lives in the hilly areas of central India (Madhya Pradesh, Orissa, and, to a lesser extent, Andhra Pradesh); in this belt, which is bounded by the Narmada River to the north and the Godavari River to the southeast, tribal peoples occupy the slopes of the region's mountains. Other tribals, the Santals, live in Bihar and West Bengal. There are smaller numbers of tribal people in Karnataka, Tamil Nadu, and Kerala, in western India in Gujarat and Rajasthan, and in the union territories of Lakshadweep and the Andaman and Nicobar Islands.

The extent to which a state's population is tribal varies considerably. In the northeastern states of Arunachal Pradesh, Meghalaya, Mizoram, and Nagaland, upward of 90 percent of the population is tribal. However, in the remaining northeast states of Assam, Manipur, Sikkim, and Tripura, tribal peoples form between 20 and 30 percent of the population. The largest tribes are found in central India, although the tribal population there accounts for only around 10 percent of the region's total population. Major concentrations of tribal people live in Maharashtra, Orissa, and West Bengal. In the south, about 1 percent of the populations of Kerala and Tamil Nadu are tribal, whereas about 6 percent in Andhra Pradesh and Karnataka are members of tribes.

There are some 573 communities recognised by the government as Scheduled Tribes and therefore eligible to receive special benefits and to compete for reserved seats in legislatures and schools. They range in size from the Gonds (roughly 7.4 million) and the Santals (approximately 4.2 million) to only eighteen Chaimals in the Andaman Islands. Central Indian states have the country's largest tribes, and, taken as a whole, roughly 75 percent of the total tribal population live there.

Apart from the use of strictly legal criteria, however, the problem of determining which groups and individuals are tribal is both subtle and complex. Because it concerns economic interests and the size and location of voting blocs, the question of who are members of Scheduled Tribes rather than Backward Classesor Scheduled Castesis often controversial. The apparently wide fluctuation in estimates of South Asia's tribal population through the twentieth century gives a sense of how unclear the distinction between tribal and nontribal can be. India's 1931 census enumerated 22 million tribal people, in 1941 only 10 million were counted, but by 1961 some 30 million and in 1991 nearly 68 million tribal members were included. The differences among the figures reflect changing census criteria and the economic incentives individuals have to maintain or reject classification as a tribal member.

These gyrations of census data serve to underline the complex relationship between caste and tribe. Although, in theory, these terms represent different ways of life and ideal types, in reality they stand for a continuum of social groups. In areas of substantial contact between tribes and castes, social and cultural pressures have often tended to move tribes in the direction of becoming castes over a period of years. Tribal peoples with ambitions for social advancement in Indian society at large have tried to gain the classification of caste for their tribes; such efforts conform to the ancient Indian traditions of caste mobility. Where tribal leaders prospered, they could hire Brahman priests to construct credible pedigrees and thereby join reasonably high-status castes. On occasion, an entire tribe or part of a tribe joined a Hindu sect and thus entered the caste system en masse. If a specific tribe engaged in practices that Hindus deemed polluting, the tribe's status when it was assimilated into the caste hierarchy would be affected.

Since independence, however, the special benefits available to Scheduled Tribes have convinced many groups, even Hindus and Muslims, that they will enjoy greater advantages if so designated. The schedule gives tribal people incentives to maintain their identity. By the same token, the schedule also includes a number of groups whose "tribal" status, in cultural terms, is dubious at best; in various districts, the list includes Muslims and a congeries of Hindu castes whose main claim seems to be their ability to deliver votes to the party that arranges their listing among the Scheduled Tribes.

A number of traits have customarily been seen as establishing tribal rather than caste identity. These include language, social organisation, religious affiliation, economic patterns, geographic location, and self-identification. Recognised tribes typically live in hilly regions somewhat remote from caste settlements; they generally speak a language recognised as tribal.

Unlike castes, which are part of a complex and interrelated local economic exchange system, tribes tend to form self-sufficient economic units. Often they practice swidden farming—clearing a field by slash-and-burn methods, planting it for a number of seasons, and then abandoning it for a lengthy fallow period—rather than the intensive farming typical of most of rural India. For most tribal people, land-use rights traditionally derive simply from tribal membership. Tribal society tends to be egalitarian, its leadership being based on ties of kinship and personality rather than on hereditary status. Tribes typically consist of segmentary lineages whose extended families provide the basis for social organisation and control. Unlike caste religion, which recognises the hegemony of Brahman priests, tribal religion recognises no authority outside the tribe.

Any of these criteria can be called into question in specific instances. Language is not always an accurate indicator of tribal or caste status. Especially in regions of mixed population, many tribal groups have lost their mother tongues and simply speak local or regional languages. Linguistic assimilation is an ongoing process of considerable complexity. In the highlands of Orissa, for example, the Bondos—a Munda-language-speaking tribe—use their own tongue among themselves. Oriya, however, serves as a lingua franca in dealings with Hindu neighbors. Oriya as a prestige language (in the Bondo view), however, has also supplanted the native tongue as the language of ritual. In parts of Assam, historically divided into warring tribes and villages, increased contact among villagers began during the colonial period and has accelerated since independence. A pidgin Assamese developed while educated tribal members learned Hindi and, in the late twentieth century, English.

Self-identification and group loyalty are not unfailing markers of tribal identity either. In the case of stratified tribes, the loyalties of clan, kin, and family may well predominate over those of tribe. In addition, tribes cannot always be viewed as people living apart; the degree of isolation of various tribes has varied tremendously. The Gonds, Santals, and Bhils traditionally have dominated the regions in which they have lived. Moreover, tribal society is not always more egalitarian than the rest of the rural populace; some of the larger tribes, such as the Gonds, are highly stratified.

Economic and Political Conditions

Most tribes are concentrated in heavily forested areas that combine inaccessibility with limited political or economic significance. Historically, the economy of most tribes was subsistence agriculture or hunting and gathering. Tribal members traded with outsiders for the few necessities they lacked, such as salt and iron. A few local Hindu craftsmen might provide such items as cooking utensils. The twentieth century, however, has seen far-reaching changes in the relationship between tribals and the larger society and, by extension, traditional tribal economies. Improved transportation and communications have brought ever deeper intrusions into tribal lands; merchants and a variety of government policies have involved tribal peoples more thoroughly in the cash economy, although by no means on the most favorable of terms. Large areas fell into the hands of nontribals around 1900, when many regions were opened by the government to homestead-style settlement. Immigrants received free land in return for cultivating it. Tribal people, too, could apply for land titles, although even title to the portion of land they happened to be planting that season could not guarantee their ability to continue swidden cultivation. More important, the notion of permanent, individual ownership of land was foreign to most tribals. Land, if seen in terms of ownership at all, was viewed as a communal resource, free to whoever needed it. By the time tribals accepted the necessity of obtaining formal land titles, they had lost the opportunity to lay claim to lands that might rightfully have been considered theirs. Generally, tribals were severely disadvantaged in dealing with government officials who granted land titles. Albeit belatedly, the colonial regime realised the necessity of protecting tribals from the predations of outsiders and prohibited the sale of tribal lands. Although an important loophole in the form of land leases was left open, tribes made some gains in the mid-twentieth century. Despite considerable obstruction by local police and land officials, who were slow to delineate tribal holdings and slower still to offer police protection, some land was returned to tribal peoples.

In the 1970s, the gains tribal peoples had made in earlier decades were eroded in many regions, especially in central India. Migration into tribal lands increased dramatically, and the deadly combination of constabulary and revenue officers uninterested in tribal welfare and sophisticated nontribals willing and able to bribe local officials was sufficient to deprive many tribals of their landholdings. The means of subverting protective legislation were legion: local officials could be persuaded to ignore land acquisition by nontribal people, alter land registry records, lease plots of land for short periods and then simply refuse to relinquish them, or induce tribal members to become indebted and attach their lands. Whatever the means, the result was that many tribal members became landless labourers in the 1960s and 1970s, and regions that a few years earlier had been the exclusive domain of tribes had an increasingly heterogeneous population. Unlike previous eras in which tribal people were shunted into more remote forests, by the 1960s relatively little unoccupied land was available. Government efforts to evict nontribal members from illegal occupation have proceeded slowly; when evictions occur at all, those ejected are usually members of poor, lower castes. In a 1985 publication, anthropologist Christoph von Fürer-Haimendorf describes this process in Andhra Pradesh: on average only 25 to 33 percent of the tribal families in such villages had managed to keep even a portion of their holdings. Outsiders had paid about 5 percent of the market value of the lands they took.

Improved communications, roads with motorised traffic, and more frequent government intervention figured in the increased contact that tribal peoples had with outsiders. Tribes fared best where there was little to induce nontribals to settle; cash crops and commercial highways frequently signaled the dismemberment of the tribes. Merchants have long been a link to the outside world, but in the past they were generally petty traders, and the contact they had with tribal people was transient. By the 1960s and 1970s, the resident nontribal shopkeeper was a permanent feature of many villages. Shopkeepers often sold liquor on credit, enticing tribal members into debt and into mortgaging their land. In the past, tribes made up shortages before harvest by foraging from the surrounding forest. More recently shopkeepers have offered ready credit—with the proviso that loans be repaid in kind with 50 to 100 percent interest after harvest. Repaying one bag of millet with two bags has set up a cycle of indebtedness from which many have been unable to break loose.

The possibility of cultivators growing a profitable cash crop, such as cotton or castor-oil plants, continues to draw merchants into tribal areas. Nontribal traders frequently establish an extensive network of relatives and associates as shopkeepers to serve as agents in a number of villages. Cultivators who grow a cash crop often sell to the same merchants, who provide consumption credit throughout the year. The credit carries a high-interest price tag, whereas the tribal peoples' crops are bought at a fraction of the market rate. Cash crops offer a further disadvantage in that they decrease the supply of available foodstuffs and increase tribal dependence on economic forces beyond their control.

This transformation has meant a decline in both the tribes' security and their standard of living.

In previous generations, families might have purchased silver jewelry as a form of security; contemporary tribal people are more likely to buy minor consumer goods. Whereas jewelry could serve as collateral in critical emergencies, current purchases simply increase indebtedness. In areas where gathering forest products is remunerative, merchants exchange their products for tribal labour. Indebtedness is so extensive that although such transactions are illegal, traders sometimes "sell" their debtors to other merchants, much like indentured servants.

In some instances, tribes have managed to hold their own in contacts with outsiders. Some Chenchus, a hunting and gathering tribe of the central hill regions of Andhra Pradesh, have continued to specialise in collecting forest products for sale. Caste Hindus living among them rent land from the Chenchus and pay a portion of the harvest. The Chenchus themselves have responded unenthusiastically to government efforts to induce them to take up farming. Their relationship to nontribal people has been one of symbiosis, although there were indications in the early 1980s that other groups were beginning to compete with the Chenchus in gathering forest products. A large paper mill was cutting bamboo in their territory in a manner that did not allow regeneration, and two groups had begun to collect for sale the same products the Chenchus sell. Dalits settled among them with the help of the Chenchus and learned agriculture from them. The nomadic Banjara herders who grase their cattle in the forest also have been allotted land there. The Chenchus have a certain advantage in dealing with caste Hindus; because of their long association with Hindu hermits and their refusal to eat beef, they are considered an unpolluted caste. Other tribes, particularly in South India, have cultural practices that are offensive to Hindus and, when they are assimilated, are often considered Dalits.

The final blow for some tribes has come when nontribals, through political jockeying, have managed to gain legal tribal status, that is, to be listed as a Scheduled Tribe. The Gonds of Andhra Pradesh effectively lost their only advantage in trying to protect their lands when the Banjaras, a group that had been settling in Gond territory, were classified as a Scheduled Tribe in 1977. Their newly acquired tribal status made the Banjaras eligible to acquire Gond land "legally" and to compete with Gonds for reserved political seats, places in education institutions, and other benefits. Because the Banjaras are not scheduled in neighboring Maharashtra, there has been an influx of Banjara emigrants from that state into Andhra Pradesh in search of better opportunities.

Tribes in the Himalayan foothills have not been as hard-pressed by the intrusions of nontribals. Historically, their political status was always distinct from the rest of India. Until the British colonial period, there was little effective control by any of the empires centered in peninsular India; the region was populated by autonomous feuding tribes. The British, in efforts to protect the sensitive northeast frontier, followed a policy dubbed the "Inner Line"; nontribal people were allowed into the areas only with special permission. Postindependence governments have continued the policy, protecting the Himalayan tribes as part of the strategy to secure the border with China.

This policy has generally saved the northern tribes from the kind of exploitation that those elsewhere in South Asia have suffered. In Arunachal Pradesh (formerly part of the North-East Frontier Agency), for example, tribal members control commerce and most lower-level administrative posts. Government construction projects in the region have provided tribes with a significant source of cash—both for setting up businesses and for providing paying customers.

Some tribes have made rapid progress through the education system. Instruction was begun in Assamese but was eventually changed to Hindi; by the early 1980s, English was taught at most levels. Both education and the increase in ready cash from government spending have permitted tribal people a significant measure of social mobility. The role of early missionaries in providing education was also crucial in Assam.

Government policies on forest reserves have affected tribal peoples profoundly. Wherever the state has chosen to exploit forests, it has seriously undermined the tribes' way of life. Government efforts to reserve forests have precipitated armed (if futile) resistance on the part of the tribal peoples involved. Intensive exploitation of forests has often meant allowing outsiders to cut large areas of trees (while the original tribal inhabitants were restricted from cutting), and ultimately replacing mixed forests capable of sustaining tribal life with single-product plantations. Where forests are reserved, nontribals have proved far more sophisticated than their forest counterparts at bribing the necessary local officials to secure effective (if extralegal) use of forestlands. The system of bribing local officials charged with enforcing the reserves is so well established that the rates of bribery are reasonably fixed (by the number of plows a farmer uses or the amount of grain harvested). Tribal people often end up doing unpaid work for Hindus simply because a caste Hindu, who has paid the requisite bribe, can at least ensure a tribal member that he or she will not be evicted from forestlands. The final irony, notes von Fürer-Haimendorf, is that the swidden cultivation many tribes practiced had maintained South Asia's forests, whereas the intensive cultivating and commercial interests that replaced the tribal way of life have destroyed the forests.

Extending the system of primary education into tribal areas and reserving places for tribal children in middle and high schools and higher education institutions are central to government policy, but efforts to improve a tribe's educational status have had mixed results. Recruitment of qualified teachers and determination of the appropriate language of instruction also remain troublesome. Commission after commission on the "language question" has called for instruction, at least at the primary level, in the students' native tongue. In some regions, tribal children entering school must begin by learning the official regional language, often one completely unrelated to their tribal tongue. The experiences of the Gonds of Andhra Pradesh provide an example. Primary schooling began there in the 1940s and 1950s. The government selected a group of Gonds who had managed to become semiliterate in Telugu and taught them the basics of written script. These individuals became teachers who taught in Gondi, and their efforts enjoyed a measure of success until the 1970s, when state policy demanded instruction in Telugu. The switch in the language of instruction both made the Gond teachers superfluous because they could not teach in Telugu and also presented the government with the problem of finding reasonably qualified teachers willing to teach in outlying tribal schools.

The commitment of tribes to acquiring a formal education for their children varies considerably. Tribes differ in the extent to which they view education positively. Gonds and Pardhans, two groups in the central hill region, are a case in point. The Gonds are cultivators, and they frequently are reluctant to send their children to school, needing them, they say, to work in the fields. The Pardhans were traditionally bards and ritual specialists, and they have taken to education with enthusiasm. The effectiveness of educational policy likewise varies by region. In those parts of the northeast where tribes have generally been spared the wholesale onslaught of outsiders, schooling has helped tribal people to secure political and economic benefits. The education system there has provided a corps of highly trained tribal members in the professions and high-ranking administrative posts.

Many tribal schools are plagued by high dropout rates. Children attend for the first three to four years of primary school and gain a smattering of knowledge, only to lapse into illiteracy later. Few who enter continue up to the tenth grade; of those who do, few manage to finish high school. Therefore, very few are eligible to attend institutions of higher education, where the high rate of attrition continues.

Practices

The influx of newcomers disinclined to follow tribal ways has had a massive impact on social relations and tribal belief systems. In many communities, the immigrants have brought on nothing less than the total disintegration of the communities they entered. Even where outsiders are not residents in villages, traditional forms of social control and authority are less effective because tribal people are patently dependent on politico-economic forces beyond their control. In general, traditional headmen no longer have official backing for their role in village affairs, although many continue to exercise considerable influence. Headmen can no longer control the allocation of land or decide who has the right to settle in the village, a loss of power that has had an insidious effect on village solidarity.

Some headmen have taken to leasing village land to outsiders, thus enriching themselves at the expense of the rest of the tribes. Conflict over land rights has introduced a point of cleavage into village social relations; increased factional conflict has seriously eroded the ability of tribes to ward off the intrusion of outsiders. In some villages, tribal schoolteachers have emerged as a new political force, a counterbalance to the traditional headman. Changes in landholding patterns have also altered the role of the joint family. More and more couples set up separate households as soon as they marry. Because land is no longer held and farmed in common and has grown more scarce, inheritance disputes have increased.

Hunters and gatherers are particularly vulnerable to these far-reaching changes. The lack of strong authority figures in most hunting and gathering groups handicaps these tribes in organising to negotiate with the government. In addition, these tribes are too small to have much political leverage.

Forced settlement schemes also have had a deleterious impact on the tribes and their environment. Government-organised villages are typically larger than traditional hunting and gathering settlements. Forest reserves limit the amount of territory over which tribes can range freely. Larger villages and smaller territories have led, in some instances, to an increase in crime and violence. Traditionally, hunters and gatherers "settled" their disputes by arranging for the antagonists simply to avoid one another; new, more circumscribed villages preclude this arrangement.

Tribal beliefs and rituals have altered in the face of increased contact with Hindus and missionaries of a variety of persuasions. Among groups in more intense contact with the Hindu majority, there have been various transformations. The Gonds, for example, traditionally worshiped clan gods through elaborate rites, with Pardhans organising and performing the necessary rituals.

The increasing impoverishment of large sections of the Gond tribe has made it difficult, if not impossible, to support the Pardhans as a class of ritual specialists. At the same time, many Gonds have concluded that the tribal gods were losing their power and efficacy. Gonds have tended to seek the assistance of other deities, and thus there has been widespread Hinduisation of Gondi belief and practice. Some tribes have adopted the Hindu practice of having costly elaborate weddings—a custom that contributes to indebtedness (as it has in many rural Indian families) and subjects them to the cash economy on the most deleterious of terms. Some families have adapted a traditional marriage pattern—that of capturing a bride—to modern conditions, using the custom to avoid the costly outlays associated with a formal wedding.

Christian missionaries have been active among sundry tribes since the mid-nineteenth century. Conversion to Christianity offers a number of advantages, not the least of which is education. It was through the efforts of various Christian sects to translate the Bible into tribal languages that those tongues acquired a written script. Christian proselytising has served to preserve tribal lore and language in written form at the same time that it has tended to change drastically the tribe's cultural heritage and belief systems. In some instances, the introduction of Christianity has driven a wedge between converts and their fellow tribal members who continue to adhere to traditional beliefs and practices

Jews and Parsis

There are several groups descended from ancient settlers in India. These groups include the Jews, the first group of whom are said to have migrated from West Asia and to have settled in Cranganore (also the traditional first site where Muslims later arrived in India) on the Malabar Coast of Kerala in the first century A.D., a second group of Jews who fled the Arabian Peninsula in the face of Muslim ascendancy in the seventh century, and the Parsis, who came to India in the eighth century A.D. to escape Muslim persecution in Persia.

Portuguese

The European powers left a small ethnic imprint on India. The Portuguese came first and left last, but at no time had they extensive dominions such as the Indian kingdoms and empires or the lands of the British in India. The Austrians, Danish, Dutch, and French had yet smaller territories for shorter periods. By the time truly large numbers of Europeans came to spend their working lives in India as part of the British Raj, racist prejudices that were largely absent in earlier centuries had developed in the Europeans. Improvements in transportation (the steamship and the Suez Canal) also had made travel swifter and safer so at least the more prosperous classes could return to Europe on leave to marry or choose brides coming on the so-called "fishing fleets" for tourism and husband-hunting.

There are around 730,000 Portuguese Indians, commonly known as Goans or Goanese, about half of whom live in the state of Goa and the others elsewhere in India. They are descended from Indians in the former Portuguese colony who assimilated to Portuguese culture and in many cases are the descendants of Indo-Portuguese marriages, which the Portuguese civil and religious authorities encouraged.

Anglo-Indians

The largest group of European Indians, however, are descendants of British men, generally from the colonial service and the military, and lower-caste Hindu or Muslim women. From some time in the nineteenth century, both the British and the Indian societies rejected the offspring of these unions, and so the Anglo-Indians, as they became known, sought marriage partners among other Anglo-Indians. Over time this group developed a number of caste-like features and acquired a special occupational niche in the railroad, postal, and customs services. A number of factors fostered a strong sense of commu-nity among Anglo-Indians. The school system focused on English language and culture and was virtually segregated, as were Anglo-Indian social clubs; the group's adherence to Christianity also set members apart from most other Indians; and distinctive manners, diet, dress, and speech contributed to their segregation.

During the independence movement, many Anglo-Indians identified (or were assumed to identify) with British rule, and, therefore, incurred the distrust and hostility of Indian nationalists. Their position at independence was difficult. They felt a loyalty to a British "home" that most had never seen and where they would gain little social acceptance. They felt insecure in an India that put a premium on participation in the independence movement as a prerequisite for important government positions. Some Anglo-Indians left the country in 1947, hoping to make a new life in Britain or elsewhere in the Commonwealth of Nations, such as Australia or Canada. Many of these people returned to India after unsuccessful attempts to find a place in "alien" societies. Most Anglo-Indians, however, opted to stay in India and made whatever adjustments they deemed necessary.

Like the Parsis, the Anglo-Indians are essentially urban dwellers. Unlike the Parsis, relatively few have attained high levels of education, amassed great wealth, or achieved more than subordinate government positions. In the 1990s, Anglo-Indians remained scattered throughout the country in the larger cities and those smaller towns serving as railroad junctions and communications centers.

Constitutional guarantees of the rights of communities and religious and linguistic minorities permit Anglo-Indians to maintain their own schools and to use English as the medium of instruction. In order to encourage the integration of the community into the larger society, the government stipulates that a certain percentage of the student body come from other Indian communities. There is no evident official discrimination against Anglo-Indians in terms of current government employment. A few have risen to high posts; some are high-ranking officers in the military, and a few are judges. In occupational terms, at least, the assimilation of Anglo-Indians into the mainstream of Indian life was well under way by the 1990s. Nevertheless, the group will probably remain socially distinct as long as its members marry only other Anglo-Indians and its European descent continues to be noted.

Africans

Still another foreign-origin group, usually known collectively as Siddhis, are the descendants of Africans brought to India as slaves. Although most African-origin Indians are descendants of the large influx of slaves brought to western India in the seventeenth century, the first Africans reportedly arrived on the Konkani Coast in the first century A.D. as a result of the Arab slave trade, and there was an important African presence, including several short-term rulers, in Bengal in the fifteenth century. Siddhis (the name means lord or prince in African usage) sometimes rose to prominent—even ruling—governmental and military positions during the Mughal and British periods. Most modern-day Siddhis are Muslims and are engaged in agricultural pursuits. They are found in Gujarat, Daman and Diu, Maharashtra, Karnataka, Andhra Pradesh, and other states and union territories, where they are designated as Scheduled Tribe members.

Regionalism

The formation of states along linguistic and ethnic lines has occurred in India in numerous instances since independence in 1947. There have been demands, however, to form units within states based not only along linguistic, ethnic, and religious lines but also, in some cases, on a feeling of the distinctness of a geographical region and its culture and economic interests. The most volatile movements are those ongoing in Jammu and Kashmir and Punjab. How the central government responds to these demands will be an area of scrutiny through the late 1990s and beyond. It is believed by some officials that conceding regional autonomy is less arduous and takes less time and fewer resources than does meeting agitation, violence, and demands for concessions.

Telangana Movement

An early manifestation of regionalism was the Telangana movement in what became the state of Andhra Pradesh. The princely ruler of Hyderabad, the nizam, had attempted unsuccessfully to maintain Hyderabad as an independent state separate from India in 1947. His efforts were simultaneous with the largest agrarian armed rebellion in modern Indian history. Starting in July 1946, communist-led guerrilla squads began overthrowing local feudal village regimes and organising land reform in Telugu-speaking areas of Hyderabad, collectively known as Telangana (an ancient name for the region dating from the Vijayanagar period). In time, about 3,000 villages and some 41,000 square kilometers of territory were involved in the revolt. Faced with the refusal of the nizam of Hyderabad to accede his territory to India and the violence of the communist-led rebellion, the central government sent in the army in September 1948. By November 1949, Hyderabad had been forced to accede to the Indian union, and, by October 1951, the violent phase of the Telangana movement had been suppressed. The effect of the 1946-51 rebellion and communist electoral victories in 1952 had led to the destruction of Hyderabad and set the scene for the establishment of a new state along linguistic lines. In 1953, based on the recommendation of the States Reorganisation Commission, Telugu-speaking areas were separated from the former Madras States to form Andhra, India's first state established along linguistic lines. The commission also contemplated establishing Telangana as a separate state, but instead Telangana was merged with Andhra to form the new state of Andhra Pradesh in 1956.

The concerns about Telangana were manifold. The region had a less developed economy than Andhra, but a larger revenue base (mostly because it taxed rather than prohibited alcoholic beverages), which Telanganas feared might be diverted for use in Andhra. They also feared that planned dam projects on the Krishna and Godavari rivers would not benefit Telangana proportionately even though Telanganas controlled the headwaters of the rivers. Telanganas feared too that the people of Andhra would have the advantage in jobs, particularly in government and education.

The central government decided to ignore the recommendation to establish a separate Telangana state and, instead, merged the two regions into a unified Andhra Pradesh. However, a "gentlemen's agreement" provided reassurances to the Telangana people. For at least five years, revenue was to be spent in the regions proportionately to the amount they contributed. Education institutions in Telangana were to be expanded and reserved for local students. Recruitment to the civil service and other areas of government employment such as education and medicine was to be proportional. The use of Urdu was to continue in the administration and the judiciary for five years. The state cabinet was to have proportional membership from both regions and a deputy chief minister from Telangana if the chief minister was from Andhra and vice versa. Finally, the Regional Council for Telangana was to be responsible for economic development, and its members were to be elected by the members of the state legislative assembly from the region.

In the following years, however, the Telangana people had a number of complaints about how the agreements and guarantees were implemented. The deputy chief minister position was never filled. Education institutions in the region were greatly expanded, but Telanganas felt that their enrollment was not proportionate to their numbers. The selection of the city of Hyderabad as the state capital led to massive migration of people from Andhra into Telangana. Telanganas felt discriminated against in education employment but were told by the state government that most non-Telanganas had been hired on the grounds that qualified local people were unavailable. In addition, the unification of pay scales between the two regions appeared to disadvantage Telangana civil servants. In the atmosphere of discontent, professional associations that earlier had amalgamated broke apart by region.

Discontent with the 1956 gentlemen's agreement intensified in January 1969 when the guarantees that had been agreed on were supposed to lapse. Student agitation for the continuation of the agreement began at Osmania University in Hyderabad and spread to other parts of the region. Government employees and opposition members of the state legislative assembly swiftly threatened "direct action" in support of the students. The Congress-controlled state and central governments offered assurances that non-Telangana civil servants in the region would be replaced by Mulkis, disadvantaged local people, and that revenue surpluses from Telangana would be returned to the region. The protestors, however, were dissatisfied, and severe violence, including mob attacks on railroads, road transport, and government facilities, spread over the region. In addition, seventy-nine police firings resulted in twenty-three deaths according to official figures, the education system was shut down, and examinations were cancelled. Calls for a separate Telangana state came in the midst of counter violence in Andhra areas bordering Telangana. In the meantime, the Andhra Pradesh High Court decreed that a central government law mandating replacement of non-Telangana government employees with Mulkis was beyond Parliament's constitutional powers.

Although the Congress faced dissension within its ranks, its leadership stood against additional linguistic states, which were regarded as "antinational." As a result, defectors from the Congress, led by M. Chenna Reddy, founded the Telangana People's Association (Telangana Praja Samithi). Despite electoral successes, however, some of the new party leaders gave up their agitation in September 1971 and, much to the disgust of many separatists, rejoined the safer political haven of the Congress ranks.

In 1972 the Supreme Court reversed the Andhra Pradesh High Court's ruling that the Mulki rules were unconstitutional. This decision triggered agitation in the Andhra region that produced six months of violence.

Throughout the 1970s, Andhra Pradesh settled into a pattern of continuous domination by Congress (R) and later Congress (I), with much instability and dissidence within the state party and constant interference from Indira Gandhi and the national party. Chenna Reddy, the erstwhile opposition leader, was for a time the Congress (I) state chief minister. Congress domination was only ended by the founding of the Telugu National Party by N.T. Rama Rao in 1982 and its overwhelming victory in the state elections in 1983.

Polls taken after the end of the Telangana movement showed a certain lack of enthusiasm for it, and for the idea of a separate state. Although urban groups (students and civil servants) had been most active in the movement, its support was stronger in rural areas. Its supporters were mixed: low and middle castes, the young and the not so young, women, illiterates and the poorly educated, and rural gentry. Speakers of several other languages than Telugu were heavily involved. The movement had no element of religious communalism, but some observers thought Muslims were particularly involved in the movement. Other researchers found the Muslims were unenthusiastic about the movement and noted a feeling that migration from Andhra to Telangana was creating opportunities that were helping non-Telanganas. On the other hand, of the two locally prominent Muslim political groups, only one supported a separate state; the other opposed the idea while demanding full implementation of the regional safeguards. Although Urdu speakers were appealed to in the agitation (e.g., speeches were given in Urdu as well as Telugu), in the aftermath Urdu disappeared from the schools and the administration.

The Telangana movement grew out of a sense of regional identity as such, rather than out of a sense of ethnic identity, language, religion, or caste. The movement demanded redress for economic grievances, the writing of a separate history, and establishment of a sense of cultural distinctness. The emotions and forces generated by the movement were not strong enough, however, for a continuing drive for a separate state. In the late 1980s and early 1990s, the People's War Group, an element of the Communist Party of India (Marxist-Leninist), renewed violence in Andhra Pradesh but was dealt with by state police forces.

Gorkhaland

The Gorkhaland movement grew from the demand of Nepalis living in Darjiling District of West Bengal for a separate state for themselves. The Gorkhaland National Liberation Front led the movement, which disrupted the district with massive violence between 1986 and 1988. The issue was resolved, at least temporarily, in 1988 with the establishment of the Darjiling Gorkha Hill Council within West Bengal.

Historically, Darjiling belonged to the kingdom of Sikkim, which had lost it several times since the eighteenth century. The ethnic identity "Gorkha" comes from the kingdom with that name that united Nepal in the late eighteenth century and was the focal point of Nepalese in the British army.

Immigration from Nepal expanded with British rule in India, and some 34 percent of the population of Darjiling in 1876 was of Gorkha (also seen as Gurkha) ethnicity. By the start of the twentieth century, Nepalese immigrants made a modest socioeconomic advance through government service, and a small anglicised elite developed among them. In 1917 the Hillmen's Association came into being and petitioned for the administrative separation of Darjiling in 1917 and again in 1928 and 1942. In 1928 the Akhil Bharatiya Gorkha League (All India Gorkha League) was formed. It gained additional support after World War II with the influx of ex-soldiers from the Gurkha regiments who had been exposed to nationalist movements in Southeast Asia during service there.

During the 1940s, the CPI organised Gorkha tea workers. In presentations to the States Reorganisation Commission in 1954, the CPI favored regional autonomy for Darjiling within West Bengal, with recognition of Nepali as a Scheduled Language. The All India Gorkha League preferred making the area a union territory under the national government.

The state of West Bengal nominally has been supportive of the use of the Nepali language. The West Bengal Official Language Act of 1961 made Nepali the official language of the hill subdivisions of Darjiling,

Kalimpong, and Kurseong, where Nepalese are a majority. The state legislative assembly passed a resolution in 1977 that led Parliament to amend the national constitution to include Nepali as a Scheduled Language. However, the Gorkhaland National Liberation Front has accused the state government of failure to actually implement use of the language.

The Gorkhaland movement distinguished Darjiling Gorkhas from nationals of Nepal legally resident in India, from Nepali-speaking Indian citizens from other parts of the country, and even from the majority in neighboring Sikkim, where Nepali is the official language. The movement was emphatic that it had no desire to separate from India, only from the state of West Bengal. Gorkhaland supporters therefore preferred to call the Gorkhas' language Gorkhali rather than Nepali, although they did not attempt to claim there is any linguistic difference from what other people call Nepali. The 1981 census of India, whether in deference to this sentiment or for some other reason, called the language *Gorkhali/Nepali*. However, when the Eighth Schedule of the constitution was amended in 1992 to make it a Scheduled Language, the term *Nepali* alone was used.

In 1986 the Gorkhaland National Liberation Front, having failed to obtain a separate regional administrative identity from Parliament, again demanded a separate state of Gorkhaland. The party's leader, Subhash Ghising, headed a demonstration that turned violent and was severely repressed by the state government. The disturbances almost totally shut down the districts' economic mainstays of tea, tourism, and timber. The Left Front government of West Bengal, which earlier had supported some form of autonomy, now opposed it as "antinational." The state government claimed that Darjiling was no worse off than the state in general and was richer than many districts. Ghising made lavish promises to his followers, including the recruitment of

40,000 Indian Gorkhas into the army and paying Rs100,000 for every Gorkha writer. After two years of fighting and the loss of at least 200 lives, the government of West Bengal and the central government finally agreed on an autonomous hill district. In July 1988, the Gorkhaland National Liberation Front gave up the demand for a separate state, and in August the Darjiling Gorkha Hill Council came into being with Ghising as chairman. The council had authority over economic development programs, education, and culture.

However, difficulties soon arose over the *panchayat*elections. Ghising wanted the hill council excluded from the national law on *panchayat* elections. Rajiv Gandhi's government was initially favorable to his request and introduced a constitutional amendment in 1989 to exclude the Darjiling Gorkha Hill Council, along with several other northeast hill states and regions (Nagaland, Meghalaya, Mizoram, and the hill regions of Manipur), but it did not pass. However, in 1992 Parliament passed the Seventy-third Amendment, which seemed to show a newly serious commitment to the idea of local self-government by *panchayats*. The amendment excluded all the hill areas just mentioned except Darjiling. Ghising insisted this omission was a machination of West Bengal and threatened to revive militant agitation for a Gorkhaland state. He also said the Gorkhaland National Liberation Front would boycott the village *panchayat* elections mandated by the amendment. A large portion of his party, however, refused to accept the boycott and split off under the leadership of Chiten Sherpa to form the All India Gorkha League, which won a sizable number of *panchayat* seats.

In 1995 it was unclear whether the region would remain content with autonomy rather than statehood. In August 1995, Sherpa complained to the state government that Ghising's government had misused hill council funds, and West Bengal chief minister Jyoti Basu promised to investigate. Both Gorkha parties showed willingness to use general shutdowns to forward their ends. The fact that so many people were willing to follow Sherpa instead of the hitherto unchallenged Ghising may indicate that they will be satisfied with regional autonomy.

Ladakh

The region of Ladakh is isolated in the Himalayas next to Tibet and differs radically from the rest of the state in that the majority of the population is culturally, ethnically, religiously, and linguistically close to Tibet. There also is a Muslim minority. The region has no interest in the separatist and Islamicist sentiments of the Vale of Kashmir.

Following several years of discontent and agitation about the position of Ladakh District in the state of Jammu and Kashmir, the central government passed the Ladakh Autonomous Hill Development Councils Act in May 1995. The 1995 act established councils for the Leh and Kargil subdistricts and allotted them powers for economic development, land use, and taxation. Elections for the Leh council were held in August 1995. Congress (I) won all twenty-two elective seats unopposed; the governor of Jammu and Kashmir was authorised to appoint four members from among minorities and women.

The Northeast

Northeastern India is made up of the states of Assam, Meghalaya, Tripura, Arunachal Pradesh, Mizoram, Manipur, and Nagaland. Certain tensions exist between these states and a relatively distant central government and between the tribal peoples, who are natives of these states, and migrant peoples from other parts of India. These tensions have led the natives of these states to seek a greater participation in their own governance, control of their states' economies, and their role in society. Emerging from these desires for greater self-governance are new regional political parties and continued insurgent movements. In addition to the more frequently analysed regional movements in Jammu and Kashmir, Punjab, and states such as Assam and Nagaland in the northeast, there are other regional movements, such as those in the Tripura and Miso tribal areas.

In May 1995, the state government of Tripura extended the area covered by the Tripura Tribal Areas Autonomous District Council, a result of the tripartite accord among the central government, the state government, and the Tripura National Volunteers movement concluded in 1988. In the elections in July 1995, the Left Front, led by the Communist Party of India (Marxist), defeated the alliance of the Congress (I) and the local Tripura Tribal Youth Association, which had controlled the council since 1990. The new council proceeded to dissolve the more than 400 development committees at various levels under its jurisdiction for corruption and inaction and promised to constitute new ones swiftly.

In June 1995, the Assam government signed an agreement with two organisations of the Mising tribe, the Mising Autonomous Demand Committee and the Mising Greater Council, to set up an autonomous council for the Misings. The council will include villages with majority tribal populations in four districts of Assam, with a total population expected to be about 315,000. However, villages in so-called Reserve Forest Areas will be included only with the approval of the central minister of state with independent charge of environment and forests. This decision is a possible source of discontent because tribals frequently feel themselves hampered by restrictions on the use of forests by the government. However, in July 1995 the Mising Bane Kebang boycotted the swearing in of the interim council because it said the Mising Autonomous Demand Committee had kept it out of its formation.

Bibliography

Ahmad, Imitiaz (ed.) 1976. *Family, Kinship and Marriage Among Muslims in India.* Manohar: New Delhi.

Ansari, Ghaus. 1959-60. Muslim Caste in Uttar Pradesh. A Study of culture contact. *The Eastern Anthropologist*, 13 (2); 1-83.

Augustine. J.S. (ed.) 1982. *The Indian Family in Transition.* Vikas Publishing House: New Delhi

Banerjee, A.C. 1983. *The Sikh Gurus and the Sikh Religion.* Munshiram Manoharlal Pvt. Ltd.: Delhi

CSWI (Committee on the Status of Women in India) 1974. *Towards Equality.* Department of Social Welfare, Government of India: New Delhi

Desai, A.R., 1984. *Rural Sociology in India.* Bombay: Popular Prakashan

Dhillon, D.S. 1988. *Sikhism: Origin and Development.* Atlantic Publishers: Delhi

Dube, Leela 1974. *Sociology of Kinship.* Popular Prakashan: Bombay

Dube, S.C. 1990.*Indian Society* New Delhi: National Book Trust, India.

Dubois, Abbe J.A. 1906. *Hindu manners, customs and ceremonies,* Oxford: Clarendon Press.

Dumont, Louis, 1980. *Homo Hierarchicus: The caste system & its implications.* Delhi: Oxford University Press.

Dutt, N.K.1986. *Origin and Growth of Caste in India,* Calcutta: Firma KLM.

Eliade M. (Ed.) 1987. *Zoroastrianism. In The Encyclopedia of Religion.* Volume 15, Macmillan Publishing: New York.

Ghurye, G.S.1961. *Caste, Class and Occupation.* Bombay: Popular Book Depot.

Gore, M.S. 1968. *Urbanization and Family Change in India.* Popular Prakashaa: Bombay

Gould, H.A. 1987. *The Hindu Caste System.* Chanakya Publications: Delhi.

Gupta, A.R., 1984. *Caste hierarchy and social change: a study of myth and reality.* New Delhi: Jyotsna.

Haugh, M. 1987. *The Parsis: Essays on their Sacred Language Writings and Religion.* Cosmo Publications: New Delhi.

Hutton, J.H., 1946, *Caste in India: Its Nature, Functions and Origins.* Cambridge: Cambridge University Press.

Jackson, Paul S.J. (ed.) 1988. *The Muslims of India: Beliefs and Practices.* Theological Publications: Bangalore, Chapter I, II & III.

Jain, Shobhita 1996. *Bharat mein Parivar, Vivah aur Natedari.* Rawat Publishers: Jaipur

Kapadia, K.M. 1972. *Industrialization and rural society: A study of Atul-Bulsar,* Bombay: Popular Books.

Karve, I. 1953. *Kinship organization in India,* Poona Deccan College.

Kolenda, Pauline 1987. *Regional Differences in Family Structure in India.* Rawat Publication: Jaipur

Madan, T.N. 1965. *Family and Kinship A Study of the Pandits of Rural Kashmir.* Asia Publishing House: New Delhi

Mayer, A.C., 1960, *Caste and kinship in central India: A village and its region.* London: Routledge & Keagan Paul

Prabhu, P.H. 1979. *Hindu Social Organisation: A Study in Socio-Psychological and Ideological Foundations.* Popular Prakashan Pvt. Ltd.: Bombay.

Radhakrishnan, S. 1979. *The Hindu View of Life.* Blackie and Son Pvt. Ltd.: Bombay.

Risley, Herbert. 1969. *The People of India,* Delhi: Oriental Book Reprint Corporation.

Saiyyed, V.V. and Mohammad, Talib 1995. *Religion and Ethnicity among Muslim.* Rawat: Jaipur

Sharma, J.B. and Sharma, S.R. 1999. *Parsis in India.* Popular Prakasan: Bombay

Singer, Milton & B.S. Cohn (eds.). 1968. *Structure and Change in Indian Society.* Philadelphia

Singh, Yogendra.1999. *Social Stratification and Change in India.* New Delhi: Manohar publications.

Singh,Gopal 1987. *The Religion of the Sikhs.* Allied Publishers Private Limited: Delhi

Srinivas, M.N. 1964. *Caste in modern India & other essays.* Bombay: Asia Publishing House,

Thapar, Romesh, (ed.). 1977. *Tribe, Caste and Religion.* New Delhi: Macmillan.

Uberoi, Patricia (ed.) 1994. *Family, Kinship and Marriage in India.* Oxford University Press: New Delhi.

Index